PRINCIPLES OF TRANSITION FINANCE INVESTING

PRINCIPLES OF TRANSITION FINANCE INVESTING

FINDING ALPHA IN A WORLD ADAPTING TO CLIMATE CHANGE

C. ROBIN CASTELLI

WILEY

Copyright © 2026 by John Wiley & Sons, Inc. All rights reserved.

Published by John Wiley & Sons, Inc., Hoboken, New Jersey.
Published simultaneously in Canada.

No part of this publication may be reproduced, stored in a retrieval system, or transmitted in any form or by any means, electronic, mechanical, photocopying, recording, scanning, or otherwise, except as permitted under Section 107 or 108 of the 1976 United States Copyright Act, without either the prior written permission of the Publisher, or authorization through payment of the appropriate per-copy fee to the Copyright Clearance Center, Inc., 222 Rosewood Drive, Danvers, MA 01923, (978) 750-8400, fax (978) 750-4470, or on the web at www.copyright.com. Requests to the Publisher for permission should be addressed to the Permissions Department, John Wiley & Sons, Inc., 111 River Street, Hoboken, NJ 07030, (201) 748-6011, fax (201) 748-6008, or online at http://www.wiley.com/go/permission.

The manufacturer's authorized representative according to the EU General Product Safety Regulation is Wiley-VCH GmbH, Boschstr. 12, 69469 Weinheim, Germany, e-mail: Product_Safety@wiley.com.

Trademarks: Wiley and the Wiley logo are trademarks or registered trademarks of John Wiley & Sons, Inc. and/or its affiliates in the United States and other countries and may not be used without written permission. All other trademarks are the property of their respective owners. John Wiley & Sons, Inc. is not associated with any product or vendor mentioned in this book.

Limit of Liability/Disclaimer of Warranty: While the publisher and author have used their best efforts in preparing this book, they make no representations or warranties with respect to the accuracy or completeness of the contents of this book and specifically disclaim any implied warranties of merchantability or fitness for a particular purpose. Certain AI systems have been used in the creation of this work. No warranty may be created or extended by sales representatives or written sales materials. The advice and strategies contained herein may not be suitable for your situation. You should consult with a professional where appropriate. Further, readers should be aware that websites listed in this work may have changed or disappeared between when this work was written and when it is read. Neither the publisher nor authors shall be liable for any loss of profit or any other commercial damages, including but not limited to special, incidental, consequential, or other damages.

For general information on our other products and services or for technical support, please contact our Customer Care Department within the United States at (800) 762-2974, outside the United States at (317) 572-3993 or fax (317) 572-4002.

Wiley also publishes its books in a variety of electronic formats. Some content that appears in print may not be available in electronic formats. For more information about Wiley products, visit our web site at www.wiley.com.

Library of Congress Cataloging-in-Publication Data:

Names: Castelli, Cino Robin author | John Wiley & Sons publisher
Title: Principles of transition finance investing : finding alpha in a
   world adapting to climate change / C. Robin Castelli.
Description: Hoboken, New Jersey : Wiley, [2026] | Includes bibliographical
   references and index.
Identifiers: LCCN 2025010515 | ISBN 9781394351732 hardback | ISBN
   9781394351756 pdf | ISBN 9781394351749 epub
Subjects: LCSH: Investments–Environmental aspects | Finance–Environmental
   aspects | Climatic changes–Economic aspects | Sustainable development |
   Financial risk management
Classification: LCC HC79.E5 C3772 2026 | DDC
   338.9/270681–dc23/eng/20250613
LC record available at https://lccn.loc.gov/2025010515

Cover Design: Wiley
Cover Images: © Vaclav Volrab/Shutterstock,
© priyo cahyo/Shutterstock
Author Photo: Courtesy of Rob Tannenbaum

SKY10119979_062825

CONTENTS

LIST OF FIGURES AND TABLES — XV

CHAPTER ONE
AN INTRODUCTION TO TRANSITION FINANCE — 1
1.1. Introduction on the principles of anthropogenic climate change — 1
1.2. Future evolution of CO_2 levels and global temperature — 9
1.3. What is the definition of transition finance? — 26
1.4. What do we mean by transition finance? — 27
1.5. What do world business and economics leaders think about transition finance? — 28

CHAPTER TWO
MODEL-BASED APPROACHES TO INVESTING — 33
2.1. Why do we need models to invest in transition finance? — 33
2.2. How do we model climate and the impact it has on the economy and society? — 37
2.3. What to model: Vendor models versus proprietary models — 46
2.4. The problem of climate data in general — 52
2.5. Data quality issues for acute physical risk — 53
2.6. Data quality issues for chronic physical risk — 55
2.7. Data quality issues for transition risk — 57
2.8. Data quality issues for climate liability risk — 61

CONTENTS

2.9.	Fat tails: Where climate risk and opportunities truly hide	64
2.10.	Are models alone enough to allow us to make informed investing decisions?	69

CHAPTER THREE
THE PROBLEM OF BACK-TESTING AND BENCHMARKING — 71

3.1.	The problem of back-testing, narratives, and validation	71
3.2.	Narratives and why we need them to be strong and explainable	72
3.3.	Back-testing: Why we really cannot do it and what to do about it	73
3.4.	Validation and why it is a challenge	75
3.5.	What to benchmark against?	77

CHAPTER FOUR
TYPES OF FUNDS IN TRANSITION FINANCE — 79

4.1.	What type of investments?	79
4.2.	Is it a static asset allocation strategy or a dynamic one?	80
4.3.	One approach versus multiple approaches	81
4.4.	Diversification and moving beyond purely emissions-based approaches	82
4.5.	Conceptual framework for quantitative investing in transition finance	85
4.6.	Positive screening	88
4.7.	Thematic investment	89
4.8.	Investing in the transition	91
4.9.	The four fund/three strategy approach	92
4.10.	The Investment Matrix	96

CHAPTER FIVE
EXAMPLES OF HOW TO BUILD AN INVESTMENT PORTFOLIO — 99

5.1.	Decide what is the climate transition scenario you believe is likely to happen	99
5.2.	Run the models based on your scenarios	103

Contents

5.3.	Challenge your model results	105
5.4.	Use subject matter expertise to apply overrides and overlays to the models	108
5.5.	Identify the set of opportunities at sector, theme, and individual name level	109
5.6.	Identify the driver for each opportunity	110
5.7.	Determine the overall Technology Readiness Level for each opportunity	111
5.8.	Determine the investment horizon for each opportunity	113
5.9.	Determine the investment maturity for each opportunity	113
5.10.	Determine the crowdedness for each opportunity	114
5.11.	Identify the root problem for each opportunity	116
5.12.	Identify what the root problem causes for each opportunity	117
5.13.	Identify what needs to happen to fix the issue for each opportunity	118
5.14.	Identify how soon the fix needs to happen for each opportunity	119
5.15.	Identify the investment opportunity for each opportunity	119
5.16.	Identify what the benefit of the investment is for each opportunity	120
5.17.	Identify the potential market size for each opportunity	121
5.18.	Identify the long-term investment vision for each opportunity	122
5.19.	Identify the trigger event for each opportunity	124
5.20.	Identify the primary fund in which each opportunity belongs	124
5.21.	Identify the primary strategy in which each opportunity belongs	126
5.22.	Select the investment theses that align with your individual risk appetite, investment horizon, and area of expertise	127
5.23.	Deep dive in investment theses of interest to identify targets and refine strategies	128
5.24.	Build your portfolio based on identified targets	129

CONTENTS

CHAPTER SIX
INVESTMENT TRIGGER EVENTS 135
- 6.1. What is an investment trigger? 135
- 6.2. How do we identify an investment trigger? 137
- 6.3. What is the likelihood and timing of a trigger and what factors affect it? 138

CHAPTER SEVEN
ABOUT HYDROGEN 139
- 7.1. The physics and chemistry of hydrogen and the effect on what role it might play 141
- 7.2. The problems with manufacturing hydrogen in volumes 144
- 7.3. The pitfalls of producing hydrogen by electrolysis 146
- 7.4. The false promise of producing hydrogen by pyrolysis 148
- 7.5. The mirage of naturally occurring hydrogen 149
- 7.6. The deceitful idea of producing hydrogen in cheap locations and shipping it to points of usage 149
- 7.7. Transporting hydrogen as ammonia is not a good idea 151
- 7.8. Hydrogen in ground transportation 152
- 7.9. Hydrogen for heating and steam generation 157
- 7.10. Ammonia-from-hydrogen uses 159
- 7.11. Hydrogen to make methanol for shipping 160
- 7.12. Hydrogen for airplanes 161
- 7.13. Hydrogen for grid energy storage 163

CHAPTER EIGHT
OVERVIEW OF PRIMARILY GROWTH FUND INVESTMENT THESES 167
- 8.1. Which opportunities are primarily growth opportunities? 168
- 8.2. BECCS: Bioenergy with carbon capture and storage 171
- 8.3. Biochar 174
- 8.4. Energy Efficiency for Buildings 178
- 8.5. DAC (Direct Air Capture) 179

8.6.	Electric airplanes	181
8.7.	Methane measure and VCM satellite monitoring	183
8.8.	MMRV (Measurement, Monitoring, Reporting, and Validation) of Voluntary Carbon Credits	185
8.9.	Novel modeling for hurricane, tornado, and wildfire impacts	187
8.10.	Ocean-based CDR	189
8.11.	Transition and physical risk E2E model providers for financial institutions	191
8.12.	VCM E2E risk transfer solutions	193
8.13.	VCM exchanges	195
8.14.	VCM insurance products	196
8.15.	Workforce retraining companies	198
8.16.	Climate litigation	200
8.17.	Vertical farming	203

CHAPTER NINE
OVERVIEW OF PRIMARILY PUBLIC STRATEGY FUND INVESTMENT THESES — 207

9.1.	Which opportunities are primarily Public Strategy Fund opportunities?	208
9.2.	Aluminum mines and smelters	210
9.3.	Copper mines	213
9.4.	Electric transportation (cars/trucks/trains/motorcycles)	215
9.5.	Insurance companies with novel modeling approaches for coastal areas	217
9.6.	Nuclear reactor manufacturers	219
9.7.	Critical mineral mines	221
9.8.	Uranium mines: Prospecting and processing	223
9.9.	HVAC manufacturers and installers	224
9.10.	Sustainable steel	226
9.11.	Emissions-free shipping	228

CONTENTS

CHAPTER TEN
OVERVIEW OF PRIMARILY INFRASTRUCTURE STRATEGY FUND
INVESTMENT THESES — 231

- 10.1. Which opportunities are primarily Infrastructure Strategy Fund opportunities? — 232
- 10.2. CCUS (Carbon Capture, Utilization, and Storage) infrastructure — 235
- 10.3. Electric grid infrastructure upgrade — 237
- 10.4. Energy storage — 239
- 10.5. Geothermal energy generation companies — 242
- 10.6. Hydroelectric power generation companies — 243
- 10.7. Sustainable Aviation Fuel — 245
- 10.8. Biofuels and waste to energy — 247
- 10.9. Tidal power generation companies — 249
- 10.10. Water — 251
- 10.11. Wind and solar power generation companies — 253
- 10.12. Sustainable concrete — 256
- 10.13. Ocean Thermal Energy Conversion (OTEC) — 258
- 10.14. Coastal tidal protection — 261

CHAPTER ELEVEN
OVERVIEW OF PRIMARILY CLIMATE ALTERNATIVES
(PHYSICAL ASSETS PLAYS) INVESTMENT THESES — 265

- 11.1. Which opportunities are primarily Climate Alternatives/Physical Assets Fund opportunities? — 266
- 11.2. Abandoned subterranean mines — 268
- 11.3. Forest land – plantation forest — 271
- 11.4. Forest land – primary forest — 273
- 11.5. Northern Latitudes Farmland — 275
- 11.6. Paper recycling facilities — 277
- 11.7. Real estate in climate sanctuary cities — 279

CHAPTER TWELVE
SAMPLE DEEP DIVE: GEOTHERMAL ENERGY — 283
- 12.1. Which is the climate driver for geothermal energy? — 283
- 12.2. Which funds do geothermal energy fall under? — 284
- 12.3. What is the TRL for geothermal? — 284
- 12.4. Determine the investment horizon for geothermal — 285
- 12.5. What is the investment maturity for geothermal? — 285
- 12.6. How crowded is geothermal? — 285
- 12.7. What is the root problem for geothermal? — 286
- 12.8. What does the root problem for geothermal cause? — 286
- 12.9. What needs to happen to fix the root problem for geothermal? — 288
- 12.10. How soon does the fix need to happen for geothermal? — 293
- 12.11. What is the investment opportunity for geothermal? — 295
- 12.12. What is the benefit from investing in geothermal? — 296
- 12.13. What is the market size for geothermal? — 296
- 12.14. What is the long-term vision for geothermal investments? — 302
- 12.15. What is the trigger for geothermal investments, and has it already occurred? — 303
- 12.16. Which new companies have been identified in early stages for geothermal (VC targets)? — 303
- 12.17. Which new companies have been identified as emerging players for geothermal (PE targets)? — 305
- 12.18. Which established players exist in geothermal (private credit targets)? — 306

CHAPTER THIRTEEN
SAMPLE DEEP DIVE: NORTHERN LATITUDES FARMLAND — 309
- 13.1. What is Northern Latitudes Farmland? — 309
- 13.2. Which is the climate driver for Northern Latitudes Farmland? — 310
- 13.3. Which funds do Northern Latitudes Farmland fall under? — 310

CONTENTS

13.4.	What is the TRL for Northern Latitudes Farmland?	311
13.5.	Determine the investment horizon for Northern Latitudes Farmland	311
13.6.	What is the investment maturity for Northern Latitudes Farmland?	312
13.7.	How crowded is Northern Latitudes Farmland?	317
13.8.	What is the root problem for Northern Latitudes Farmland?	318
13.9.	What does the root problem for Northern Latitudes Farmland cause?	318
13.10.	What needs to happen to fix the root problem for Northern Latitudes Farmland?	319
13.11.	How soon does the fix need to happen for Northern Latitudes Farmland?	320
13.12.	What is the investment opportunity for Northern Latitudes Farmland?	320
13.13.	What is the benefit from investing in Northern Latitudes Farmland?	320
13.14.	What is the market size for Northern Latitudes Farmland?	348
13.15.	What is the long-term vision for Northern Latitudes Farmland Investments?	354
13.16.	What is the trigger for Northern Latitudes Farmland investments, and has it already occurred?	355
13.17.	Which geographies have been identified for Northern Latitudes Farmland?	356

CHAPTER FOURTEEN
SAMPLE DEEP DIVE: ENERGY EFFICIENCY FOR BUILDINGS 359

14.1.	Which is the climate driver for Energy Efficiency for Buildings?	359
14.2.	Which funds do Energy Efficiency for Buildings Energy fall under?	360
14.3.	What is the TRL for Energy Efficiency for Buildings?	360

14.4.	Determine the investment horizon for Energy Efficiency for Buildings	361
14.5.	What is the investment maturity for Energy Efficiency for Buildings?	361
14.6.	How crowded is Energy Efficiency for Buildings?	361
14.7.	What is the root problem for Energy Efficiency for Buildings?	362
14.8.	What does the root problem for Energy Efficiency for Buildings cause?	362
14.9.	What needs to happen to fix the root problem for Energy Efficiency for Buildings?	363
14.10.	How soon does the fix need to happen for Energy Efficiency for Buildings?	364
14.11.	What is the investment opportunity for Energy Efficiency for Buildings?	369
14.12.	What is the benefit from investing in Energy Efficiency for Buildings?	373
14.13.	What is the market size for Energy Efficiency for Buildings?	373
14.14.	What is the long-term vision for Energy Efficiency for Buildings Investments?	383
14.15.	What is the trigger for Energy Efficiency for Buildings investments, and has it already occurred?	383
14.16.	Which new companies have been identified in early stages for Energy Efficiency for Buildings (VC targets)?	384
14.17.	Which emerging companies have been identified as emerging players for Energy Efficiency for Buildings (PE targets)?	395
14.18.	Which established players exist in Energy Efficiency for Buildings (private credit targets)?	402

INDEX	405

LIST OF FIGURES AND TABLES

Figures

Figure 1.1	The average temperature on land: Global 1750–2020.	2
Figure 1.2	Compilation of CO_2 records and EPICA Dome C temperature anomaly over the past 800,000 yr.	4
Figure 1.3	Atmospheric CO_2 concentration (ca) through time.	6
Figure 1.4	Global CO_2 concentrations in the last 800,000 years.	7
Figure 1.5	Monthly mean CO_2 concentration at Mauna Loa observatory, 1958–2021.	8
Figure 1.6	Aggregate view of SSP pathways.	19
Figure 1.7	SSPs by mitigation and adaptation challenge levels.	23
Figure 1.8	Changes in power production by climate change scenario.	25
Figure 2.1	A visualization of the Spherical Cow Critique.	34
Figure 2.2	Workflow example of an optimization-based IAM.	42
Figure 2.3	DICE Model projections on 2016 data.	44
Figure 2.4	Generalized End-to-End climate modeling flowchart.	45
Figure 2.5	Generalized Climate Premium Evaluation Model flowchart.	46
Figure 2.6	ECS values from the 40 CMIP6 models available as of May 2020 where necessary experiments to calculate ECS (using the Gregory method) are currently available.	56

LIST OF FIGURES AND TABLES

Figure 2.7	Warming influence of greenhouse gases, 1980–2022.	60
Figure 2.8	Climate litigation cases in the United States by year, 2004–2022.	63
Figure 3.1	The trifecta of challenges with climate modeling.	72
Figure 4.1	Idealized views of characteristics of transition finance investing.	80
Figure 4.2	Conceptualizations on static or dynamic allocations.	81
Figure 4.3	Conceptualizations on single or multiple approaches.	82
Figure 4.4	Conceptualizations on factors impacting complexity in transition finance investing.	83
Figure 4.5	The Transition Finance Investment Thesis Identification Process.	85
Figure 4.6	Graphical visualization of principles of positive screening.	89
Figure 4.7	Graphical visualization of principles of thematic investment.	90
Figure 4.8	Graphical visualization of investing in the transition.	91
Figure 4.9	The four types of funds in transition finance.	93
Figure 4.10	Graphical visualization of time horizon considerations for transition finance.	94
Figure 4.11	The 4 × 3 investment matrix of funds and strategies.	96
Figure 5.1	The transition finance investing flowchart.	100
Figure 5.2	Example of energy investment from NGFS Phase IV scenarios.	103
Figure 5.3	Example of solar use and carbon sequestration involving BECCS projections from NGFS Phase IV scenarios.	104
Figure 5.4	Example of comparison for carbon sequestration projections between NGFS scenarios Phase III and Phase IV using REMIND IAM model.	105
Figure 5.5	The model results challenge process.	106
Figure 5.6	The subject matter experts overrides and overlays process.	108
Figure 5.7	The identification of opportunities at driver, theme, and topic level, exemplified for geothermal energy.	109
Figure 5.8	The four climate risk drivers: Acute physical risk, chronic physical risk, transition risk, and climate liability risk.	110

List of Figures and Tables

Figure 5.9	The process for market size identification.	121
Figure 5.10	The nested markets.	122
Figure 5.11	An idealized vision of long-term investment vision identification.	123
Figure 5.12	A conceptualization of the long-lasting effects of trigger events.	125
Figure 5.13	The four funds in transition finance investing.	126
Figure 5.14	The three strategies for transition finance investing.	127
Figure 5.15	The risk pyramid.	128
Figure 5.16	The process of deep diving into investment theses.	129
Figure 5.17	An idealized diversified portfolio.	133
Figure 8.1	Market growth projections for transition finance Growth Fund opportunities, 2024–2032 baseline scenario.	171
Figure 8.2	Representative views of BECCS.	172
Figure 8.3	Schematic cycle for BECCS.	173
Figure 8.4	Representative views of biochar.	175
Figure 8.5	Representative views of Energy Efficiency for Buildings.	178
Figure 8.6	Representative views of Direct Air Capture.	180
Figure 8.7	Representative views of electric airplanes.	181
Figure 8.8	Representative views of methane measure and VCM satellite monitoring.	183
Figure 8.9	Representative views of MMRV of VCM.	185
Figure 8.10	Representative views of novel modeling for hurricane, tornado, and wildfire impacts.	187
Figure 8.11	List of ocean-based CDR with potentials and characteristics.	189
Figure 8.12	Characteristics of transition and physical risk E2E modeling for financial institutions.	191
Figure 8.13	Flowchart for End-to-End Voluntary Carbon Markets risk transfer.	194
Figure 8.14	Representational views of VCM exchanges.	196

LIST OF FIGURES AND TABLES

Figure 8.15	Interconnections for Voluntary Carbon Markets insurance products.	197
Figure 8.16	Notional representations of workforce retraining.	199
Figure 8.17	Notional representations of climate litigation.	201
Figure 8.18	Examples of vertical farming companies.	203
Figure 9.1	Market growth projections for transition finance Public Strategy Fund opportunities, 2024–2032 baseline scenario.	211
Figure 9.2	Representational images for aluminum mining and smelting.	211
Figure 9.3	Representational images for copper mining.	213
Figure 9.4	Representational images for electric transportation.	215
Figure 9.5	Examples of novel modeling approaches for physical risk insurance companies.	218
Figure 9.6	Representational images for nuclear reactor manufacturers.	220
Figure 9.7	Representational images for critical minerals mining.	222
Figure 9.8	Representational images for uranium mining: Prospecting and processing.	223
Figure 9.9	Representational images for HVAC manufacturing and installation.	225
Figure 9.10	Representational images for sustainable steel and examples of companies in the space.	226
Figure 9.11	Examples of companies in the emissions-free shipping space.	228
Figure 10.1	Market growth projections for transition finance Infrastructure Strategy Fund opportunities, 2024–2032 baseline scenario.	235
Figure 10.2	Representational views of CCUS infrastructure.	236
Figure 10.3	Representational views of electric grid infrastructure upgrade.	238
Figure 10.4	Examples of companies in the energy storage space.	239
Figure 10.5	Representational views of geothermal energy.	242
Figure 10.6	Representational views of hydroelectric power generation.	244

List of Figures and Tables

Figure 10.7	Representational views of Sustainable Aviation Fuel.	245
Figure 10.8	Representational views of biofuel and waste to energy.	247
Figure 10.9	Examples of companies in the tidal and wave energy space.	249
Figure 10.10	Representational views of water infrastructure.	252
Figure 10.11	Representational views of wind and solar power generation.	254
Figure 10.12	Examples of companies in the sustainable concrete space.	256
Figure 10.13	Examples of companies in the OTEC space.	258
Figure 10.14	Examples of use cases in the coastal tidal protection space.	261
Figure 11.1	Market growth projections for transition finance Climate Alternatives and Physical Assets Plays Fund opportunities, 2024–2032 baseline scenario.	268
Figure 11.2	Representational views of abandoned subterranean mines.	269
Figure 11.3	Representational views of forest land – plantation forest.	271
Figure 11.4	Representational views of forest land – primary forest.	273
Figure 11.5	Representational views of Northern Latitudes Farmland and changes in US hardiness zones, 1990–2012.	275
Figure 11.6	Representational views of paper recycling facilities.	277
Figure 11.7	Representational views of climate sanctuary cities.	280
Figure 12.1	Descriptive views of geothermal energy applications.	284
Figure 12.2	NGFS Phase IV scenarios.	289
Figure 12.3	Temperature evolution, global CO_2 emissions and shadow carbon price for NGFS Phase V scenarios.	291
Figure 12.4	Growth of geothermal globally and by selected countries, 2000–2022.	292
Figure 12.5	Global utilization and installed capacity for geothermal heating and cooling, 1995–2020.	293
Figure 12.6	Installed capacity for geothermal energy, by region.	294
Figure 12.7	NGFS Phase 4 geothermal energy projections, 2025–2055 averages of 6 IAM models for Net Zero 2050 scenario.	294

LIST OF FIGURES AND TABLES

Figure 12.8	NGFS Phase 4 geothermal energy projections, 2025–2055 averages of 6 IAM models for transition scenario.	295
Figure 12.9	Projected geothermal power market size, 2023–2032.	297
Figure 13.1	Descriptive views of Northern Latitudes Farmland.	310
Figure 13.2	Polar amplification at northern latitudes.	313
Figure 13.3	Changes in plant growth over 1983–2013 in northern latitudes.	315
Figure 13.4	Shifting of hardiness zones in North America - a) Hardiness zones for the US 1971–2000 and projection 2041–2070. b) Global warming and potential northward expansion of wheat mega-environment 6 in North America by 2050.	316
Figure 13.5	Cropland select US states, value per acre (US$) 1996–2024.	324
Figure 13.6	Cropland select US states, value YOY Change % 1996–2024.	324
Figure 13.7	Irrigated cropland select US states, value per acre (US$) 1996–2024.	325
Figure 13.8	Cropland irrigated, select US states, value YOY change % 1996–2024.	326
Figure 13.9	Non-irrigated cropland select US states, value per acre (US$) 1998–2024.	326
Figure 13.10	Non-irrigated cropland, select US states, value YOY change % 1998–2024.	327
Figure 13.11	Pastureland select US states, value per acre (US$) 1998–2024.	328
Figure 13.12	Pastureland, select US states, value YOY Change % 1998–2024.	329
Figure 13.13	Rent-to-value ratio, all cropland, select US states 1996–2024.	330
Figure 13.14	Rent-to-value ratio, irrigated cropland, select US states 1996–2024.	331
Figure 13.15	Rent-to-value ratio, non-irrigated cropland, select US states 1996–2024.	332
Figure 13.16	Rent-to-value ratio, pastureland, select US states 1996–2024.	332
Figure 13.17	Risk-Adjusted Returns, all cropland, selected states 1998–2024.	335

List of Figures and Tables

Figure 13.18	Risk-Adjusted Returns, irrigated cropland, selected states 1998–2024.	337
Figure 13.19	Risk-Adjusted Returns, non-irrigated cropland, selected states 1998–2024.	338
Figure 13.20	Risk-Adjusted Returns, pastureland, selected States 1998–2024.	339
Figure 13.21	Baseline and projections of hardiness zones for the United States in low and high climate-change scenarios.	342
Figure 13.22	Twenty-year trends for farmland in the United States.	349
Figure 13.23	Farmland as percent of land area by county, 2022.	350
Figure 13.24	Distribution of US Farms by size and % of farmland owned.	351
Figure 13.25	1961–2050 Population and arable land per capita data (and projections).	353
Figure 13.26	NASA GISS temperature trend, 2000–2009.	356
Figure 14.1	Descriptive views of Energy Efficiency for Buildings.	360
Figure 14.2	French DPE and GES certification example.	363
Figure 14.3	BEMS market projection, 2022–2032, by end user.	374
Figure 14.4	BEMS market by geography, 2022.	376
Figure 14.5	Global building thermal insulation market, 2022, share by end user.	377
Figure 14.6	US BTI market projections, 2020–2030.	378
Figure 14.7	Global BTI market projections, 2020–2030, largest and fastest growing markets.	378
Figure 14.8	Projections for global HVAC market, 2024–2032.	380
Figure 14.9	Projections for North America HVAC market, 2024–2032.	381
Figure 14.10	2023 Global segmentation of HVAC market by region.	382

Tables

Table 1.1	Examples of climate risks from the TCFD report.	14
Table 1.2	SSPs and relative narratives.	20

LIST OF FIGURES AND TABLES

Table 2.1	Types of models needed for each step of the modeling process, recommended approach, and rationale for the recommendation.	47
Table 5.1	Technology Readiness Levels as defined by the EU.	112
Table 5.2	Maturity for investment as used for transition finance investing opportunity grading.	114
Table 5.3	Investment crowdedness as used for transition finance investing opportunity grading.	115
Table 5.4	Root problem examples for geothermal, HVAC manufacturers and installers, and Northern Latitudes Farmland.	116
Table 5.5	Root problem effect examples for geothermal, HVAC manufacturers and installers, and Northern Latitudes Farmland.	117
Table 5.6	Fix examples for geothermal, HVAC manufacturers and installers, and Northern Latitudes Farmland.	118
Table 5.7	Fix timing examples for geothermal, HVAC manufacturers and installers, and Northern Latitudes Farmland.	119
Table 5.8	Investment opportunity definition examples for geothermal, HVAC manufacturers and installers, and Northern Latitudes Farmland.	120
Table 5.9	Investment benefit examples for geothermal, HVAC manufacturers and installers, and Northern Latitudes Farmland.	121
Table 5.10	Deep dive source examples for geothermal.	130
Table 7.1	Hydrogen versus gasoline energy content and energy density.	142
Table 8.1	List of Growth Fund investment theses.	168
Table 8.2	Market projections for baseline scenario 2024–2032, for Growth Fund opportunities and comparison to aggregate values for all funds.	170

List of Figures and Tables

Table 9.1	Primarily Public Strategy Fund opportunities.	209
Table 9.2	Market projections for baseline scenario 2024–2032, for Public Strategy Fund opportunities and comparison to aggregate values for all funds.	210
Table 10.1	Primarily Infrastructure Strategy Fund Opportunities.	233
Table 10.2	Market projections for baseline scenario 2024–2032 for Infrastructure Strategy Fund opportunities and comparison to aggregate values for all funds.	234
Table 11.1	Primarily Climate Alternatives and Physical Assets Strategy Fund opportunities.	267
Table 11.2	Market projections for Climate Alternatives and Physical Assets Plays Fund opportunities, baseline scenario 2024–2032, and comparison to aggregate values for all funds.	267
Table 13.1	Reference return rates, 1996–2024.	333
Table 13.2	Risk-Adjusted Returns: All cropland and selected benchmarks, 1998–2024.	336
Table 13.3	Risk-Adjusted Returns: Irrigated cropland and selected benchmarks, 1998–2024.	336
Table 13.4	Risk-Adjusted Returns: Non-irrigated cropland and selected benchmarks, 1998–2024.	338
Table 13.5	Risk-Adjusted Returns: Pastureland and selected benchmarks, 1998–2024.	340
Table 13.6	Value per acre and increase in value by average hardiness zone at state level.	343
Table 13.7	Projected increases in land value due to hardiness zone improvements, 2023–2040.	344
Table 13.8	Estimated CAGR due to projected shifts in hardiness zones, 2024–2040 for selected states within the NLF investment opportunity, based on RCP 4.5.	345

LIST OF FIGURES AND TABLES

Table 13.9	Aggregate effect of 1998–2024 average RAR for farmland coupled with projected impact of shift in hardiness zones for selected NLF states in the United States.	346
Table 13.10	Farms and farmland key metrics and changes, 2017–2022.	349
Table 13.11	Land use for farmland in the United States, 2022.	350
Table 13.12	Farm Specialization in the United States in 2022, by land usage.	351
Table 13.13	Land ownership by percentage of farms and land.	352
Table 14.1	Select list of Energy Efficiency for Buildings laws by countries/regions.	365
Table 14.2	Examples of Energy Efficiency for Buildings (EEB) opportunities.	370
Table 14.3	Early-stage players in the Energy Efficiency for Buildings space.	384
Table 14.4	Emerging players in the Energy Efficiency for Buildings space.	395
Table 14.5	Established players in the Energy Efficiency for Buildings space.	403

CHAPTER ONE

AN INTRODUCTION TO TRANSITION FINANCE

How transitioning from an oil-based economy to a net-zero economy represents the third industrial revolution

1.1 INTRODUCTION ON THE PRINCIPLES OF ANTHROPOGENIC CLIMATE CHANGE[1]

The unabated emissions of greenhouse gases (GHG) in the atmosphere since the industrial revolution in the late 1700s has led to an increase in temperature, compared to the global average of around 2°C since pre-industrial times.

---

[1] This section borrows heavily from *Quantitative Methods for ESG Finance*, 1st edition. Wiley. (December 1, 2022).

The observation of the atmospheric temperatures on earth, which has been logged directly at meteorological stations around the world, with reliable and sufficiently granular data starting in the early 19th century (the oldest series of temperature measurements on record is the Central England temperature data series, which starts in 1659 and can be freely downloaded at https://www.metoffice.gov.uk/hadobs/hadcet/), has shown a marked and steady increase of approximately 1.1 °C since 1880 to 2020. Note that 1880 was already ~ 1.0 °C warmer than 1760 (i.e., before the industrial revolution).

The increase in temperature might seem, in and of itself, modest and protracted over a relatively (by human standards) long period of time. This proves, however, not to be the case, if we actually look at the shape of the average temperature curves, as shown in Figure 1.1, taken from the Berkley Earth project, as we rapidly notice how the entirety of the

Figure 1.1 The average temperature on land: Global 1750–2020.
Source: Berkeley Earth/ https://berkeleyearth.org/temperature-region/global-land / last accessed February 18, 2025.

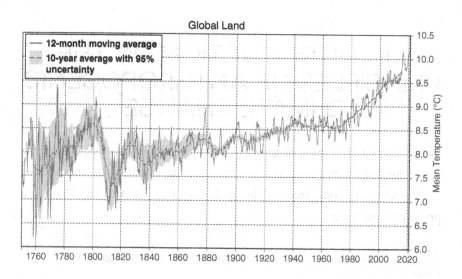

temperature increase has occurred between 1980 (when the temperature was, effectively, very similar to the late 1700s) and 2021, and that the slope of this increase is distinctly different from previous changes in the record.

Additionally, it is important to notice how this is an *average temperature for all land-based meteorological stations*, and the local changes are larger in scope (and, as the earth is in a meta-stable equilibrium, changes in base conditions of seemingly small magnitude can catalyze much larger chains of events via feedback and feed-forward mechanisms, which are typical of complex, chaotic systems).

The data, at this point, no longer allows for viable alternative hypotheses and conjectures to deny the measured facts that the planet has indeed entered an accelerated warming stage, and the question shifts to the causes behind it and what action, if any, can, and should, be taken to mitigate or reverse this trend.

For the purposes of this book, we have chosen to source some of our data from the Global Change Data Lab, a nonprofit organization which publishes *Our World in Data* (www.ourworldindata.org), a freely accessible online resource focused on increasing the use of data and evidence to make progress against the world's largest problems.

We will intentionally keep this discussion very brief, so we can focus more directly on the financial consequences of this phenomenon and how to apply the concepts that we shall present to investing in transition finance.

As a general rule of thumb, the atmospheric concentration of CO_2 is directly correlated with the average global temperature, with increasing concentrations correlating to increases in temperatures and decreasing concentrations correlating to decreases in temperatures, as can be seen in the 800,000-year record from Antarctic ice cores, shown in Figure 1.2.

Figure 1.2 Compilation of CO_2 records and EPICA Dome C temperature anomaly over the past 800,000 yr.

Source: Lüthi, D. et al. 2008 - High-resolution carbon dioxide concentration record 650,000-800,000 years before present, 453 DO - 10.1038/nature0694 / Springer Nature Limited.

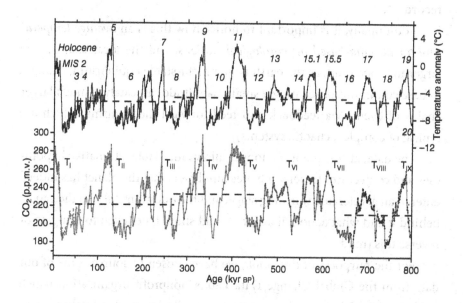

The Historical Record of Atmospheric CO_2

Atmospheric CO_2 has varied with cycles of different periodicity over the last 600 million years (for which there is accurately reconstructed data), through the effects of multiple naturally occurring cycles and processes. As a data point, the highest estimated value on record (for life-bearing epochs) for CO_2 in the atmosphere is ~5,000 ppm during the Cambrian period (~500 million years ago), and the lowest is ~170 ppm during the Pleistocene glaciation (approximately 2 million years ago). It is estimated by experimental results that a level of atmospheric CO_2 of around 150 ppm or lower would no longer allow plant life to survive, as there would not be enough carbon in the air to sustain photosynthesis and plants would go dormant and start dying out rapidly.[2]

There are different ways to measure past atmospheric CO_2 levels. The easiest method is direct measurement of air bubbles in Antarctic ice, available for about 800,000 years. The longest method is alkenone–pCO_2, using algal biomarker carbon isotopes. Other consistent techniques include stomatal indices, paleosol carbonate compositions, and boron isotopes in foraminifera.

By looking at the data from all the various sources, as summarized in Figure 1.3, we can see how the CO_2 concentration in the atmosphere has changed dramatically over time, as was originally pointed out by in the 19th century by John Ball in his *Proceedings of the Royal Geographical Society and Monthly Record of Geography*,[3] where he noted how "all the coal in the Carboniferous deposits that were being mined at the time, must have been extracted from the atmosphere."

Figure 1.3 (from Peter J. Franks et al. in "Sensitivity of plants to changing atmospheric CO_2 concentration: from the geological past to the next century")[4] summarizes in a single, easy to comprehend, graph the record of the last 600 million years, with three separate detailed windows for the last 800,000 years, last 2,000 years, and last 100 years.

Please note how the graph shows the emergence of major plant adaptations over geological time (appearance of embryophytes, or land plants, evolution of stomata, or leaf pores, emergence of angiosperms, or flowering plants, and arrival of grasses).

---

[2] Gerhart, L. and Ward, J. (2010). Plant responses to low [CO_2] of the past. *New Phytologist*, 188(3), pp. 674–695; and Tolbert, N., Benker, C., and Beck, E. (1995). The oxygen and carbon dioxide compensation points of C3 plants: possible role in regulating atmospheric oxygen. *Proceedings of the National Academy of Sciences*, 92(24), pp.11230–11233.

[3] Ball, John. *Proceedings of the Royal Geographical Society and Monthly Record of Geography*, Vol. 1, No. 9, Sep., 1879, pp. 564–589. Wiley.

[4] Franks, Peter J., et al. (2013). Sensitivity of plants to changing atmospheric CO_2 concentration: from the geological past to the next century. *New Phytologist*. 25 January 2013. Wiley. https://doi.org/10.1111/nph.12104

PRINCIPLES OF TRANSITION FINANCE INVESTING

Figure 1.3 Atmospheric CO₂ concentration (ca) through time.

Source: Clarke et al., 2011, Edwards et al., 1998, Strömberg, 2011.

Note: (a) From 560 to 10 million yr ago simulated by the GEOCARBSULF model (Berner, 2008; parameterised for basalt/granite weatherability = 2, NV = 0.015, fB0 = 5) connecting discrete values (open squares) with straight lines. Also indicated are proposed timings of appearances of embryophytes and angiosperms (815–568 and 240–175 million yr ago, respectively; Clarke et al., 2011), stomata (Edwards et al., 1998), grasses (Strömberg, 2011) and C4 plants (Sage et al., 2012). (b) High-resolution atmospheric CO₂ concentration values from Antarctic ice cores as compiled by Luthi et al. (2008) for the period 800,000–1000 yr ago and from the DSS Antarctic ice core for the period 1006–1954 C.E. (Etheridge et al., 1996). That ice core record is extended with annual mean measured *in situ* values at the Mauna Loa Observatory (1959–1979; Tans & Keeling, 2012) and globally averaged marine surface annual mean measurement data (1980–2011; Conway & Tans, 2012). Discrete values are connected with straight lines. The arrow indicates the lowest CO₂ concentration reported from an ice core measurement (171.6 ppm). (c) Measured values since year 1 C.E. as given in (b) but with ice core values shown as discrete points and with the Mauna Loa and global marine surface time series jointly labeled "NOAA." The measured time series is continued (extrapolated) with the four "representative concentration pathways" (RCPs) scenarios RCP2.6, RCP4.5, RCP6.0 and RCP8.5 (Moss et al., 2010), for the period 2015–2100 C.E. (d) Values for the period 1900–2100 C.E. from (c), but at greater resolution.

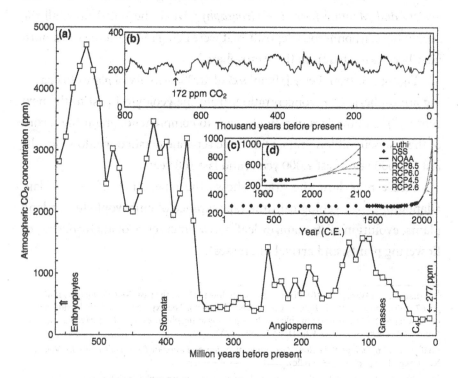

An Introduction to Transition Finance

The amplitude of the fluctuations has declined significantly since the Carboniferous period (~360 to ~300 million years ago) to which Ball referred to in his paper, due in part to the large depositions of fossil fuels, with fluctuations around the 1,000 ppm level during the Cretaceous period (~100 million years ago) and then decreasing constantly through the entire Cenozoic era (66 million years ago to today). As we have seen in previous data, for the last several million years, the concentration has been fluctuating periodically between a minimum recorded level of 172 and ~300 ppm, with a series of nine glacial periods where it remained steady at the lowest values for tens of thousands of years at a time.

If we look at the more granular data, taken from the direct measurement of the trapped atmosphere in the ice core samples from Antarctica, we can zoom into the last 800,000 years, as shown in Figure 1.4, within the oscillating equilibrium period (Milankovitch cycles), and clearly see

Figure 1.4 Global CO$_2$ concentrations in the last 800,000 years.
Source: Adapted from NOAAA Antarctic Ice core samples.

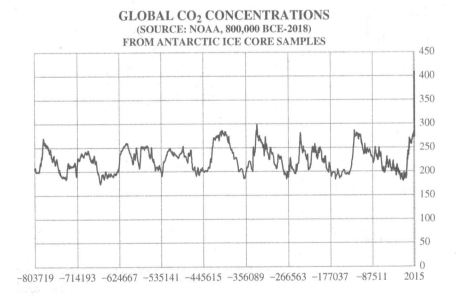

the cyclical oscillation between ~170 and ~280 ppm, which is tied to the ice age cycles, and the very recent spike up to 400+ which starts with the industrial revolution in the 1700s (which happened to coincide with a peak in the ice age cycle).

If we look at a much shorter timescale, for example at the data measured at the Mauna Loa observatory between 1958 and 2021, as shown in Figure 1.5, we can see, besides the seasonal variation pattern that is

Figure 1.5 Monthly mean CO$_2$ concentration at Mauna Loa observatory, 1958–2021.

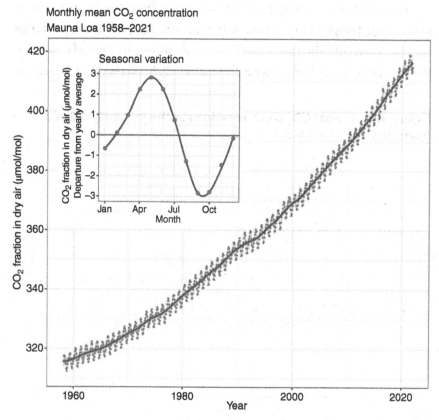

Data: Dr. Pieter Tans, NOAA/ESRL (https://gml.noaa.gov/ccgg/trends/) and Dr. Ralph Keeling, Scripps Institution of Oceanography (https://scrippsco2.ucsd.edu/). Accessed 2021-12-16
https://w.wiki/4ZWn

most evident and provides a sigmoidal change of ± 3% over the yearly average, a clear and monotone increase of approximately 100 ppm (or roughly 1/3 of the starting level) in atmospheric CO_2 concentration over the last 60 years.

1.2 FUTURE EVOLUTION OF CO_2 LEVELS AND GLOBAL TEMPERATURE

As much as it is clear that CO_2 levels and global thermal anomalies are steadily rising, the situation becomes harder to assess once we pose the question of CO_2 and temperature in a future tense, not in terms "shall they continue to rise" (to which the answer, at least in the short term, is an obvious yes), but "which profile of rising will they follow?" and, more poignantly, "what impact can current and future policy have on GHG and temperature levels in the decades and centuries to come?"

The answer to both of these questions is strongly predicated on a series of assumptions that can be modeled (how much fossil fuel will be burned in the coming years?, how much more the world will rely on renewable energy sources?, how more efficient processes will become?, which policies will be enacted and how successful governments worldwide will be at enforcing them?, etc.) and several others that either cannot yet be modeled accurately or are, at the moment, highly speculative or present very large margins of error in the current models (for example, the amount, speed and feed-forward effect of release of methane and CO_2 trapped in arctic permafrost that is undergoing accelerated thawing).[5]

---

[5] https://www.thearcticinstitute.org/permafrost-thaw-warming-world-arctic-institute-permafrost-series-fall-winter-2020

As a result, there are multiple scenarios that are being proposed, which predict, based on a series of assumptions that we shall look at later in this chapter, global temperature rises between 1.3 °C and 5.1 °C, on average, by the year 2100.

While this data alone is worthy of concern, as investors, we must be able to identify, and quantify, what risks such scenarios would bring to the financial and economic systems, to allow ourselves a way to better understand the differential impact that these climate-related risks might have on one corporation or entity versus another. In order for us to do so, we first require a common taxonomy of climate-related risks, that we shall take from the "Recommendations of the Task Force on Climate-Related Financial Disclosures,"[6] which, albeit not focused specifically on financial risks, provides very good classification for financial and nonfinancial entities alike.

Physical Risks Versus Transition Risks. All climate-related risks are divided in two categories, "physical" risks and "transition" risks, based on the nature of their action.

Physical Risks. These are risks resulting by direct action due to changes in climate patterns, which can be immediate and event-driven, in which case they are characterized as "acute risk" or long-term climate-pattern shift driven, in which case they are characterized as "chronic risk." The way physical risks manifest themselves is typically through direct action on assets owned by organizations, such as damage to facilities and infrastructure, or by indirect action, such as impact on supply chains. In a similar fashion, physical risks can also disrupt an organization's financial performance by changing the underlying conditions that are necessary for it to be a viable business, for example by reducing or changing the availability and quality of water supply, reducing the availability of

---

[6] https://assets.bbhub.io/company/sites/60/2020/10/FINAL-2017-TCFD-Report-11052018.pdf

food supplies for workforce needs and/or extreme temperature events affecting premises, storage facilities, operations, supply chains, transport needs, and employee safety. Specifically:

Acute Physical Risk. Examples of acute physical risks include increased severity of extreme weather events, such as cyclones, tornadoes, hurricanes, or floods, as well as heat/cold waves and seasonal drought,

Chronic Physical Risk. Examples of chronic physical risks are, for example, protracted higher temperatures leading to sea level rise, seasonal pattern shifts making fertile areas turn into deserts, winter heating of skiing resorts which results in temperatures too high to allow snow to persist on the ground, changes in ocean currents/temperature disrupting fisheries, or chronic heat waves leading to crop failures.

Transition Risks. These are risks resulting from the requirements due to the transition from present-day, carbon-intensive practices, to the end-state of a lower-carbon economy. The types of risks that are covered by this category include extensive policy, legal, technology, and market changes that might occur as a response to, and to mitigate the effects of, climate change.

Depending on what these specific risks are, how fast they materialize and make their effects felt, and what they focus on, these transition risks may pose different levels of financial and reputational threat to organizations. A few examples of transition risks that are relevant to the Transition Finance Investor are the following:

Market Risk. The ways in which climate change can, and will, affect the global markets are varied, complex, and hard to predict. These include, beyond any doubt, the appearance of shifts in supply and demand for certain commodities, products, and services, as the climate changes and old patterns disappear while new ones emerge. It is expected that risks and opportunities that are climate-related will rapidly increase over time, as we shall see in more detail in later portions of this book.

Policy Risk. The regulatory environment regarding climate change is in a state of constant flux, as policies and laws continue to evolve at a rapid pace. The objectives of these policies are generally of two kinds, actions which attempt to reduce the adverse effects of climate change (for example by limiting the amount of GHG emissions) and actions which seek to foster adaptation to impending changes in climate patterns in different countries and jurisdictions. A few examples of the first category include carbon-pricing mechanisms (aimed to reduce GHG emissions); incentives to shifts in energy sources toward renewable energy/lower emission sources; imposition of stringent energy efficiency standards for construction of new buildings, introduction of laws, rules, and regulations to improve efficiency in water usage; and promotion of sustainable land-usage practices. The risks that are associated with policy risks, and the financial impact that they can have on corporations, are typically highly dependent on the nature of the policy measures that are implemented and the timing of the implementation (i.e., major change with fast implementation will have much higher cost that minor change with slow implementation, as is intuitive).

Litigation Risk. This category of risk covers litigation and legal risks that are linked to climate-related issues. In recent years there has been an increasing trend in climate and environmental related litigation claims against corporations, having been brought forward by property owners, municipalities, states, insurers, shareholders, and public interest organizations (NGOs). Often these claims have been based on failure of corporations to mitigate impacts of climate change, adapt to climate change, and/or fully disclose materially relevant financial risks related to climate/environmental risks to shareholders and the general public. Given the expectation of continued, and accelerated, climate change in the years to come, the nature, size, and quantity of these claims is very likely to increase significantly in the near future.

Technology Risk. This category of risk covers technological innovation requirements that will be needed by corporations to adapt to a lower-carbon, more energy-efficient economic system than the one in which they currently operate. These improvements and innovations will come at a cost and are likely to have significant impacts on how organizations operate and turn profits. As an example of technology risk, we can see how the development and use of emerging technologies such as renewable energy sources will require a significant investment in batteries and other energy storage infrastructure, improvements in energy efficiency, and potentially carbon capture and storage, all of which will affect the competitiveness and bottom line of many organizations, by adding to production and distribution costs, and impacting the demand for their products and services by the customers. Very often, as was the case with the emergence of the automobile which replaced the horse and buggy industry, the new technologies will displace older ones and disrupt some portions of the incumbent economic systems, leading to the emergence of winners and losers from this process of "creative destruction." While it is clear that these transitions will have to occur, the timing of the development of the technologies required, and their fielding, is still unclear, and, therefore, adds to the uncertainty, exacerbating the potential impact of this type of risk on corporations.

Reputation Risk. Since climate change is a very visible, and high priority, topic in most countries around the world, many corporations, especially those that are publicly traded, will be under tight scrutiny from public opinion on how they manage the challenges and requirements that derive from it. As a result, there is significant reputational risk if a corporation is perceived, by customers or the general public, as being lax in the way it handles the climate change transition and/or too slow/uncommitted to transition to a lower-carbon economy.

Table 1.1, taken from the report from the Task Force on Climate-Related Financial Disclosures (TCFD), provides some more detailed examples of physical risks and transition risks.

Table 1.1 Examples of climate risks from the TCFD report.

Type	Climate-Related Risks	Potential Financial Impacts
Transition Risks	**Policy and Legal**	
	• Increased pricing of GHG emissions	• Increased operating costs (e.g., higher compliance costs, increased insurance premiums)
	• Enhanced emissions-reporting obligations	• Write-offs, asset impairment, and early retirement of existing assets due to policy changes
	• Mandates on and regulation of existing products and services	• Increased costs and/or reduced demand for products and services resulting from fines and judgments
	• Exposure to litigation	
	Technology	
	• Substitution of existing products and services with lower emissions options	• Write-offs and early retirement of existing assets
	• Unsuccessful investment in new technologies	• Reduced demand for products and services
	• Costs to transition to lower emissions technology	• Research and development (R&D) expenditures in new and alternative technologies
		• Capital investments in technology development
		• Costs to adopt/deploy new practices and processes
	Market	
	• Changing customer behavior	• Reduced demand for goods and services due to shift in consumer preferences
	• Uncertainty in market signals	• Increased production costs due to changing input prices (e.g., energy, water) and output requirements (e.g., waste treatment)

Type	Climate-Related Risks	Potential Financial Impacts
	• Increased cost of raw materials	• Abrupt and unexpected shifts in energy costs
		• Change in revenue mix and sources, resulting in decreased revenues
		• Re-pricing of assets (e.g., fossil fuel reserves, land valuations, securities valuations)
	Reputation	
	• Shifts in consumer preferences	• Reduced revenue from decreased demand for goods/services
	• Stigmatization of sector	• Reduced revenue from decreased production capacity (e.g., delayed planning approvals, supply chain interruptions)
	• Increased stakeholder concern or negative stakeholder feedback	• Reduced revenue from negative impacts on workforce management and planning (e.g., employee attraction and retention)
		• Reduction in capital availability
	Acute	• Reduced revenue from decreased production capacity (e.g., transport difficulties, supply chain interruptions)
	• Increased severity of extreme weather events such as cyclones and floods	• Reduced revenue and higher costs from negative impacts on workforce (e.g., health, safety, absenteeism)

(Continued)

Table 1.1 (Continued)

Type	Climate-Related Risks	Potential Financial Impacts
Physical Risks	Chronic	• Write-offs and early retirement of existing assets (e.g., damage to property and assets in "high-risk" locations)
	• Changes in precipitation patterns and extreme variability in weather patterns	• Increased operating costs (e.g., inadequate water supply for hydroelectric plants or to cool nuclear and fossil fuel plants)
	• Rising mean temperatures	• Increased capital costs (e.g., damage to facilities)
	• Rising sea levels	• Reduced revenues from lower sales/output
		• Increased insurance premiums and potential for reduced availability of insurance on assets in "high-risk" locations

SOURCE: Adapted from https://www.tcfdhub.org/risk-management/.

If we look at the published works from the Bank of England (BoE) we see how Mark Carney, the former governor of the bank, classified the risks slightly differently in his 2018 speech, as "three channels through which climate risk affects financial stability":

- **Physical risks** that arise from the increased frequency and severity of climate- and weather-related events that damage property and disrupt trade;
- **Liability risks** stemming from parties who have suffered loss from the effects of climate change seeking compensation from those they hold responsible; and
- **Transition risks** that can arise through a sudden and disorderly adjustment to a low carbon economy. Independently of whether we consider liability risks as part of transition risks or as their own self-standing category, the transition risks for markets and financial

entities are a major driver for transition finance. We shall also define *carbon risk* as the risk of financial losses resulting from GHG emissions (generally as a result of any one, or combination of more than one, channels identified by Carney previously).

Another important definition that we have to bring into the picture at this moment is that of *stranded assets*. These are a risk category, which is defined as "assets that have suffered from unanticipated or premature write-downs, devaluations or conversion to liabilities."

Amongst the most significant environment-related drivers that can result in stranded assets we can list are:

- **Direct environmental drivers** (climate change, ecosystem degradation, changes in marine currents/temperatures, droughts, etc.)
- **Drivers that derive from changes to resources** either via scarcity or modification of equilibria (e.g., shale-gas abundance, phosphate scarcity)
- **Policy and regulatory drivers** (new laws, carbon pricing, air pollution standards, etc.)
- **Changing costs for renewable energies** (reducing costs for solar, Eolic, electric vehicles, etc.)
- **Social/behavioral drivers** (divestment campaigns from fossil fuels, changes in consumer habits and behaviors, increased demand for sustainable products, etc.)
- **Litigation drivers** (GHG liabilities) and changing interpretations of corporate statutory duties (e.g., fiduciary duties, disclosure requirements, social responsibilities, etc.)

As a typical example of stranded assets risk due to drivers in this list, we can look at the case of large underground deposits of fossil fuels, which are currently on the balance sheets of oil and gas companies, as untapped assets. These deposits might have to remain underground, if their extraction becomes uneconomical or unpalatable to shareholders in the future (whether due to direct regulation or a shift in demand for these fuels), and thus have to be written down on the balance sheet.

Projected Scenarios for CO_2 and Temperature for the Remainder of the Century

As we have seen earlier on in this chapter, there are several different assumptions used to calibrate the models that provide the possible pathways for CO_2 and temperature for the next 80 years.

Most of these assumptions, as well as the models and the science behind them, fall under the mandate of the IPCC[7] (Intergovernmental Panel on Climate Change), which is a United Nations body for assessing the science related to climate change, and is one of the international organizations most relevant to climate change analysis. The IPCC was created to provide policymakers with regular scientific assessments on climate change, its implications, and potential future risks, as well as to put forward adaptation and mitigation options.

Using a large number of parallel climate models, the IPCC gathered a working group to project RCPs (Representative Concentration Pathways) to describe several different GHG emissions trajectories, and consequent average surface temperatures, which could take place over the next 80 years.

The working group resulted in a projection of five separate pathways, shown in Figure 1.6, spanning a relatively broad range of outcomes between 2020 and 2100, all of which were purposefully published without the inclusion of socioeconomic narratives (as these were beyond the scope of the panel).

---

[7] https://www.ipcc.ch

Figure 1.6 Aggregate view of SSP pathways.
Source: Adapted from https://www.carbonbrief.org.

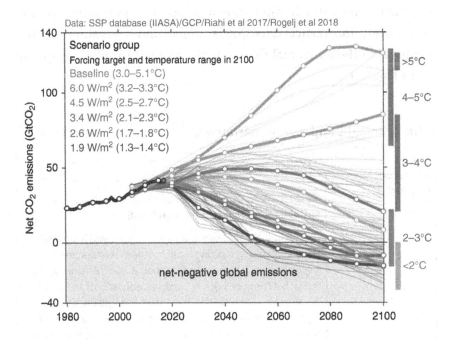

A parallel and complementary IPCC effort, called SSPs (Shared Socioeconomic Pathways), analyzed five different ways in which the world might evolve in the absence of shared climate policies, as well as how different levels of climate change mitigation results might be achieved if the mitigation targets from the RCPs were to be combined with the SSPs (see Table 1.2). The SSPs have specific narratives that describe which socioeconomic trends and policies are required for the pathway to occur, and how these would affect future societies. The goal of these different narratives is to cover the range of plausible, if not all the possible, future outcomes (Riahi et al., 2017).[8]

---

[8] Riahi, K., Van Vuuren, D., Kriegler, E., et al. (2017). The Shared Socioeconomic Pathways and Their Energy, Land Use, and Greenhouse Gas Emissions Implications: An Overview. *Global Environmental Change*, 42, 153–168. https://doi.org/10.1016/j.gloenvcha.2016.05.009

In order to visualize the amount of mitigation challenge and adaptation challenge that is required in each of the five SSPs it is very helpful to visualize them in a bi-dimensional graph, with mitigation requirements being the vertical axis (low to high) and adaptation requirements being the horizontal (low to high from left to right), as we can see in Figure 1.7.

Table 1.2 SSPs and relative narratives.

Shared Socioeconomic Pathway	Narrative
SSP1	**Sustainability (Taking the Green Road)** The world shifts gradually, but pervasively, toward a more sustainable path, emphasizing more inclusive development that respects perceived environmental boundaries. Management of the global commons slowly improves, educational and health investments accelerate the demographic transition, and the emphasis on economic growth shifts toward a broader emphasis on human well-being. Driven by an increasing commitment to achieving development goals, inequality is reduced both across and within countries. Consumption is oriented toward low material growth and lower resource and energy intensity.
SSP2	**Middle of the road** The world follows a path in which social, economic, and technological trends do not shift markedly from historical patterns. Development and income growth proceeds unevenly, with some countries making relatively good progress while others fall short of expectations. Global and national institutions work toward but make slow progress in achieving sustainable development goals. Environmental systems experience degradation, although there are some improvements and overall the intensity of resource and energy use declines. Global population growth is moderate and levels off in the second half of the century. Income inequality persists or improves only slowly and challenges to reducing vulnerability to societal and environmental changes remain.

Shared Socioeconomic Pathway	Narrative
SSP3	**Regional rivalry (A Rocky Road)**
	A resurgent nationalism, concerns about competitiveness and security, and regional conflicts push countries to increasingly focus on domestic or, at most, regional issues. Policies shift over time to become increasingly oriented toward national and regional security issues. Countries focus on achieving energy and food security goals within their own regions at the expense of broader-based development. Investments in education and technological development decline. Economic development is slow, consumption is material-intensive, and inequalities persist or worsen over time. Population growth is low in industrialized and high in developing countries. A low international priority for addressing environmental concerns leads to strong environmental degradation in some regions.
SSP4	**Inequality (A Road Divided)**
	Highly unequal investments in human capital, combined with increasing disparities in economic opportunity and political power, lead to increasing inequalities and stratification both across and within countries. Over time, a gap widens between an internationally connected society that contributes to knowledge- and capital-intensive sectors of the global economy, and a fragmented collection of lower-income, poorly educated societies that work in a labor intensive, low-tech economy. Social cohesion degrades and conflict and unrest become increasingly common. Technology development is high in the high-tech economy and sectors. The globally connected energy sector diversifies, with investments in both carbon-intensive fuels like coal and unconventional oil, but also low-carbon energy sources. Environmental policies focus on local issues around middle- and high-income areas.

(Continued)

Table 1.2 (Continued)

Shared Socioeconomic Pathway	Narrative
SSP5	**Fossil-Fueled Development (Taking the Highway)**
	This world places increasing faith in competitive markets, innovation and participatory societies to produce rapid technological progress and development of human capital as the path to sustainable development. Global markets are increasingly integrated. There are also strong investments in health, education, and institutions to enhance human and social capital. At the same time, the push for economic and social development is coupled with the exploitation of abundant fossil fuel resources and the adoption of resource and energy intensive lifestyles around the world. All these factors lead to rapid growth of the global economy, while global population peaks and declines in the 21st century. Local environmental problems like air pollution are successfully managed. There is faith in the ability to effectively manage social and ecological systems, including by geo-engineering if necessary.

SOURCE: Adapted from https://www.carbonbrief.org.

The Intergovernmental Panel on Climate Change (IPCC) periodically issues reports covering aspects of scientific, technical, and socio-economic relevance on the topic of climate change. The Seventh Assessment Report (AR7) is structured in three working groups (WG) which assess three major aspects of climate change and a synthesis report. Working Group I focuses on the physical science basis; Working Group II is on impacts, adaptation, and vulnerability; and Working Group III reviews mitigation of climate change. The synthesis report of the Seventh Assessment Report will be produced after the completion of the working group reports and released by late 2029.

Figure 1.7 SSPs by mitigation and adaptation challenge levels.
Source: Adapted from https://www.carbonbrief.org.

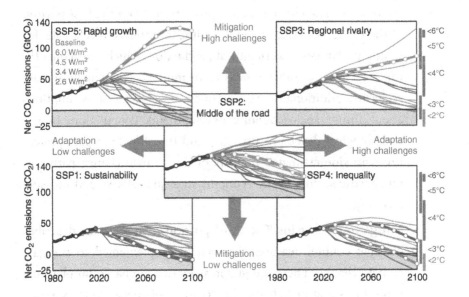

A good online resource to provide context and comprehension of climate scenarios is the SENSES Project (http://senses-project.org/), a nonprofit organization dedicated to the popularization of climate change scenarios. SENSES supports the understanding of climate change scenarios through sharing of data and visualization tools, which include an online "toolkit" composed of three main portions:

1 **Projections of climate change** This portion provides quantitative information (i.e., temperature, precipitation, frequency of extreme climatic events) on how the climate is expected to evolve in response to specific projected levels of atmospheric CO_2.

2 **Projections of climate change impact on the economy** This portion describes the potential impacts that the different scenarios

would have on specific sectors. These can include water economy, agriculture, fisheries, marine ecosystems, coastal infrastructure sectors, etc. The climate change projections from the first portion of the toolkit are used as input for impact models to calculate, for example, changes in agricultural production, which, subsequently, can be drivers of other downstream models. The climate impact scenarios, additionally, are dependent on a series of assumptions about future socioeconomic developments (population, policy, technological developments, etc.) and the climate impact projections provide estimated impacts of the climate change pathways on specific sectors of the economy in a quantitative and measurable way.

3 **Mitigation scenarios** The third portion of the toolkit describes possible countermeasures that can be implemented to mitigate climate change. These mitigation scenarios are based on plausible projections that include the development of energy sources, economies, changes in land use and emissions across the globe. They are constrained by the goal of not allowing the global mean temperature to exceed a particular temperature threshold (i.e., the model first postulates the threshold, and then what mitigation is required to achieve the goal, if the goal can be achieved). Again, all the projections depend on a series of assumptions on future socioeconomic developments, and the mitigation scenarios describe the macroeconomic investments, technology costs, changes in land use, and other postulated requirements needed to remain within specific set levels of climate change.

SENSES also curates a "finance track" online resource at https://climatescenarios.org/finance-portal which, as an example, discusses impact to the power industry under different possible climate change scenarios. Figure 1.8 shows a sample of projections on how volumes of power generation from different sources are expected to change under the assumptions of the 2 °C warming scenario. Notice how sectors are projected both to decrease (Coal, Gas without CCS), stay relatively stable (Hydro), grow significantly (Nuclear, Solar, Wind), or follow idiosyncratic patterns (Gas with CCS, where there is a growth followed by a decrease).

Figure 1.8 Changes in power production by climate change scenario.
Source: https://climatescenarios.org/power-sector/last accessed February 18, 2025.

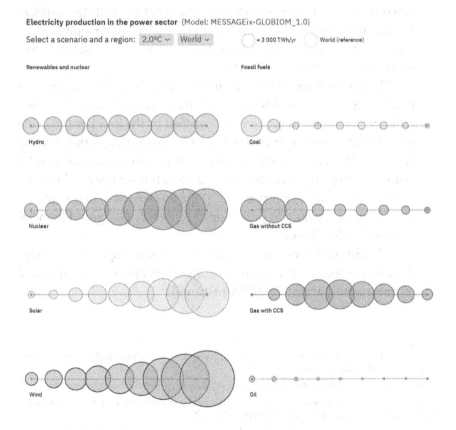

1.3 WHAT IS THE DEFINITION OF TRANSITION FINANCE?

Transition finance is a *new and developing field*, with multiple definitions, depending on the source:

"Transition finance is understood as *finance raised or deployed by corporates to implement their net-zero transition*, in line with the temperature goal of the Paris Agreement and based on a credible corporate climate transition plan." **(OECD)**[9]

"Transition finance is any financing including lending, capital markets and other financing solutions provided to clients for activities (including technologies) that support greenhouse gas emission reduction, directly or indirectly, in high-emitting and hard-to-abate sectors towards a 1.5C pathway." **(Barclay's)**[10]

"Transition finance: Investment, financing, insurance, and related products and services that are necessary to support an orderly, real economy transition to net zero as described by the four key financing strategies that finance or enable 1) entities and activities that develop and scale climate solutions; 2) entities that are already aligned to a 1.5 degrees C pathway; 3) entities committed to transitioning in line with 1.5 degrees C-aligned pathways; or 4) the accelerated managed phase-out of high-emitting physical assets." **(GFANZ, Glasgow Financial Alliance for Net Zero)**[11]

"Transition finance is any form of financial support that helps decarbonize high emitting activities or enables the decarbonization of other economic activities." **(CFA Institute)**[12]

---

[9] https://www.oecd.org/content/dam/oecd/en/publications/reports/2022/10/oecd-guidance-on-transition-finance_ac701a44/7c68a1ee-en.pdf

[10] https://home.barclays/our-sustainability-/barclays-climate-strategy/financing-the-transition

[11] https://assets.bbhub.io/company/sites/63/2022/09/Recommendations-and-Guidance-on-Financial-Institution-Net-zero-Transition-Plans-November-2022.pdf

[12] https://rpc.cfainstitute.org/-/media/documents/article/industry-research/transition-finance.pdf

1.4 WHAT DO WE MEAN BY TRANSITION FINANCE?

Transition finance in the context of this book is defined as:

"All the financial activities, including Investment, Financing, Insurance and Financial products and services, that will be required as a result of the global macroeconomic system adapting to a transition from the current carbon-intensive economy to a net-zero, or carbon-negative end state"

Some examples of what can constitute transition finance are:

- Financing for Carbon Dioxide Removal (CDR) and Voluntary Carbon Markets (VCM)
- Financing for development of improved CAT models for hurricanes, tornados, and wildfires
- Investment in workforce retraining
- Investment in transition-critical metals and mining
- Investment in alternative energy sources
- Investment in electric grid improvements
- Net-zero transportation (electric vehicles, airplanes, trains, motorcycles, etc.)
- Green cement
- Green steel
- Innovative climate-related insurance products
- Emissions-free shipping
- Energy storage
- Coastal tidal protection
- Farmland in northern latitudes
- Timberland

1.5 WHAT DO WORLD BUSINESS AND ECONOMICS LEADERS THINK ABOUT TRANSITION FINANCE?

Since the recognition of global temperature changes and their impacts on countries, economies, and societies, many opinions have emerged about the effects on investments and financial opportunities.

It is unnecessary to analyze all these opinions in detail. Instead, we will focus on two main areas: the *risks posed by climate change* and the *opportunities it presents*.

On the climate risk side, there is frequent news about climate-driven disasters, which have been acknowledged by regulators, insurance companies, and governments due to the significant risks they pose to businesses.

Most of the climate risk that is more obvious to the casual observer is, typically, physical risk, as it has direct, measurable, and often dramatically striking effects. Transition risk, on the other side, is less visible, almost mirroring the invisible nature of the GHGs themselves, but is no less real, albeit on a longer timeframe. Climate liability risk, on the other side, is becoming increasingly common, with multiple lawsuits being filed (and often won) around the world (as a recent example, we can quote the Swiss Elders for Climate Protection who won a case in the European Court of Human Rights against the Swiss Government, for violating their right to a healthy environment and exposing older citizens to increased health risks).[13]

On this background of well-recognized risk, and action being undertaken by many multilateral organizations such as the NGFS[14] (Network for

---

[13] https://www.weforum.org/videos/swiss-women-sued-government
[14] https://www.ngfs.net/en

Greening the Financial System), TCFD[15] (Task Force on Climate-Related Financial Disclosures), IPCC[16] (Intergovernmental Panel on Climate Change), and furthered by events such as the yearly COP[17] (Conference of Parties) conferences, NY Climate Week,[18] and many others, we will only quote a couple of notable opinions on the risk side of climate change, to avoid repeating concepts that have been heard many times before.

The first quote on Climate Risk is by Larry Fink, the CEO of BlackRock[19] the New York–based asset manager, which had, as of YE 2023, over $11.5 trillion in AUM. He has been well aware of the risks due to climate change, and in January 2020 declared:

"Climate Risk is Investment Risk."

Moving on to a representative of a sector that is very much exposed to climate risk, we can now see the opinion of Jerome Heageli, group chief economist for Swiss RE, one of the worlds largest, and oldest, reinsurance companies. In October 2021, he said:

"Climate change is the No. 1 long-term risk out there."

Jerome's opinion was further solidified by action when, in December 2023, Swiss RE acquired[20] leading climate flood risk modeling company Fathom[21] for an undisclosed sum.

If we now shift our attention to the Climate Opportunities side of the coin, for the sake of space and elegance, we shall also reduce the citations to just two, of significant heft.

---

[15] https://www.fsb-tcfd.org
[16] https://www.ipcc.ch
[17] https://unfccc.int/process/bodies/supreme-bodies/conference-of-the-parties-cop
[18] https://www.climateweeknyc.org
[19] http://blackrock.com
[20] https://www.swissre.com/press-release/Swiss-Re-acquires-Fathom-a-leader-in-water-risk-intelligence/4af5e0d7-e065-404a-b80d-6f32955f0fbe
[21] https://www.fathom.global

The first voice we shall quote, as it is from an older interview, is that of Bill Gates, co-founder of Microsoft, at one time, world's richest man (and currently fourth in the ranking), international philanthropist and global technological icon. In an interview that he gave to CNBC[22] as part of the virtual SOSV Climate Tech Summit in October 2021, he stated:

> *"Climate Tech will produce 8 to 10 Teslas, a Google, an Amazon, and a Microsoft."*

In addition to the creation of this plethora of new unicorns, he stated that "future returns in climate investing will be comparable to what the biggest tech companies have produced" and that the "gains will be spread out over a wider swath of companies, beyond the electric vehicle space." He concluded his interview with a note of caution, "We will have a high failure rate," but there are enough ideas that "have a likelihood of substantial success."

To conclude this section, the best quote is one from a speech that Janet Yellen, at the time US Treasury secretary, and previously chair of the US Federal Reserve (2014–2018), gave in July 2024,[23] specifically on the topic of Transition Finance. This speech, delivered in Brazil after meeting with G20 finance ministers to discuss economic development, is relevant both in the recognition of the importance of Transition Finance as an investment opportunity, as well as for the sizing of it both in dollar values and duration.

> *"The single-greatest economic opportunity of the 21st century."*
> **Janet Yellen**, *U.S. Treasury Secretary, speaking on transition finance, July 2024*

---

[22] https://www.cnbc.com/2021/10/20/bill-gates-expects-8-to-10-teslas-and-a-google-amazon-and-microsoft.html
[23] https://home.treasury.gov/news/press-releases/jy2504

Besides highlighting the unique prevalence of Transition Finance over all other opportunities in the 21st century, Yellen stated that "neglecting to address climate change [...] is bad economic policy" and quantified that "the transition will require no less than **$3 trillion in new capital** from many sources **each year between now and 2050.**"

CHAPTER TWO

MODEL-BASED APPROACHES TO INVESTING

Leveraging quantitative models to identify investment theses in transition finance

2.1 WHY DO WE NEED MODELS TO INVEST IN TRANSITION FINANCE?[1]

The world is facing an unprecedented climate change emergency affecting the global economy. Most current economic models predict the future by analyzing past events through methods like regressions and correlations.

---

[1] This section borrows heavily from *Quantitative Methods for ESG Finance*, 1st edition. Wiley. (December 1, 2022).

While this approach works for stable conditions, it is not suitable for handling changing conditions, stress events, or significant shifts as the ones that will derive from climate change.

The reasons for using these kinds of models in economics and finance over the past century have mostly been due to the need to simplify a set of very complex interactions and adapt existing techniques from abstract fields such as physics and mathematics to the very real-world problems of the economy and the markets.

A good example of this way of thinking, and overly simplified approaches to modeling complex systems, is the well-known joke about spherical cows (see Figure 2.1):

> Milk production at a dairy farm was low, so the farmer wrote to the local university, asking for help from academia. A multidisciplinary team of professors was assembled, headed by a theoretical physicist, and two weeks of intensive on-site investigation took place. The scholars then returned to the university, notebooks crammed with data, where the task of writing the report was left to the team leader. Shortly thereafter the physicist returned to the farm, saying to the farmer, "I have the solution, but it works only in the case of spherical cows in a vacuum."

Figure 2.1   A visualization of the Spherical Cow Critique.

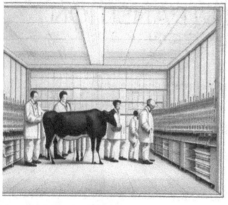

Generated with AI using Perchance

Looking at more mainstream quotes, we can see that, when Robert Solow, winner of the 1987 Nobel Prize in economics, was asked to testify at the 2010 Congressional Hearing on macroeconomic modeling aiming to investigate why macroeconomists failed to foresee the financial crisis of 2007–2010, his commentary was very much aligned to the Spherical Cow Critique:

> I do not think that the currently popular DSGE models pass the smell test. They take it for granted that the whole economy can be thought about as if it were a single, consistent person or dynasty carrying out a rationally designed, long-term plan, occasionally disturbed by unexpected shocks, but adapting to them in a rational, consistent way. [...]
>
> The protagonists of this idea make a claim to respectability by asserting that it is founded on what we know about microeconomic behavior, but I think that this claim is generally phony. The advocates no doubt believe what they say, but they seem to have stopped sniffing or to have lost their sense of smell altogether.

The reasons that underpin this failure of neoclassical economics models to actually predict regime changes and shifts (which are critical for ESG and climate change modeling) are that these models have biases and assumptions that are so far removed from practical conditions to make the entire modeling exercise not applicable to the world in which we live in.

Some examples of these assumptions, for what is called "economic man," are:

- Perfect rationality
- Possession of complete information about all prices, now and in the future
- Living in a world with perfect competition

As it is immediately clear to any of our readers, all three assumptions fail the most basic of tests, as irrational behavior is widespread, information about prices is far from complete, and competition is nowhere near perfect in most of the markets and countries in the world (thanks to the existence of monopolies, tariffs, barriers to entry, etc.).

If we take a cursory look at the most commonly used models in the econometric space, we notice how both DSGE (Dynamic Stochastic General Equilibrium) models and CGE (Computable General Equilibrium) models share the same major flaws (based on the design of the models and the equations which govern them) that result in:

- Incapability of predicting regime changes
- Incapability of accounting for emerging behaviors and new patterns
- Incapability of describing nonlinear dynamics of economic fluctuations

Current approaches, overall, try to predict the future by looking at the past, and regularly fail to foresee crisis events ahead of time.

While it is easy to understand where this kind of modeling and academic school of thought derives from, it is also quite clear that it cannot be of much use for work in the Climate space, where the requirement is for modeling of entirely novel situations, interactions and emerging properties, brought into existence by the complex, and generally unpredictable, interactions of many different agents engaged in a real-time exercise on the global stage.

The traditional paradigm that has been applied in modeling economic and financial systems has generally been one of pre-determined relationships, correlations, and strict laws (with strong assumptions underpinning the models). This is a framework that postulates intelligence, intelligent behavior, and complex mathematics to solve it, and does not allow for detection of chaotic, unusual events and/or emerging properties. Recent studies in multiple fields, however, have shown how most of these assumptions and postulates do not hold true, or aren't strictly necessary to optimally solve complex problems in an efficient manner (including fascinating new research by A. Boussard et al.,[2] which shows that single-celled organisms with no nervous system can actually solve complex problems such as mazes and network optimization, which were previously thought to require high-level intelligence and/or massive computational power).

Given the complexities of climate change and the impact it has on societies, macroeconomic variables, and financial players, it is imperative to use a science-based approach to gain insight into the likely paths that lie ahead of us, as opposed to relying on subject matter expertise, intuition, and "gut feeling."

There are multiple existing frameworks that can be used for this purpose, which are currently being applied to stress testing and climate scenario analysis, both from a risk management perspective, and can be easily converted into very useful tools for Transition Finance Investing, as we shall see in the following paragraphs and chapters.

2.2   HOW DO WE MODEL CLIMATE AND THE IMPACT IT HAS ON THE ECONOMY AND SOCIETY?

The methodologies for modeling climate change, such as those that are used for the generation of the scenarios that we have seen in the previous chapter, are various and of different degrees of complexity, based on the timeframes that are being modeled, the granularity of data inputs and outputs, and the kind of accuracy and sensitivity that is necessary.

---
[2] Boussard, A., et al. (2021). Adaptive behaviour and learning in slime moulds: the role of oscillations. *Phil. Trans. R. Soc. B* 376: 20190757

While climate models are not part of the scope of this book, we shall, however, take a cursory look at the most common types of methodologies that are used in the field, to provide a better understanding of the subject to our readers (especially considering that the climate premium models use the output from climate change models as their own input).

While there are several qualitative models for climate, we shall focus exclusively on the quantitative ones, as these are the ones that are used for the purposes of climate change modeling as intended for transition finance.

The common characteristic of all numerical climate models is to use quantitative methodologies, of one kind or another, to model the interactions of different drivers for climate, such as atmosphere, land surface, oceans, and ice coverage, and produce estimates of resulting effects, given initial postulated assumptions. These models can be used for multiple purposes and in different timescales, from weather predictions all the way to overall long-term climate change.

All these models look at the earth as a closed system, with a set amount of incoming energy from the sun, in the form of short-wave electromagnetic radiation (mostly in the visible and short-wave near-infrared and infrared spectrum), and a set amount of outgoing radiating energy in the infrared electromagnetic spectrum. In the most simplistic of models, an imbalance between the incoming calories and the outgoing ones, in favor of the incoming ones, will lead to an increase in temperature, and the opposite will lead to a decrease.

The simplest models look at the earth as a single unified radiant heat transfer model, and average outgoing and incoming energy to predict temperature changes. As can be easily imagined, these models are not very precise, and can only be used for order-of-magnitude types of assessments.

There are also models that couple atmosphere-ocean-sea ice into one aggregated system and solve full equations for mass and energy transfers and radiant exchange, which provide more precise estimates and data projections.

The most used types of climate models currently in use fall into the following general categories (in increasing order of complexity):

Zero-dimensional models The zero-dimensional ("0d") Energy Balance Model simply models the balance between incoming and outgoing radiation at the Earth's surface, modeling the earth as a mathematical point in space — i.e., there is no explicit accounting for latitude, longitude, or altitude. This is a very simplistic model, and includes the effective radiative temperature of the earth (including clouds and atmosphere) and provides an estimated average of the earth of 15 °C. This type of model relies heavily on earth reflectivity (albedo) and is capable of rapidly determining the impact of changes in solar output, earth albedo (such as if we were to increase aerosols in the atmosphere) or earth radiance on average earth temperature. It is, however, not useful, in pointing out the causes behind these changes and the temperature distribution on the planet, as it has no capability to address energy transfer within the global system.

Box models These models are the simplest of climate models, excluding 0d models, and they reduce the global environment to a simplified set of boxes (also known as reservoirs) that are interconnected and exchange calories between each other. There are many assumptions in these models (homogenous mixing, free flow, uniform concentration of chemical species, etc.), to allow easy computation. Simple versions (small number of chemical species and reduced number of boxes) can be solved analytically, but most models are generally too complex for this type of approach and require solving by numerical techniques.

Radiative-convective models Radiative-convective models add the geographical dimension to the zero-dimensional models, and are capable of predicting, fairly accurately, globally and seasonally averaged surface and atmospheric temperatures. These models include the well-known and documented surface temperature/ H_2O amount in the atmosphere feedback mechanism. Despite the higher degree of granularity that these models pose, they still have several significant drawbacks and are far from perfect. A comprehensive review of these models can be found by V. Ramanathan and J. A. Coakley.[3]

Higher-dimension models This is an expansion of the zero-dimensional model, to integrate manually specified horizontal transport of energy in the atmosphere (i.e., hot equator and cold poles, for example). It allows better zonal averages than a pure zero-dimensional model, but is lacking in any dynamics (i.e., is entirely static).

EMICs (Earth-system Models of Intermediate Complexity) EMICs are mainly used to investigate climate on long timescales at reduced computational cost. These models are mostly classified by their resolution, parametrization, and "integration." There are four generally recognized EMIC categories, dependent on the type of atmospheric simplification used:

- Statistical dynamic models
- Energy moisture balance models
- Quasi-geostrophic models
- Primitive equation models

As a data point, out of 15 models included in the IPCC's fifth assessment report, 26% were statistical dynamic (4/15), 46% were energy moisture balance (7/15), and 13% each quasi-geostrophic and primitive equations models (2/15 each).

---

[3] Ramanathan, V. and Coakley, J.A. (1978). Climate modeling through radiative-convective models, *Rev. Geophys.*, 16(4), 465–489. doi:10.1029/RG016i004p00465

GCMs (Global Climate Models, or General Circulation Models)
The GCMs are the most complex climate models currently in use. These models divide the atmosphere and oceans into discrete cells, each of which is treated as a separate computational unit (similar to how agent-based models operate). Individual cell-level processes are modeled directly, and the interface between cells is then calculated by specific rules and boundary conditions. There are models that only focus on the atmosphere (AGCMs) and ones that couple the atmosphere with the ocean (AOGCMs).

In addition to the climate change models that we have just seen, there are also models that *assess the impacts and damages of the changes on the economy and on specific sectors*. The combination of these two types of models creates a new class of models called Integrated Assessment Models (IAM). The IAMs are what is used to generate the SSP projections both for physical parameters (Temperature, GHG emissions) and macroeconomic variables (GDP and similar). Most IAMs are general equilibrium (optimization) models, but there are also more traditional econometric models in use as well as Agent-Based models (refer to Chapter 6 of *Quantitative Methods for ESG Finance* for a more detailed coverage).

A typical workflow of an optimization-based IAM is shown in Figure 2.2.

Most IAMs are built by combining two modules, an economic module, and a climate module, which feed off each other, and are used to maximize a specific utility function.

Typically the modules fall along the following lines:

Economic Module: defines the production function (GDP), including the impact of climate change on GDP (mitigation and adaptation costs, physical damage costs); the quantitative impact is calculated as a function of the average temperature, which is provided by the climate module.

Figure 2.2 Workflow example of an optimization-based IAM.

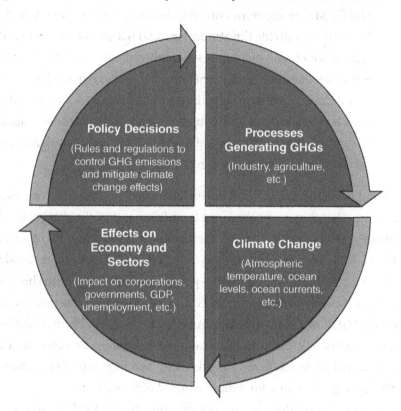

Climate Module: a model of atmospheric and oceanic temperature distribution, including the dynamics of GHG emissions, based on assumptions and scenarios, some of which are exogenous (*ab initio* parameters) and others deriving from the economic module itself.

We can now take a rapid look at a couple of modeling approaches, to allow our readers to transition from a generic, theoretic view, to some examples of real-world applications that are relevant for ESG practitioners in their day-to-day work.

DICE Model

Perhaps the most well-known IAM is the Dynamic Integrated Model of Climate and Economy (DICE) by Nordhaus (1992 https://cowles.yale.edu/sites/default/files/files/pub/d10/d1019.pdf), who received a Nobel memorial prize for his IAM work.

The model maximizes present value of global utility, as follows:

$$\{\mu_t\} = argmax \sum_t U_t(1 + r)^{-t}$$

where

$$U_t = P_t \frac{1}{1-\alpha}(c_t^{1-\alpha} - 1)$$

and

P_t is the global population at time t

c_t is the consumption per capita at time t

α is close to 1, and is a measure of societal inequality aversion

μ_t is a control variable path that represents policies affecting the amount of GHG emissions.

The optimization is subject to several types of constraints which we shall now examine in detail in this book.

The projections of the DICE model, based on 2016 data, can be seen in Figure 2.3. Please note that we are showing this model for illustrative purposes only (as it was a precursor model and won the Nobel Prize), and it is not a model currently used for practical purposes.

Most of the currently used models project the probability of average warming by more than 2 °C by the end of the century as approaching 100%. It is noteworthy to notice how many of these models only include human emissions of fossil fuels, and do not include releases of other GHGs (such as methane and CO_2 trapped in permafrost) which could induce a feed-forward mechanism that would result in faster and larger scale

Figure 2.3   DICE Model projections on 2016 data.

Source: Le Guenedal, Theo. (2019). Economic Modeling of Climate Risks. 10.13140/RG.2.2.13263.30882 / with permission of Elsevier

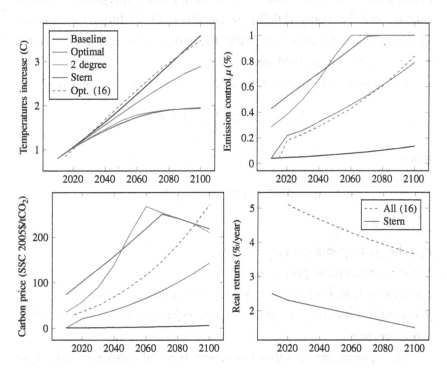

warming. Given the high degree of uncertainty that is tied to outcomes of warming above the 2° level, the long-time horizons involved, the large number of assumptions to be made, and the complexities of the financial markets' feedback loops into the macroeconomy, it is inherently difficult to take these projections directly into financial models and convert them to future losses.

For the purposes of climate scenario analysis, an example of which is the recently completed 2023 Federal Reserve Board FRB CSA[4] (for which

---

[4] https://www.federalreserve.gov/publications/climate-scenario-analysis-exercise-results.htm

Model-based Approaches to Investing

the author of this paper was responsible for modeling the Citi portfolio for transition risk), a generalized approach that goes from scenario selection to loss estimation at aggregate portfolio level is presented in Figures 2.4 and 2.5. Note how the core of the model is the Climate Premium Evaluation Model, as this is where the actual impact of the climate variables is estimated on the companies being evaluated.

GCM and IAM models are upstream to the schematic in Figure 2.5, and feed the drivers (mainly at Sector GVA Projection level) Physical risk models, including CRE (Commercial Real Estate) and RRE (Residential Real Estate) models are also upstream and their compounded effects are calculated in the third column in the Climate Drivers section.

For the LGD portion, there is no added value in developing any proprietary model, as there is very little climate-specific LGD consideration to be modeled, and what exists (stranded assets) can be added as an obligor-level overlay from the stranded assets model.

Figure 2.4 Generalized End-to-End climate modeling flowchart.
Source: © C.R. Castelli 2024.

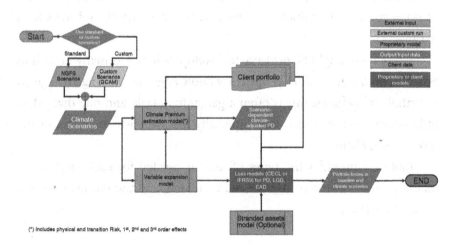

Figure 2.5   Generalized Climate Premium Evaluation Model flowchart.
Source: © C.R. Castelli 2024.

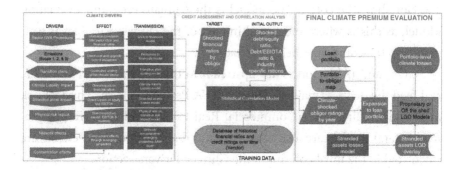

2.3   WHAT TO MODEL: VENDOR MODELS VERSUS PROPRIETARY MODELS

When looking at transition finance investing as a business proposition, it is necessary to decide which models/processes are to be external (vendor or open-source) and which ones have to be internalized, and for which reasons.

While there might be pressure to develop in-house as many models as possible, on the grounds of proprietary knowledge and gaining an edge on potential competitors, this is often a gargantuan task, and one that offers little return on the investment, especially for the upstream parts of the model value chain.

Table 2.1 provides the types of models needed for each step of the modeling process, the recommended approach, and the rationale for the recommendation.

Table 2.1 Types of models needed for each step of the modeling process, recommended approach, and rationale for the recommendation.

Effects Modeled	Model	Recommended Approach	Rationale	Options
Climate-to-Climate / Climate to Macro	General Circulation Models (GCM), Integrated Assessment Models (IAM)	Open-Source Models	These are extremely onerous and large models, being developed (and freely made available to the public) by Universities and NGOs worldwide and requiring huge computing power to run. They are the high-level climatological models as presented earlier, and there is no practical advantage for an investor to try to replicate these models in-house.	There are multiple models that can be used, such as: GCAM (https://gcims.pnnl.gov/modeling/gcam-global-change-analysis-model), REMIND-MagPIE (https://www.pik-potsdam.de/en/institute/departments/transformation-pathways/models/remind), -MESM (https://globalchange.mit.edu/research/research-tools/earth-system-model), IMAGE (https://www.iamconsortium.org/resources/model-resources/image/), MESSAGEix-GLOBIOM (https://www.iamconsortium.org/resources/model-resources/message-globiom/), -WITCH-GLOBIOM (https://www.witchmodel.org/)

(Continued)

Table 2.1 (Continued)

Effects Modeled	Model	Recommended Approach	Rationale	Options
Climate-to-Macro	Climate Liability Models	In-House or Vendor	These models are computation-based and require a fair amount of data to predict: • Likelihood of a company being sued on climate grounds • Likelihood of loss of the lawsuit • Duration of lawsuit • Amount of liquidating damages Data is available via various sources, but needs compiling and aggregating into a model.	At the time of writing, the author is not aware of any vendor offering a turnkey solution for modeling Climate Liability projections, and therefore the only current option is in-house modeling.
Climate-to-Macro	Variable Expansion Models	Vendor or Internal	These models take the high-level set of Macroeconomic Variables (MeV) produced by the IAMs, and expand them to regional and sectoral granularity, to allow downstream models (typically PD/LGD/EAD models) to use the granular variables.	There are a variety of academic publications, as well as vendors (such as Moody's, https://www.moodys.com/web/en/us/capabilities/economic-data.html) which can be chosen for this purpose, as this is a well-established practice that is used for CCAR, ICAAP, and many other stress testing exercises across the banking system.

Climate-to-Macro	Physical Risk Impact Assessment Models	Vendor	These are highly specialized climate-driven models, which estimate the likelihood of extreme weather events hitting specific areas and the kind of damage that will result. They require very specialized skillsets that are not typically found in the financial sector, and are highly intensive both computationally and in terms of manpower required to run and maintain them.	There are multiple models that can be used, such as: AON-TCS (https://www.aon.com/en/insights/articles/how-companies-are-using-climate-modeling-to-improve-risk-decisions) Reask (https://reask.earth/) Karen Clark and Co (https://www.karenclarkandco.com/) IBM Environmental Intelligence Suite (https://www.ibm.com/products/environmental-intelligence-suite/climate-risk) Moody's (https://www.moodys.com/web/en/us/capabilities/climate-risk.html) S&P (https://www.spglobal.com/esg/solutions/physical-climate-risk)
Macro-to-Financials	Climate Liability Impact Model	In-House	This model needs to take the inputs from the climate liability models and overlay them to the individual companies in the overall simulation, as part of the climate premium estimation. As such, it is relatively simple but needs to be tailored to the overall approach and implementation and cannot be realistically outsourced.	N/A

(Continued)

Table 2.1 (Continued)

Effects Modeled	Model	Recommended Approach	Rationale	Options
Macro-to-Financials	Transition Risk Climate Premium Model	Internal or Hybrid Internal/Vendor	This model is the core of the climate modeling exercise and brings in multiple components into one cohesive estimation of the impact of climate, decoupled from the impact of the MeV pathway that the scenario postulates. As such, it requires a certain amount of customization and aggregation that cannot be done by vendors alone.	For the Direct Impact Assessment of Climate (which is one component of the Climate Premium Evaluation Model, but not the entire model, as seen in previous sections), there are some vendor options: Oliver Wyman Climate Credit Analytics Model CCA/ S&P (https://www.oliverwyman.com/our-expertise/solutions/climate-credit-analytics.html) QuantFoundry (https://quantfoundry.com/climate-change/) Vivid Economics/McKinsey – Planetrics – (https://www.mckinsey.com/capabilities/sustainability/how-we-help-clients/planetrics) PWC Climate Excellence – (https://www.pwc.de/en/sustainability/climate-excellence-making-companies-fit-for-climate-change.html) Baringa + Blackrock Climate Change Scenario Model – (https://www.baringa.com/en/insights/climate-change-sustainability/climatechangescenariomodel/)

| Macro-to-Financials | Physical Risk Damage Assessment Models | Vendor | Damage assessment is generally done using CAT models, which are standard insurance models, with a long track record. There are multiple options available. | Moody's (https://www.rms.com/catastrophe-modeling) Verisk (https://www.air-worldwide.com/models/About-Catastrophe-Modeling/) Fathom (https://www.fathom.global/) Oasis Loss Modeling Framework (https://oasislmf.org/) AON (https://www.aon.com/attachments/reinsurance/models_if_brochure.pdf) JBA (https://www.jbarisk.com/) KatRisk (https://www.katrisk.com/) Risk Frontiers (https://riskfrontiers.com/) Temblor (https://temblor.net) ARA (https://www.ara.com/hurloss/) Royal Haskoning (https://www.royalhaskoningdhv.com/en/twinn/sectors/financial-services) |

2.4 THE PROBLEM OF CLIMATE DATA IN GENERAL

As the father of computer science, Charles Babbage,[5] once said:[6]

> On two occasions I have been asked, "Pray, Mr. Babbage, if you put into the machine wrong figures, will the right answers come out?" ... I am not able rightly to apprehend the kind of confusion of ideas that could provoke such a question.

This seminal concept from the dawn of mechanical computation, translates into the currently popular GIGO (Garbage-In, Garbage-Out) framework that most of our readers are certainly more familiar with.

The Garbage-In, Garbage-Out rule applies in a steadfast manner to climate modeling, both at the model/relationships/rules level, which is part of the modeling framework section of this book, as well as the climate data, and financial data, that the models ingest to produce the results that are then used for the purposes of Transition Finance Investing.

We shall not go into too much detail on the traditional data that is common to any other modeling (such as mortgage modeling, wholesale credit modeling, etc.), as there is nothing that differentiates climate modeling from the usual vanilla modeling being applied across the financial services on a routine basis, and a treatise of data quality for financial modeling is outside the scope of our discussion.

We shall, on the other hand, review the climate-specific datasets that are required to estimate the climate premium, and the data quality challenges that are particular to each of them.

---

[5] https://en.wikipedia.org/wiki/Charles_Babbage

[6] Babbage, Charles. (1864). *Passages from the Life of a Philosopher*, p. 67. Longman and Co.

2.5 DATA QUALITY ISSUES FOR ACUTE PHYSICAL RISK

When the modeling is focused on acute physical risk, we are effectively modeling the impact of extreme weather events on properties and assets, which is then used in downstream models to assess the overall effects on balance sheets and income statements (or directly on the value of collateral). As a result, the focus of the data that is needed for this exercise is at the asset level itself, the physical characteristics of the asset, and the underlying data that is used to run and calibrate the CAT models that drive the estimation of likelihood of impact and magnitude of damages.

Specifically, we face the following major challenges:

Need for precise asset geo-location data: Modeling physical risk is all about estimating the damage that could occur to assets when specific extreme weather events were to occur. As these events are created as complex simulations, they are, for practical purposes, "synthetic" hurricanes, floods, wildfires, and other events, and have specific pathways and geo-locations. Consequently, it is critical to have precise geo-locations for assets, as, for example, it can make a dramatic difference to the outcomes of the model run, if the address of a company is listed as a Delaware PO box not at risk of a major hurricane (the legal address), as opposed to a coastal Florida town in the middle of Hurricane Alley (the actual operating address).

Need for accurate altitude data for assets: The altitude of an asset is also a major data point that is necessary, especially for hurricanes and coastal flooding, as significant portions of the damages that can be incurred by buildings often stem from flooding, and a few feet in altitude can make the difference between hundreds of thousands of dollars of damage, and an asset offline for months, and a minor inconvenience that will only last a few days. As such, it is important to ensure that, besides the precise geo-location for assets, updated and accurate altitude data is available. For the United States, the Federal Emergency Management Agency (FEMA, https://www.fema.gov/) provides accurate floodplain mapping for the whole country,[7] while for the rest of the world a more piecemeal approach is required (Google Maps offers an Elevation API[8] that allows developers to access elevation data for any location in the world, but precision is still somewhat debatable).

Need for detailed building characteristics: The characteristics of a building (whether it is concrete, wood framing, brick, etc.) are critical data points for proper estimation of physical risk, and to run models correctly. Often this data is not available, or incorrect, and needs to be estimated via different methodologies (from a simple proxy on the age of the building, to AI-based approaches that take street views and deduct the building type from them). Some of the information needed is very specific (for example, does the building have a basement? If it does, is it where servers and computers are located?) and has a direct bearing on the vulnerability and damages that would occur in specific types of events (i.e., hurricanes and coastal flooding), and is generally hard to obtain, unless third-party vendors are used.

Type of global physical risk models and their drivers: The variables and drivers that the models use to predict the pathways for the extreme weather events is a critical aspect for the production of the results that are used downstream for Transition Finance Investing. For this reason it is key that new, science-based models are used, as opposed to older, statistically based ones, as the older models routinely fail in predicting accurate pathways for the extreme weather events, given they are calibrated on weather patterns and conditions that are no longer the ones that are driving the phenomena today. This is the fundamental reason

---

[7] https://msc.fema.gov/portal/home
[8] https://developers.google.com/maps/documentation/elevation/start

why many insurance companies are failing to correctly price hurricane, coastal flooding, and wildfire risks in many communities, and choosing to exit potentially profitable markets (and/or raising prices to unnecessarily high levels, to compensate for the uncertainty).

2.6 DATA QUALITY ISSUES FOR CHRONIC PHYSICAL RISK

Once the modeling focus shifts to chronic physical risk, we now care to understand the effects of long-term weather changes on properties, assets, and (indirectly) corporations, which is then used in downstream models to assess the overall effects on balance sheets and income statements (or directly on the value of collateral).

While a good number of data challenges are common to acute physical risk, with some slight modifications, there are a set of specific ones that are not brought into play, as we can see in the following list:

Need for precise asset geo-location data: This is the same need that we reviewed for acute physical risk.

Need for accurate altitude data for assets: This is the same need that we reviewed for acute physical risk.

Need for detailed building characteristics: This is the same need that we reviewed for acute physical risk.

Type of global physical risk models and their drivers: The models used for chronic physical risk are different from the acute physical risk, as these are the Global Circulation Models, which estimate the impact on the weather of the postulated rises in GHG emissions that are provided by the scenarios (with the feedback loops shown in Figure 2.2). It is noteworthy that the choice of IAM will generate significantly different outcomes, as there is a

Figure 2.6 ECS values from the 40 CMIP6 models available as of May 2020 where necessary experiments to calculate ECS (using the Gregory method) are currently available.
Source: Carbon Brief Ltd / https://www.carbonbrief.org/cmip6-the-next-generation-of-climate-models-explained / last accessed February 18, 2025
Note: Models with an ECS above the IPCC AR5 likely range are shown in light shading. All models shown are independent, as some modeling groups – such as CESM2 – have multiple versions. Chart by carbon brief using Highcharts.

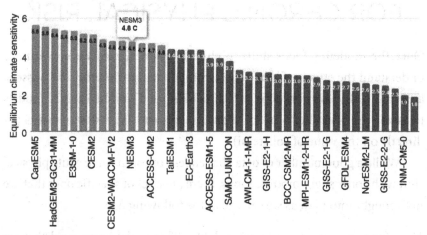

nontrivial spread within the different models in so far as estimated amount of forcing (i.e., heating) that set amounts of GHG emissions cause. Figure 2.6 shows the sensitivity to climate (ECS, Equilibrium Climate Sensitivity) in 40 different CMIP6 models, as of May 2020, evaluated using the Gregory Method,[9] which provides a visual explanation of how much variance is to be expected between models.

---

[9] Gregory, J.M., Ingram, W.J., Palmer, M.A. et al. (2004). A new method for diagnosing radiative forcing and climate sensitivity. *Geophys. Res. Lett.*, 31, L03205, doi:10.1029/2003GL018747. https://agupubs.onlinelibrary.wiley.com/doi/full/10.1029/2003gl018747

Data on company facilities and operations: The information on where facilities are located (factories, warehouses, supply chains, etc.) is necessary and critical for chronic physical risk, as this is one of the key channels of risk transmission, especially for the second order impacts, and incorrect/missing data will lead to underestimation of risk (or underestimation of opportunities, depending on what data is missing). Examples of opportunities that could be missed are large agricultural businesses having holdings in northern latitudes, which are bound to become more productive and valuable over time.

Granularity of General Circulation Models being used: The size of the cell that is being projected by the GCM matters significantly for projections of impact on individual assets. The spatial resolution of a General Circulation Model (GCM) refers to the size of the grid cells used. These cells can differ in size, but a standard GCM usually has a horizontal resolution ranging from 250 to 600 km. To illustrate, a GCM with a resolution of 4.5° latitude by 7.5° longitude at 40° N latitude would feature grid cells measuring 500 km by 640 km. As these are very large cells, they need to be further expanded at higher resolutions to provide impacts that are useable at asset level, and this process adds additional uncertainty and data challenges, depending on how it is done, and what data the process relies upon for the expansion of the impacts.

2.7 DATA QUALITY ISSUES FOR TRANSITION RISK

Looking at what is required for transition risk, in terms of data, we see how the focus now is on corporate data, and an entirely different dataset from what we have, up to now, concentrated on.

The transition risk data quality issues, as presented, come with a unique set of challenges and idiosyncrasies, which need to be understood and addressed adequately to be able to properly model and comprehend the impacts of climate change on obligors and CRE (Commercial Real Estate)/RRE (Residential Real Estate) that derive from the effects of societal responses to climate change.

Granularity of data used in the models: When looking at transition risk models, the granularity of data issues that we have observed, to some extent, for physical risk, are brought into full focus. This is due to the fact that the output of the IAMs is generally high-level variables, produced at country/regional level as the most granular level, and cannot be used, as is, for regional/local modeling. As a consequence, variable expansion modeling is required, to go from high-level MeV (MacroEconomic Variable)/country time-series to granular sectoral GVA (Gross Value Added)/regional projections, thus adding levels of uncertainty and concerns about the quality of models and data used to calibrate them.

Reliability of emissions data: Within transition risk, the first order impact estimates often are driven by the direct impact of the shadow carbon price on companies and assets via their Scope 1, Scope 2, and Scope 3 emissions. This mechanism relies heavily on self-reporting by companies, as well as vendor-reported data, which often produce contradictory emissions values for the same company, exacerbated by multiple vendors reporting different values (especially in the highly inconsistent Scope 3 emissions, which tend to be estimates at best). Given these emission values are the drivers for the model, and often are entirely missing for many companies, it becomes clear how this dataset is critical for the overall modeling effort, and requires careful review and challenge, as well as effective imputation algorithms for missing data (typically based on company characteristics, size, footprint, and sectoral averages) for the models to remain robust.

Reliability/availability of energy class data for buildings: For transition risk, the focus is not on the building characteristics in the optics of damage functions, but rather in terms of energy efficiency and energy usage. This data is often not available easily, and has to be proxied via regional aggregate statistics, coupled to publicly available data on individual assets (such as the age of a building, which can generally be correlated with energy efficiency, with more recent buildings being more energy efficient than older ones). There are several resources available for the purposes of fine-tuning the data needed for the buildings in scope of the modeling, from third-party vendor surveys which provide certain datasets (typically regional and limited), to industry and government-wide aggregated survey data (such as the EPA GHG emissions factors by regions and sub-regions in the United States).[10]

Timeliness of financial reporting: As the focus on most of the transition risk modeling is on financial impacts on corporates or on real estate (typically CRE, which is treated as an income-generating proposition), the availability, timeliness, and accuracy of the financial information used for the modeling is a critical factor in producing useable results. Given the climate premium is applied to an underlying substrate of economic and financial considerations at individual company/asset level, any major changes that occur at T_0 have the potential to change the overall trajectory of the specific company/asset being modeled, in a material way. It follows, therefore, that subscribing to high-quality third-party suppliers of financial data is a key aspect of any transition risk modeling effort, as it underpins the entire framework, and bad/late/incomplete data in this dimension can have far-fetched impacts on the overall quality of the output being generated.

Additional complexity of methane emissions data: The GHG emissions landscape is often, simplistically, reduced to CO_2 alone, but it has several other major components, including methane, nitrous oxide, and fluorinated

---

[10] https://www.epa.gov/climateleadership/ghg-emission-factors-hub

Figure 2.7 Warming influence of greenhouse gases, 1980–2022.
Source: Adapted from The NOAA Annual Greenhouse Gas Index (AGGI), NOAA.gov, National Oceanic and Atmospheric Administration (NOAA). Spring 2023.

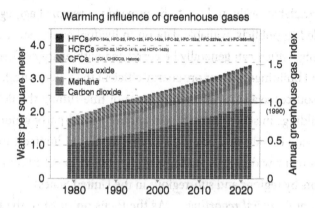

compounds, as illustrated in Figure 2.7. While nitrous oxide and the fluorinated compounds are well understood and included in the projections, methane (CH_4) presents some unique challenges as well as unaccounted for potential for feedback loops that could drastically accelerate global warming to unprecedented levels. This is due to the higher potency of methane as a GHG if compared to CO_2 (depending on the timeframe we consider, methane can be between 30 and 90 times more powerful than CO_2 as a GHG) and the difficulty of accurately tracing the emissions of methane from agricultural sources (due to their diffuse nature, which makes it hard to measure directly) and oil rig venting (due to inaccurate and conflicted self-reporting, which can, however, be remediated by satellite monitoring, as these emissions are highly concentrated). Besides the anthropogenic methane emissions, which account for 12–20% of the overall GHG emissions,[11] there is an extremely large reservoir or methane, and CO_2, trapped in permafrost in the Arctic latitudes, which is not accounted in any of the

---

[11] https://www.globalmethane.org/documents/gmi-mitigation-factsheet.pdf

current scenarios, and is a materially significant risk factor in potentially accelerating the warming cycle to unprecedented levels. The Artic latitudes hold a vast amount of CO_2 and CH_4 in the oldest component of permafrost (called the Yedoma, this is a type of permafrost that was formed between 1.8 million and 10,000 years ago and is particularly rich in organic material). While studies are underway on the mechanisms that characterize both thawing and thermokarst, which is a fast process of permafrost degradation that leads to rapid thawing of the ancient deposits, the fact that the area is warming up at a 33% faster rate than what was currently estimated, as discovered by a study on Nature Geoscience in May 2022,[12] raises the risk rating of methane to new heights. To put things into perspective, according to a recent European Space Agency-ESA article,[13] the Arctic permafrost stores almost 1,700 billion tons of carbon, the release of which, through feedback loops, could cause a highly accelerated warming (which has not been modeled in any of the current scenarios).

2.8 DATA QUALITY ISSUES FOR CLIMATE LIABILITY RISK

Once we move to analyzing the situation for climate liability risk, and the data that it requires for proper modeling, an entirely novel set of challenges is revealed to us.

Climate liability modeling, in the sense of trying to establish a likelihood that an individual entity will be sued for climate-related matters in any given year, the likely duration of the lawsuit, the likelihood of losing

---

[12] Zhou, W., Leung, L.R. and Lu, J. (2024). Steady threefold Arctic amplification of externally forced warming masked by natural variability. *Nat. Geosci.* https://doi.org/10.1038/s41561-024-01441-1 https://www.nature.com/articles/s41561-024-01441-1

[13] https://www.esa.int/Applications/Observing_the_Earth/FutureEO/Permafrost_thaw_it_s_complicated

the lawsuit (or of settling), and the amount of liquidating damages paid in the case of a loss or settlement, requires access to a series of datasets (both directly related to climate, and to be used as proxies) that the traditional quant modeler is usually not familiar with. These datasets have, among others, the data quality issues presented in the following list.

Lack of long enough historical climate litigation precedents for model training: When modeling climate litigation we need to produce computational simulations to estimate the probability of a specific company (or governmental entity) falling victim to a climate-based lawsuit. In order to build such a model, we need to have a certain amount of data that relates to previous climate litigation to be able to determine the likelihood of lawsuits by jurisdictions and sectors, and evaluate the role of prior litigation (if any). This endeavor requires carefully going through legal cases databases, such as the one maintained by the Sabin Center for Climate Change Law at Columbia University, and categorizing the cases by type, outcome, sector, and any other relevant metric, as per the example shown in Figure 2.8.

Small sample size for climate lawsuits that have reached settlement/final sentencing stages: Once we have built a model that can determine, for any given year, the (scenario-dependent) probability for a specific company to be sued over climate-related matters, it is necessary to be able to estimate what the likelihood of losing the lawsuit or settling might be, which reduces the (already small) sample that we have at our disposal for model training.

Need for proxying for damages: The long duration and relatively recent nature of climate litigation translates into a very limited set of cases which have reached compensation/damage determination stage, which is an additional data problem for modeling climate liabilities, and requires the model developers to shift to proxies/law approaches to estimate the damages that successful litigation will result in. For some cases this estimate can be quite straightforward (for example, where the EU

Figure 2.8 Climate litigation cases in the United States by year, 2004–2022.
Source: Adapted from C.R. Castelli based on data from Sabin Center for Climate Change Law.

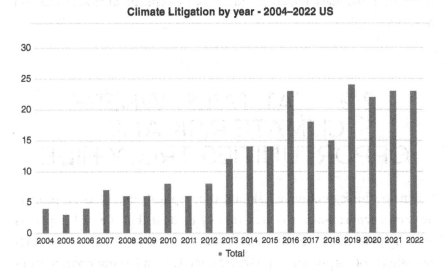

Green Claims directive mandates a 4% of annual revenue penalty for greenwashing), while in other cases, it might be necessary to see what courts did in similar cases (such as tobacco litigation, or the recent oxycodone litigation) to build a credible framework. Damage compensation from acute/chronic physical events, on the other hand, is more easily calculated, as it can be tied to directly measurable factors (the damage incurred), and individual companies can be held accountable based on their percentage of historical cumulative emissions.

Subjective nature of case interpretation: The databases being used to train the models are typically devoid of many details on specific cases, and the model developers and analysts need to review the data to be able to categorize cases within a generalized taxonomy that is useful for modeling climate liabilities. This is, by definition, a subjective task, and different analysts could, and will, produce somewhat different historical time series to train the models on. Likewise, there is a subjective nature of the prediction of future cases, and how they will pan out, and climate liability modeling should be approached as the *implied cost of self-insuring against climate litigation* by individual companies and not as a specific prediction of a lawsuit or another.

2.9 FAT TAILS: WHERE CLIMATE RISK AND OPPORTUNITIES TRULY HIDE

When we think of climate risk and the implications it has on properties and corporations, it is very rapidly evident that the real impact is unlikely to be due to the direct costs of the carbon price hitting the balance sheets of corporations via their Scope 1, 2, and 3 emissions, or from the direct damage inflicted by acute physical risk on real estate holdings. This is very clear when the aggregate results of the 2023 Federal Reserve Board (FRB) Climate Scenario Analysis[14] are reviewed, and the underwhelming nature of the losses that the exercise highlighted is taken into account (the results were even lower than would have been expected due to the FRB choosing to only look at the first 10 years of a 30-year climate scenario).

The true risks (and, conversely, opportunities) for climate, which constitute the fat tails in the climate outcomes distribution, lie in the second, and third, order effects of global warming, and the responses that it will elicit in societies around the world. Nominally, these second and third order impacts can be summarized in the following sections.

---

[14] https://www.federalreserve.gov/publications/files/csa-exercise-summary-20240509.pdf

Physical Risk in Transition Risk

While the direct impact of physical risk on assets such as commercial real estate, or residential real estate is a (fairly) straightforward exercise, which is somewhat complicated by considerations of cost and availability of insurance, and pass-through rates for costs of upgrades, preparation, and hardening of assets, the indirect impacts require an additional layer of modeling which is asset and company specific. The indirect impact of physical risk in transition risk can be exemplified by the case of a hurricane, wildfire, or coastal flooding event hitting a factory owned by a corporation. While the direct impact to the facility has been considered in the physical risk model and is, likely, covered by specific insurance (which would have a growing cost over the scenario), the true, long-term, impact to the company is due to the asset being offline for a significant period of time (which is subject to modeling assumptions on the severity of the event, and data assumptions tied to the building itself) and the consequent losses of future inventory, market shares, and opportunities that can be far reaching and difficult to model in a generalized way. The same kind of concept applies to weather events affecting the supply chains, in ways that are similar to what has been recently seen for the Covid-19 pandemic. In order to model this additional layer of risk appropriately, it is necessary to have a significant amount of data available for the company (location of assets, as well as information on the supply chains on which it relies), and computational models, which allow running multiple iterations of simulations to determine the distribution of impacts that is likely to occur (as this is a statistical event, it does not depend directly from the scenario being run, and therefore can only be estimated computationally over very large numbers of simulations).

Stranded Assets

When we look at any company today, or at certain types of real estate assets, we typically have a set of assumptions that we can rely on for the estimation of what the LGD would be for each of them, which are typically tied to certain conversion factors being used for assets having to be liquidated. If we take shale oil reserves, for example, and assume a liquidation that occurs in 2025, the likely value that will be obtained is probably in the range of 95 cents to each dollar on the balance sheet, or not very far off. If we, however, think about this same situation in a scenario where the date is 2035 and we are on a net-zero transition, that very same asset is likely to have a much lower value (if any value at all), and the net present value of the asset is therefore scenario-dependent (given the underground assets cannot be instantaneously extracted, and the scenario postulates a decreasing value and a hard stop date). A similar situation presents itself for above ground assets, both in the energy sector (for example coal utilizing power plants) and in the real estate sector (buildings with poor energy efficiency, which will be increasingly at risk of falling afoul of rental regulations). All of these types of stranded assets need to be modeled, and integrated into the projections, in addition to the direct effects of emissions, as they have the potential to impact PD and LGD values in a material way.

Climate Litigation Risk

In its 2022 report, the Intergovernmental Panel on Climate Change (IPCC) acknowledged for the first time the impact of litigation on "the outcome and ambition of climate governance." The Climate Change Laws of the World (CCLW) database shows that there has been a sharp rise in the number of climate change–related lawsuits filed worldwide over time. A wide variety of corporate industries are the targets of growing numbers of lawsuits brought against the largest corporate carbon emitters. Fifty-four percent of cases had outcomes that were in favor of taking action on climate change, according to an analysis of the CCLW database results. The following categories are typically included in litigation cases against corporations:

- Future Damages
  - Greenwashing
  - Failure to enforce climate standards
  - Failure to adapt
- Past/Current Damages
  - Damage compensation due to acute or chronic physical risk effects

As a result, it is necessary to incorporate the likelihood, and potential impact, of successful lawsuits tied to climate litigation into the overall modeling framework, as the penalties that existing legislature has put in place in several jurisdictions are of such a magnitude to pose existential challenges to many companies, if they were to be levied as written.

Concentration Risk

Concentration risk for the purposes of climate risk is to be seen as the effects that stem from being in an area or sector of concentrated climate risk, either physical or transition risk, which acts in addition to the standard direct effects. Examples of climate concentration risk are those of businesses supporting the economy of agricultural areas that will become non-productive because of droughts due to climate change, or services and entertainment businesses in towns that are highly concentrated in manufacturing of components for internal combustion engines, which are indirectly exposed to climate risk via concentration effects.

Contagion Risk

By contagion risk we mean the risk that is indirectly transferred to a corporation via suppliers/clients/workforce, independently of a specific corporation's emissions profile. Examples of this can include service providers for high-emitting companies, or companies who indirectly rely on suppliers who are high emitters and are likely to either go out of business or raise prices dramatically.

Network Effects

Network effects, for the purposes of Transition Finance in this book, are intended as effects of climate-driven defaults that are transferred via the networks in a systemic way, with typically more than two nodes of separation between the defaulter and the company being affected by the default. This can be seen as the effects of potential defaults of key players in local markets affecting multiple companies and assets in a cascading manner, which is typically difficult to model and predict (this can be as indirect as a large company going out of business, vacating a significant number of office space and depressing the value of commercial real estate on the local market, and, consequently, causing losses to a regional REIT). This is also a very difficult effect to measure and model, as it requires significant amounts of data and a computational framework of models to run very large numbers of simulations (ideally an agent-based model framework).

Migration Effects

This last effect is extremely high-level yet has dramatic potential for impacting local communities and economies. As the impact of acute and chronic physical risk manifests itself over the years, it is expected that certain areas of the globe will become less adapted to permanent habitation, while others will become more appealing, and migratory fluxes will ensure as a result (both within countries and between countries). These aspects need to be modeled initially via the GCM/IAM models, and then specifically by using dedicated population models for migration estimation such as the ones presented in Atesmachew et al. (2018),[15] where the authors present an agent-based model, called OMOLAND-CA, which explores the impact of climate change on the adaptive capacity of rural communities in the South Omo Zone of Ethiopia. The purpose of the model is to answer research questions on the resilience and adaptive capacity of rural households with respect to variations in climate, socioeconomic factors, and land use at the local level. Results from the model show that successive episodes of extreme events (e.g., droughts) affect the adaptive capacity of households, causing them to migrate from the region.

2.10 ARE MODELS ALONE ENOUGH TO ALLOW US TO MAKE INFORMED INVESTING DECISIONS?

The models alone are not sufficient to allow us to proceed directly to investment decisions, as transition finance investing is a complex endeavor which requires detailed review and challenge stages, SME-based edits, overlays, overrides, etc.

---

[15] Atesmachew et al. (2018). An agent-based model of rural households' adaptation to climate change. *Journal of Artificial Societies and Social Simulation*, 21(4)4, 2018. Doi: 10.18564/jasss.3812. http://jasss.soc.surrey.ac.uk/21/4/4.html

CHAPTER THREE

THE PROBLEM OF BACK-TESTING AND BENCHMARKING

How to tackle the uncharted waters that lie in front of us

3.1 THE PROBLEM OF BACK-TESTING, NARRATIVES, AND VALIDATION

When looking at climate modeling in general, and climate scenario analysis specifically, both of which are critical to transition finance investing, we are faced with structural characteristics that give rise to the trifecta of challenges represented by narratives, back-testing, and validation, as shown in Figure 3.1.

In order to understand these three problems, and what we can do about them, it is important that we understand where they originate, and

Figure 3.1 The trifecta of challenges with climate modeling.

we embrace them, as opposed to trying to fight them and trying to fit a square peg into a round hole.

Let's look at each of these three problems individually, determine what it is, where it originates from, and how to tackle it.

3.2 NARRATIVES AND WHY WE NEED THEM TO BE STRONG AND EXPLAINABLE

Modeling climate is a nascent science and is strongly predicated on first principles and scientific bases to the models being used, as we have seen in Chapter 2.

Consequently, most of the parties involved in the review, challenge, and utilization of results that the models produce are not familiar with the techniques, challenges, strengths, and weaknesses that these models have. It is therefore important that the model developers, and the PM and investment team, are capable of generating clear, concise, consistent, and transparent narratives to explain how results were produced, which variables and relationships were the main drivers of what is being presented, and why the results make sense.

This is particularly important if the results are being discussed and reviewed with internal reviewers such as model risk management and internal audit (or external reviewers such as regulators, if applicable) and other parties (such as bankers in the case of models being used for wholesale credit) who have competing interests.

Narratives need to be strong and explainable as:

- Regulators, model risk management, and internal audit will expect stronger impacts than what is produced.
- Business owners and bankers will push for weaker impacts.
- Model developers need to justify the results in a convincing manner and resist the diverging pressures coming from these two sets of stakeholders.

3.3 BACK-TESTING: WHY WE REALLY CANNOT DO IT AND WHAT TO DO ABOUT IT

Climate change is an unprecedented event, at least within the human timeframe for which we have economic data to compare against, and one that entails a transition in state from a well-known state (i.e., the current fossil fuel–driven global economy) to a new state (a carbon-negative economy) that is unprecedented in the history of modern technological mankind.

This very nature of the phenomenon that we are trying to model leads to two complementary effects.

The first effect is that it is not possible to look to the past to predict the future, as the past holds little, if no, predictive value for the purposes of understanding where we are headed, and, most importantly, when to expect acceleration in the speed of change (i.e., trigger events). This also means that the very popular AI-driven approaches that are being used across multiple fields in recent years, hold little potential, as the basic principles behind AI are based upon pattern recognition, analysis of big datasets to find hard-to-detect associations and correlations, and, effectively, very good predictions of the future from very large sets of past events.

Given there are no real past events of climate change as a regime change that can be used to train an AI model to predict climate change pathways, the AI engines will be incapable of predicting anything different from what has already occurred (i.e., at best, a linear projection of the current change trends, and never a sigmoid curve, which is what is actually predicted by all behavioral/computational models).

The second effect, which is closely linked to the first, is that *it becomes impossible to back-test any model against historical data using traditional stochastic techniques*, since there is no historical record to test against (besides the initial flat part of the projected sigmoidal curve, which holds no informational value). To put it in other words, we cannot do what we do in standard stress testing, i.e., look at the 2008 Financial Crisis, or the 1970s Oil crisis as previous examples of what we are trying to model, and see how our model would have performed then, with the available data (as there is no prior climate change event to use).

The lack of the possibility for traditional back-testing requires that we change our paradigm for reviewing and challenging our results, and become more rigorous than we otherwise would be. Typically, we should implement, at least, the following best practices:

- Check results against external ones as a benchmark
- Have robust understanding of result drivers and narratives
- Produce detailed sensitivity testing for all models (i.e., understand what variables, drivers, and assumptions have impacts on the model output)
- Deep-dive on any surprising results to fully understand where the results come from

- Do not focus on false precision, keep in mind the directionality of results (winners/losers)
- Be ready to make changes and apply overlays/overrides for results that are hard to explain

3.4 VALIDATION AND WHY IT IS A CHALLENGE

When we look at things from the side of the model validators, all the considerations we have discussed earlier in this chapter coalesce into an overall difficulty to validate climate models in general. These are also compounded by some climate-specific issues which we shall address as follows.

The reasons for the challenging validation for climate models can be summarized along these lines:

Data is not good. As we have touched upon earlier, there are significant data quality issues with the models at large, which pose material challenges for validators when trying to assess the impact that these have on the overall results.

We cannot look to historical precedents to gain insights. As per section 3.3, it is not possible to use historical precedent to evaluate the performance of the models, thus depriving Model Risk Management of one of the principal tools used to gauge model performance in BAU (Business-As-Usual) processes.

The models are new and don't have long track records. The majority of models that MRM is used to validating are typically well established and have been in use, as a framework, for a long time (for example, PD/LGD/EAD models, ALM models, or VAR models), while climate models are fairly new, having been only in use in financial institutions for a short number of years at best. This short track record, and rapid evolution of the state of the art during the years in which it was established, makes it hard to compare current results to past results in a meaningful way, and further complicates the task at hand for MRM.

The modeling assumptions can make huge differences in the results. Since many of the models being used are forward projections of responses to complex scenarios, they are, by design, very sensitive to specific assumptions and relationships being modeled into the framework. Small changes in these variables and formulae can lead to major jumps in output for the model, and, if using vendor models, the relationships and underlying elasticities and sensitivities are often not fully divulged, in order to protect intellectual property. As a consequence of this, it is hard for MRM to be able to pinpoint which variables and assumptions drive the results, and which do not, and the validation work is therefore made harder.

Scenarios and IAM input have very large uncertainty bands. Projecting financial statements and performance 30 years into the future is no easy task, and has an intrinsically large margin of error, that is often not fully clear to the users of the model data. In addition to this uncertainty, there is an underlying uncertainty of the IAM models themselves, which has to be added to the model uncertainty, leading to a compounded effect. It is therefore difficult to look at results which are, by definition, produced as precise numbers, without falling into the pitfall of discussing them as if they indeed represent a precise estimate of reality at $T_0 + x$ years, as opposed to considering all the uncertainty that is associated with them, and evaluating the directionality and overall magnitude of the moves while not focusing on the (false) precision of the output. In the validation stages, it is often hard for MRM to correctly estimate these two concurrently operating uncertainty bands, and the impact that they can have on the overall model performance.

Model risk management is not familiar with the novel modeling techniques required for climate modeling. While for some portions of the E2E (End-to-End) climate modeling cycle as presented in Figure 3.1, MRM has a well-established familiarity with the models (for example the loss models), and the validation effort is limited to the idiosyncrasies of their use for climate applications, for others MRM has virtually no prior experience at all. This is clearly visible with the GCM/IAM portion of the modeling cycle, where the models are highly complex, computational, and include large portions that pertain to earth sciences and climatology, neither of which is a skillset that a model validator in the financial services is expected to be familiar with. While these models are unlikely to be validated at all (i.e., they are taken as external SME inputs), there are others, such as the models required for the computation of second- and third-order impacts within the climate premium estimation, that fall squarely within the mandate of the financial sector, but are still almost as alien to the run-of-the-mill validator as the climate models are. These models are based on agent-based model frameworks and computational frameworks based on behavioral rules, which are very rarely, if ever, used in traditional finance (the closest modeling technique to these models being Monte Carlo simulations), and therefore, when presented to MRM for validation, they create a unique set of challenges and questions.

3.5 WHAT TO BENCHMARK AGAINST?

Given the novel nature of transition finance investing, and the difficulty of back-testing any model and strategy, the question of what to benchmark an investor's performance against is not a trivial one. Effectively, we can generate a series of risk-adjusted returns (RAR) over time (and this should be looked at over the 20-year investment horizon for the funds in transition finance investing, and not on shorter durations), but how can we tell if these returns are good, average, or bad?

At the time of writing, this is still an unanswered question that requires some research to come up with a definitive answer, but there are a few options for metrics that could be used as starting points.

For private equity investing funds, performance can be evaluated through various metrics, including the internal rate of return (IRR), the multiple of invested capital (MOIC), and the public market equivalent (PME). To gauge the performance of private equity investments, it is common to use public market indexes like the S&P 500 as benchmarks. Additionally, these benchmarks can be adjusted by adding a premium, such as 4 to 6% to the S&P 500.[1]

A more advanced approach to assessing the performance of a private equity fund is by utilizing the public market equivalent (PME) method. This method involves comparing the cash flows and returns of a private equity fund with those of a public market index, such as the S&P 500 or the MSCI World. By employing the PME technique, a more comprehensive evaluation of a private equity fund's performance can be achieved. As an example the Russell 2000 public equity index is often considered as a good index for comparison of public equity returns across strategies.[2]

---

[1] https://www.northerntrust.com/documents/brochures/asset-servicing/private-equity-benchmarking.pdf
[2] https://www.chronograph.pe/private-equity-benchmarking-deep-dive

CHAPTER FOUR

TYPES OF FUNDS IN TRANSITION FINANCE

The varied ecosystem of investment opportunities in the transition finance space

4.1 WHAT TYPE OF INVESTMENTS?

Transition finance is a multifaceted and vast ecosystem of investment opportunities, which span from early-stage VC deals in emerging technology, to PE deals in rising players in growing markets, to equities and debt investing in publicly traded companies engaged in large-scale projects needed to sustain the transition from an oil and fossil-fuel based economy to one based on alternative energy and carbon-negative (Figure 4.1).

The resulting types of investments, therefore, are as varied as the opportunities that fall under this new industrial revolution that we are

Figure 4.1 Idealized views of characteristics of transition finance investing.

starting to enter, and have different time horizons, strategies, returns, and risk profiles, allowing the portfolio managers to tailor solutions based on their overall risk appetite and investment goals.

4.2 IS IT A STATIC ASSET ALLOCATION STRATEGY OR A DYNAMIC ONE?

Asset owners must be ready for the opportunity set to change due to the magnitude of the energy transition and the length of time required to go from fossil fuels to renewable energy sources. Traditional sector/industry classifications, for instance, might not be as helpful in the future as they are today, and new technologies, services, and companies might emerge, which have not yet been identified by current, state of the art, modeling approaches (see Figure 4.2). A transition finance portfolio that is climate-driven is likely to include a range of industries (such as industrials,

Figure 4.2 Conceptualizations on static or dynamic allocations.

technology, utilities, and consumer staples) and real asset plays, and this list is expected to change over time, producing a multisector opportunity set that will adapt dynamically over the years.

4.3 ONE APPROACH VERSUS MULTIPLE APPROACHES

Current ESG investing strategies typically focus on one specific KPI or metric to base the investment strategy upon, be this ESG ratings ("green vs. brown" portfolio theory), pure emissions (Weighted Average Carbon Intensity, WACI), Implied Temperature Rise (ITR), or Science Based Target Initiative alignment (SBTI). These approaches are used, and have some merit, to build equities and bond portfolios, where the goal is to create algorithmic exclusion/inclusion principles, and trade on relatively short-term returns from the stock markets.

For the purposes of transition finance investing, on the other hand, the approach has to be, by definition, one of multiple metrics and models, used

Figure 4.3 Conceptualizations on single or multiple approaches.

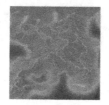

concurrently and compounded by subject matter expertise, to enrich the capability of making informed decisions over which opportunities (and which specific targets within the opportunity set) are to be part of the portfolio. See Figure 4.3.

This approach results in a much clearer and transparent enunciation of the rationale for each and every investment made and provides justification that can be used to track performance against stated objectives, as well as for capital raising/marketing purposes.

4.4 DIVERSIFICATION AND MOVING BEYOND PURELY EMISSIONS-BASED APPROACHES

A purely emissions-based approach to estimating the impact of transition risk, and by extension transition finance investing, severely underestimates both the impact and opportunities that derive from climate change, due to a convergence of factors (Figure 4.4) such as:

Incomplete nature of Scope 2 and Scope 3 emissions: for large numbers of companies, and data quality issues with the figures that are available.

Figure 4.4 Conceptualizations on factors impacting complexity in transition finance investing.

Generated with AI using Perchance

Lack of consideration for complex interactions typical of climate risk: that go beyond the first-order effects (i.e., emissions and effects of MeV pathways) such as:

Effects of Physical Risk in Transition Risk: the future losses that acute weather events cause to companies, beyond the immediate damages that derive from the event itself. This can be in the form of assets being offline for protracted periods of time, supply chain disruptions, losses of market share, losses of opportunities, etc.

Effects of Stranded Assets on Corporates and Real Estate: These are potential losses and worsening of balance sheets brought upon corporate entities or individuals by changes in regulation that lead to assets losing value at an accelerated time. Examples of this are below ground fossil fuel reservoirs, such as Tar Sands, which would become effectively worthless at a certain point in time in transition scenarios, above ground assets such as coal plants, which would not be allowed to operate and would require significant CapEx to be reconverted, and real estate with poor energy efficiency, which, as is already happening in various countries in the EU, would no longer be allowed to be rented out, leading to losses in value.

Effects of Climate Litigation Risk on Corporates and Munis/Sovereigns: the future losses that corporates are likely to suffer due to climate litigation, either as the result of incurred damages, resulting from acute or chronic physical risk, or future damages, from greenwashing and/or failure to enforce climate standards/adapt.

Effects of Concentration Risk: the potential losses that a corporate or a real asset can experience due to being in a concentrated area or sector that is indirectly exposed to transition or physical risk. An example is businesses supporting the economy of a ski resort which is likely to face decreasing skiing days due to climate change, or services and entertainment businesses in areas that specialize in coal mining, which are indirectly exposed to the risk of their source of income disappearing.

Contagion Risk: the losses that a corporate can be subjected to not due to the direct exposure to climate transition risk per se, but via the risk that comes via suppliers/clients/workforce being affected by transition risk and affecting the corporate in an indirect way. An example of this could be represented by a service provider, which has low or negligible emissions, but is servicing primarily companies that depend on emissions intensive clients, and which are at risk of losing business/defaulting when these high emitters are impacted.

Network Effects: These are potential losses deriving from network-driven effects due to climate-caused defaults, which, if sufficiently concentrated either geographically or by sector, have the potential to reach apparently unrelated corporates and businesses, and cause losses.

Migration Effects: these are losses due to the impact on macroeconomic variables, such as GDP, unemployment, and housing demand, driven by migratory fluxes caused by physical risk, both acute and chronic, and/or transition risk. Examples of this can be migration of population from areas that become chronically affected by coastal flooding or drought, or are displaced by technological innovation, as in the case of communities centered around fossil fuel extraction and refining sites, especially the ones that have the worst emission profiles, such as coal.

4.5 CONCEPTUAL FRAMEWORK FOR QUANTITATIVE INVESTING IN TRANSITION FINANCE

The overall conceptual framework for transition finance investing is shown in Figure 4.5. It differs from traditional ESG-themed investing by being quantitative-model driven, systematic, and transparent.

Figure 4.5 The Transition Finance Investment Thesis Identification Process.

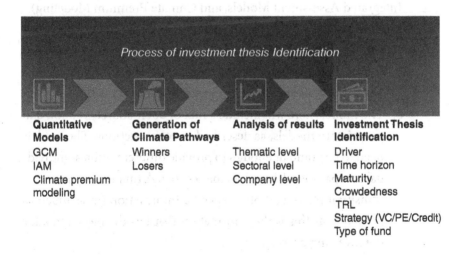

It uses the same principles of stress testing for financial institutions, which are widespread and in use across the majority of financial regulators worldwide and expands them to be used for investment decision making.

While traditional stress testing, with which the reader is likely familiar (CCAR, EBA stress tests, PRA stress tests, etc.), are focused on simulating the ability of a financial institution of dealing with an unexpected crisis or event (a "one-in-fifty" or "one-in-one-hundred" shock scenario, followed by a reversion to mean within typically three years), and are thus unsuitable for investment purposes, **climate scenario analysis** (which are the climate version of stress tests), as they focus on a series of likely transition scenarios (in fact, the entire gamut ranging from "do nothing" to "go net-zero as aggressively as humanly possible, starting tomorrow") **are extremely well suited to be used for the purposes of identification of investment opportunities**.

The Transition Finance Investment Thesis Identification Process (Figure 4.5) is therefore composed of the following four stages:

I. **Running the Quantitative Models** (General Circulation Models, Integrated Assessment Models, and Climate Premium Modeling)
   a. This portion of the process includes the decision of which transition scenario is thought to be the most likely (note: this is a key step, as a current policies projection will be very different from a Net Zero 2050 one, or from a custom scenario run).
   b. The models here will include a mix of open-source, vendor, and proprietary models, as described in other sections. The models need to be granular enough to provide differentiation at individual company level, based on the company's financials, emissions, transition plans, and other specific information (in as much as possible), as this is the information that has the most value for the investing process.

II. Generating the Climate Pathway Winners and Losers
   a. This portion of the process deals with the identification of companies that will benefit and companies that will be negatively affected by the climate scenario being run.
   b. The process allows us to identify the first slate of existing companies that are potential targets, but it is typically limited to publicly traded companies, that are already well established and have financials, emissions, and (ideally), transition plans available. For smaller companies, and new companies, the identification needs to come from subject matter expertise from steps III and IV.
III. Analyzing the Results
   a. This portion of the process focuses on reviewing the initial results and evaluating them at sectoral, geographical, and individual name level, to ensure that the model results are correct and align with the SME knowledge.
   b. Overlays and overrides are added to the results at this stage, to produce a final set of results that are used for investment thesis identification in step IV.
IV. Identifying the Investment Theses
   a. This portion of the process covers the translation of the analytic results from the models into multiple investment theses.
   b. The detailed process for investment theses identification is covered in Chapter 5, but the high-level steps are the following:
      i. Identify the set of opportunities at sector, theme, and individual name level.
      ii. Identify the driver for each opportunity.
      iii. Determine the overall technology readiness level for each opportunity.
      iv. Determine the investment horizon for each opportunity.
      v. Determine the investment maturity for each opportunity.
      vi. Determine the crowdedness for each opportunity.

vii. Identify the root problem for each opportunity.
viii. Identify the root problem causes for each opportunity.
ix. Identify what needs to happen to fix the issue for each opportunity.
x. Identify how soon the fix needs to happen for each opportunity.
xi. Identify what the investment opportunity is for each opportunity.
xii. Identify what the benefit of the investment is for each opportunity.
xiii. Identify the potential market size for each opportunity.
xiv. Identify the long-term investment vision for each opportunity.
xv. Identify the trigger event for each opportunity.
xvi. Identify the primary fund in which each opportunity belongs.
xvii. Identify the primary strategy in which each opportunity belongs.
xviii. Select the investment thesis that aligns with your individual. risk appetite, investment horizon, and area of expertise.
xix. Deep dive in investment theses of interest to identify targets and refine strategies.
xx. Build your portfolio based on identified targets.

4.6 POSITIVE SCREENING

In the transition finance investing strategy, one of the approaches used is positive screening (Figure 4.6), where the portfolio managers actively target companies that are leaders within the individual transition finance opportunity and align to a specific individual investment thesis.

Figure 4.6 Graphical visualization of principles of positive screening.

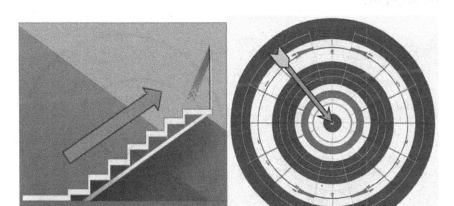

This screening allows for a transparent and explainable focus on companies and assets that are well positioned to meet the challenges of the scenario that has been identified as most plausible and has a direct correlation to measurable metrics and goals.

There is a flipside, as positive screening will reduce the total number of companies and assets that are available to invest in, and, if investing in PE or private credit, runs the risk of missing out on companies and assets that are the right bets, but not yet mature for the investing strategy being pursued. This flipside is mitigated by the four fund/three strategy approach that we shall cover in subsequent sections.

4.7   THEMATIC INVESTMENT

In addition to positive screening, transition finance investing, as a strategy, also includes thematic investment (Figure 4.7), where companies and assets that can benefit from specific climate-driven themes and trends are identified and selected, using a model-based approach.

Figure 4.7 Graphical visualization of principles of thematic investment.

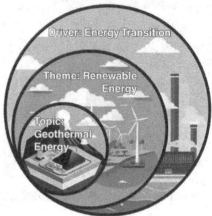

Thematic investment gives the overall strategy the added benefit of deriving revenues and alpha from the higher pricing power and increased potential revenue flows that come with the predicted growth of the specific market or asset class that the transition opportunity refers to.

The negative aspect of thematic investment, which however is common across transition finance investment for the reasons that we have seen in Chapter 3 on back-testing and benchmarking, is the challenging nature of finding relevant benchmarks to evaluate how the investments are performing. Additionally, but this again is aligned to many transition finance opportunities in general, the timelines for thematic investment tend to be long, and there can be debate on how well specific companies align to a specific theme (for example, is an oil and gas company that has 10% of their output in geothermal, aligned to the "geothermal" theme or not?).

Types of Funds in Transition Finance

4.8 INVESTING IN THE TRANSITION

Another strategy that is part of transition finance investing is investing in the transition (Figure 4.8), where investments are made in specific companies, from high emitting sectors which are committed to serious transition plans and/or possessing technology that is relevant to transition finance. An example of this is leading oil and gas companies in the

Figure 4.8 Graphical visualization of investing in the transition.

CCUS (Carbon Capture Usage and Storage) space, or the hypothetical oil and gas company from section 4.7 that has started differentiating in geothermal (assuming this is part of a long-term decarbonization strategy).

This approach provides access to potentially undervalued assets from sectors that are not typically being invested in, as well as generating real-world impact on high emitters, which is a key aspect of achieving a successful transition. It also allows a good amount of differentiation within the portfolio, as these assets tend to be uncorrelated to the rest of the assets that would be included in the portfolio.

The negative side of this approach is, besides the long-term duration of the investments which is common across the strategy, mostly one of perception of the investments not being "green" enough, coupled with the risk that the companies that become targets of investment end up not following up with the plans and/or not being receptive to guidance and advice from the transition finance investors, thus nullifying the effort.

4.9 THE FOUR FUND/THREE STRATEGY APPROACH

Transition finance investing, by the nature of the technologies, assets, and themes that arise from it, requires a multi-asset, multi-strategy setup, which we have formalized in a four fund/ three strategy approach.

The four funds (Figure 4.9) are: 1. The Growth Strategy Fund, 2. The Public Strategy Fund, 3. The Infrastructure Strategy Fund, 4. The Climate Alternatives/Physical Assets Plays Strategy Fund.

There are three types of strategies that are applicable in transition finance investing: 1. Venture capital, 2. Private equity, 3. Private credit.

Types of Funds in Transition Finance

Figure 4.9   The four types of funds in transition finance.

Types of proposed funds

| Growth Fund | Public Strategy | Infrastructure Strategy | Climate Alternatives (Physical Asset Plays) |

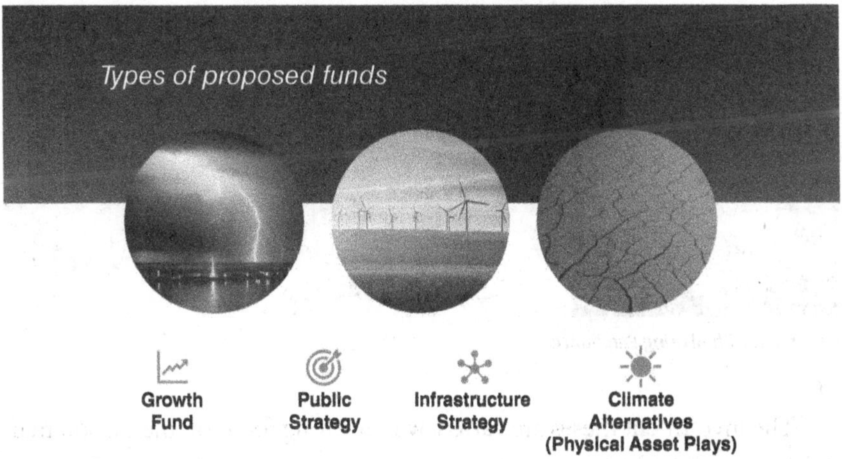

Generated with AI using Perchance

The Time Horizon for Transition Finance Funds

The time horizon for transition finance funds is, by definition, one characterized by a long duration, and often looks at a 20-year life span, even if certain theses and investments are likely to have shorter durations and earlier liquidation events (Figure 4.10).

Transition finance investing is a strategy that is suited to patient and flexible investors, who are playing the long game, and focusing on long-term benefits, as opposed to short-term gains.

The evaluation of the fund's performance over time will be, generally, risk-adjusted returns over the investment horizon.

The Growth Strategy Fund

This fund includes companies primed for rapid revenue or earnings growth, outpacing either industry peers or the market overall.

Figure 4.10 Graphical visualization of time horizon considerations for transition finance.

Generated with AI using Perchance

The investment theses are varied, with a strong focus on the carbon markets space (VCM exchanges, VCM insurance, VCM E2E risk transfer, VCM MMRV) and the carbon dioxide removal technology itself (BECCS, Biochar, DAC, ocean-based CDR). Additionally, there is a focus on growth sectors of transportation (electric airplanes), opportunistic responses to higher temperatures and economy transitions (*Energy Efficiency for Buildings*, workforce retraining and climate litigation) and modeling/compliance solutions (Methane measure, novel modeling of hurricanes and tornado impacts, transition risk E2E modeling for financial institutions). The investment model is *purchase and hold, or purchase, grow, and exit*, depending on the area of focus.

The Public Strategy Fund

The public strategy focuses on publicly traded companies, to lend capital as private credit and invest/co-invest in joint ventures with publicly traded companies. It also focuses on understanding the risks and identifying the opportunities of climate change in the transition finance space, as applicable to public companies.

The investment theses range from traditional plays such as various types of metals and mining, and the energy sector (nuclear reactor manufacturers), to more climate-specific ones, such as insurance companies with novel modeling approaches for coastal areas, HVAC manufacturers and installers, and cutting-edge transportation sector technology companies, such as EVs (cars and motorcycles), electric trucks, Mag-lev trains, and emissions-free shipping.

The investment model is *purchase and hold*, or *purchase, grow, and exit*, depending on the area of focus.

The Infrastructure Strategy Fund

The infrastructure fund invests in climate-driven public assets and services that are essential for a functioning society, such as power, transport, water and waste.

The climate change drivers are acting in unison with traditional drivers such as population growth, aging infrastructure, GDP growth in developing countries and governmental subsidies to increase the attractiveness of the sector.

The investment theses range from traditional infrastructure deals in the water space, hydroelectric power space, wind and solar power generation, and the electric grid upgrade space, to more transition-focused energy plays such as Carbon Capture Utilization and Storage (CCUS) facilities, energy storage companies, geothermal energy, Sustainable Aviation Fuel (SAF), and tidal power, to physical risk–driven plays such as tidal zone protection technology infrastructure.

The investment model is *purchase and hold*, or *purchase, grow, and exit*, depending on the area of focus.

The Climate Alternatives/Physical Assets Plays Strategy Fund

This fund includes compelling climate-driven investment theses in the physical assets space, which include a range of investments from traditional property transactions in the farmland and agriculture space and the timberland space, to more transition-focused plays such as paper-recycling facilities and abandoned subterranean mines, for usage for long-term carbon sequestration and carbon credits.

The revenue model is buy *and hold*, which can be broken down into *buy and operate*, and *buy and lease* (or some combination thereof).

4.10 THE INVESTMENT MATRIX

The investment matrix (Figure 4.11) for transition finance investing crosses the four funds with the three investing strategies, to highlight the Primary/Initial focus, and the Secondary/Later focus. It also shows which strategies

Figure 4.11 The 4 × 3 investment matrix of funds and strategies.

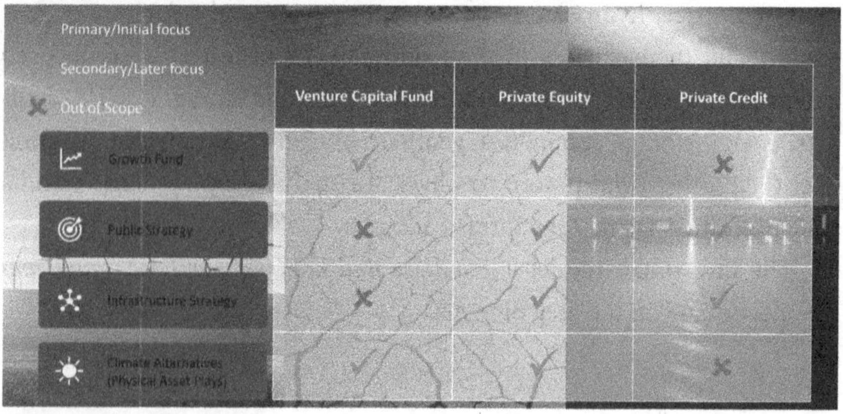

	Venture Capital Fund	Private Equity	Private Credit
Growth Fund	✓	✓	✗
Public Strategy	✗	✓	✓
Infrastructure Strategy	✗	✓	✓
Climate Alternatives (Physical Asset Plays)	✓	✓	✗

Legend: Primary/Initial focus; Secondary/Later focus; ✗ Out of Scope

are out of scope (for example Venture Capital in the Infrastructure Strategy Fund, or Private Credit in the Climate Alternatives/Physical Assets Plays).

By observing the matrix we see how all four funds have Private Equity as their Primary Focus (which is understandable, as transition finance investing is primarily a PE strategy), and the Growth Fund and the Climate Alternatives have a secondary VC component (but not a Private Credit one), while the Public Strategy and the Infrastructure Strategy have an immediate Private Equity component, in addition to the PE one, but no VC component.

The matrix allows for the entire coverage of the universe of transition finance opportunities, and could be, ideally, covered by a single entity, or, alternatively, by a group of co-investing funds sharing the same vision and methodology.

CHAPTER FIVE

EXAMPLES OF HOW TO BUILD AN INVESTMENT PORTFOLIO

How to identify the potential winners and what to do about it

5.1 DECIDE WHAT IS THE CLIMATE TRANSITION SCENARIO YOU BELIEVE IS LIKELY TO HAPPEN

This step in the process shown in the flowchart (see Figure 5.1) is the most critical one, as everything else depends on the outcome of this decision, and not enough stress can be placed on how important it is that the appropriate scenario (or scenarios) be selected for modeling.

PRINCIPLES OF TRANSITION FINANCE INVESTING

Figure 5.1   The transition finance investing flowchart.

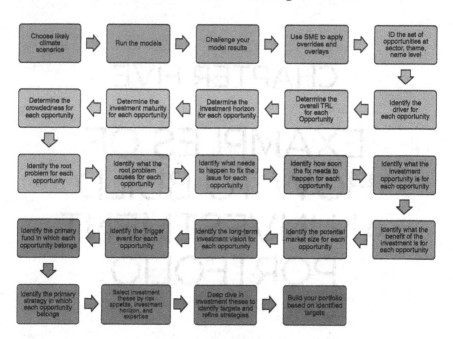

As a best practice, it is good to run at least three different scenarios, to be able to assess the sensitivity of the results to scenario assumptions, and the timing of trigger events (one of these scenarios should always be the "Current Policies/Do Nothing" scenario and the other one should be a "Net Zero 2050/ Immediate Transition" kind of scenario, to have a bookending set of scenarios to compare to the one that is chosen as the most likely one). *The time-horizon* on which the scenarios should be run, given the dynamics of climate change and transition finance, *should always be 30 years into the future* (so, if we are running in 2025, it should be a 2026–2056 projection).

This decision must be based on up-to-date information on the state of global geo-political events, the ongoing efforts of decarbonization across the world, and the measured speed at which GHG levels are increasing, as well as the frequency of extreme weather events.

The last item in the list, the increasingly frequent extreme weather events, is particularly relevant, as it holds the potential to be one of the big drivers in determining aggressive climate action in major economies, such as the United States, South East Asia, Mexico, Japan, and certain areas of Central and South America, due to the potential knock-on effects that repeated climate disasters (such as hurricanes, coastal floods, wildfires, etc.) leading to failures of insurance companies would have on public opinion, and consequently government and policy. This mechanism can be compared to what was observed during the Covid-19 pandemic, where the initial response was muted indifference and minimization of the impact of the epidemic, rapidly followed by a public opinion swing (and policy swing) once the mortality numbers started becoming significantly large, which led to the implementation of extreme policy decisions (blanket lockdowns), which would have been unimaginable only a few months before.

As part of the decision process of determining the best scenario to use, it is necessary to consider which scenario approach to follow:

- Use pre-prepared scenarios (such as NGFS)
- Use customized scenarios run through IAMs (such as GCAM)

Both options have pros and cons, which we can quickly address as follows:

Pre-prepared Scenarios

Pros

- These scenarios come with a lot of pre-existing work done by world-renowned SMEs in economics, climate, social sciences, etc.
- Narratives exist and are clearly enunciated and easily explained.
- Most practitioners, academics, and investors in the ESG and climate field are familiar with the scenarios and narratives.

- Vendor models typically can process these scenarios without any need for customization.
- There is no requirement for deep-diving into the complexities of scenario generation to be able to benefit from the scenarios.

Cons

- The scenarios are pre-set and cannot be changed.
- There are many assumptions and built-in views in the scenarios that the portfolio managers might disagree with, and could result in significantly different pathways.
- The scenarios use a limited set of IAMs, thus limiting the choice of models for the portfolio manager (PM).

Customized Scenarios

Pros

- Scenarios that fully match the portfolio manager's views on likely events can be integrated into the investment framework.
- The PM has complete control on assumptions and views that are included into the scenario.
- The PM can choose to use newer and potentially more relevant IAMs than what is used in the pre-prepared scenarios.

Cons

- Usage of custom scenarios requires significant amounts of specialized work for scenario generation, execution, and implementation.
- Narratives need to be written for any custom scenario in order to explain what is being projected to investors.
- Given this is a rare approach, most of the investing, academic, and climate community would not be familiar with it.
- If using vendor models, there would be potentially a need for significant customization to allow intake of custom scenarios.

Examples of How to Build an Investment Portfolio

There is no clear winner in this case, and the decision needs to be made by the investment team, based on the following considerations:

- Available resources and skillsets for custom versus pre-prepared scenarios
- Cost/benefit analysis
- Alignment of pre-existing scenarios with your own views of most likely scenario
- Timing considerations and other practical considerations

5.2 RUN THE MODELS BASED ON YOUR SCENARIOS

Once the decision has been made on what scenario to use (as per section 5.1), the next step is to run the scenario and models, to generate the results of the scenarios that have been chosen (Figure 5.2).

Figure 5.2 Example of energy investment from NGFS Phase IV scenarios.
Source: Adapted from https://www.ngfs.net/ngfs-scenarios-portal/

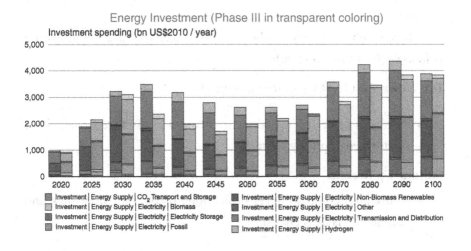

Figure 5.3 Example of solar use and carbon sequestration involving BECCS projections from NGFS Phase IV scenarios.
Source: Adapted from https://www.ngfs.net/ngfs-scenarios-portal/

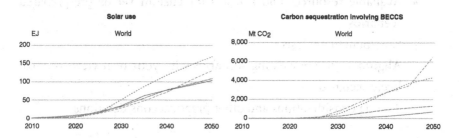

The models, as described in Chapter 2, will provide a set of projections (Figure 5.3) by country, geography, sector, and select individual corporate names (based on availability of data and relevance of companies, the methodologies and techniques for these selections being outside the scope of this book), or projected impacts of climate risk on specific asset classes by location (for example CRE and RRE, if in scope for the fund). Additionally, there will also be the results of the IAMs themselves, which will include the overall projections for multiple climate and MeV variables (Figure 5.4) that are critical to the investment process too (these are used for the identification of growing sectors and opportunities; see Chapter 12 on geothermal for an example).

These results will come in the form of projected timeseries that differ as follows (for transition risk):

Top-Down Results (by sector/geography)

- Series of projected variations in changes in distance to default by sector/geography by scenario

Bottom-Up Results:

- Individual company level projections of relevant financials and climate KPIs by scenario

Figure 5.4 Example of comparison for carbon sequestration projections between NGFS scenarios Phase III and Phase IV using REMIND IAM model.
Source: Adapted from https://www.ngfs.net/ngfs-scenarios-portal/

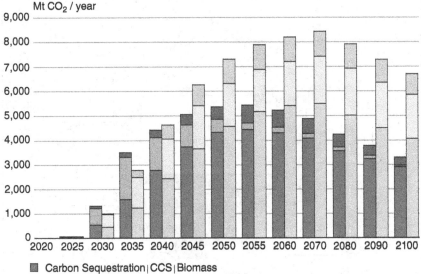

These results will be directly generated by the modeling framework without any manual intervention, and need to be reviewed and challenged by the modeling/investing team, as per section 5.3.

5.3 CHALLENGE YOUR MODEL RESULTS

Model results cannot be taken "as is" and acted upon. There are often results that are unintuitive, incorrect, or perplexing that are mixed in with valid ones, and these need to be identified, analyzed, and highlighted.

Figure 5.5 The model results challenge process.

As shown in Figure 5.5, the reasons for these results are typically the following (and there might be others too):

Bad/missing data: In many cases, certain companies/assets have data that is either missing or wrong, which leads to nonsensical results being generated. Given the large volumes of data being processed, it is easier to catch these results at the end of the process, as opposed to preemptively checking each and every data point before running the models. These cases are often fairly easy to identify as they lead to outcomes that are dramatically outside the average sectoral/geographical performance, and can be resolved with fairly straightforward analysis.

Modeling assumptions/misalignments: These are cases where the data is accurate, but the model is not using it in the correct way, and therefore is generating inaccurate/incorrect results. These are often systemic in nature and follow recognizable patterns (for example, you might notice that all of the Japanese companies in the simulation are being hit dramatically). The reasons are often harder to understand (the model might not be trained to read Japanese accounting standards, and therefore assume companies have no capital reserves), and require more workarounds to diagnose and fix.

Lack of company/sector-specific data in the model: These are cases where the model is projecting outcomes based on the knowledge and data that are available to it, and the PM/modelers are aware of additional circumstances that make the projection outdated (for example, the model might be projecting a power company to be severely hit by a shift to net zero because it is currently using coal plants for 90% of their power generation, but the PM and the investors are aware that the CEO and board have started a plan to shift completely to geothermal within a certain timeframe, which is not being addressed in the model).

Model uncertainty: The models always have large bands of uncertainty, and the results should mostly be used for indications of directionality rather than precise target end states. Often, some amount of the variability of the results can derive by how the computational components of the model have been run in a specific simulation, and results that are puzzling call for a repetition of the computational parts at higher numbers of simulations, to confirm/invalidate the results.

5.4 USE SUBJECT MATTER EXPERTISE TO APPLY OVERRIDES AND OVERLAYS TO THE MODELS

Once the challenging of the model results has been finalized, as per section 5.3, the PM, model developers, and any additional SME as needed, determine the final set of overrides and overlays to be applied to the model results, to produce the final set of approved results for transition finance opportunity identification (Figure 5.6).

This step is a relatively straightforward one, where the output from the models is modified, using the agreed-upon changes, and produces a final set of data that can be reviewed and presented at various levels of granularity.

This is an important step of the process, as these results are what the investment process relies upon for the decision making, and are likely to be shared (at aggregate level) with investors at some point in the fundraising/reporting cycles.

Figure 5.6 The subject matter experts overrides and overlays process.

5.5 IDENTIFY THE SET OF OPPORTUNITIES AT SECTOR, THEME, AND INDIVIDUAL NAME LEVEL

This step is the one that requires the most cross-sectional amount of work and is generally characterized by being a blend of analytics, subject matter expertise, and intuition. It also requires the PM and the rest of the investment team to be dynamically adjusting this set to new developments and updated model runs, as we have discussed in section 5.2.

The way the identification process is performed is by systematically going through the scenario narratives and variable pathways, and translating them into the sectoral, thematic, and individual company level insights that are the foundational blocks of the transition finance investing method (Figure 5.7).

This work requires a vast amount of research and prior expertise in the field, to be able to read the scenarios and model results in a coherent

Figure 5.7 The identification of opportunities at driver, theme, and topic level, exemplified for geothermal energy.

way, as well as cross-reference the growth opportunities that the scenarios implicitly identify by variables (such as growing price of carbon, volume of carbon dioxide removal, projected amount of geothermal energy production, etc.), with real-world target companies that exist today, and are at the right stage of their corporate development to benefit from the future growth that the scenarios predict.

Chapter 12 will provide a case study of how this method is applied to the example opportunity of geothermal, to give our readers a hands-on feeling of how the process works and what the output is in the real world.

5.6　IDENTIFY THE DRIVER FOR EACH OPPORTUNITY

For each transition finance opportunity, the main driver needs to be identified. This is, fundamentally, the risk transmission channel that is driving the opportunity (after all, risk is the flipside of opportunity).

As a refresher, the four risk transmission channels (Figure 5.8) for climate risk are:

1. **Acute Physical Risk:** Risks resulting from the increased frequency of extreme weather events deriving from GHG-driven climate change.

Figure 5.8　The four climate risk drivers: Acute physical risk, chronic physical risk, transition risk, and climate liability risk.

Generated with AI using Perchance

2. **Chronic Physical Risk:** Risks deriving from the permanent changes in weather patterns deriving from GHG-driven climate change.
3. **Transition Risk:** Risks deriving from the adaptation to new policies, technologies, and market trends, deriving from GHG-driven climate change.
4. **Climate Litigation Risk:** Risks deriving from increased stakeholder litigation and regulatory enforcement, resulting from GHG-driven climate change.

Most opportunities will be driven by a single driver (for example, "HVAC Manufacturing and Installation" is driven by chronic physical risk, as the warming up of the planet will increase the demand for air conditioning in areas where it currently isn't required), but there is no specific reason to assume that this is a steadfast rule that will always apply, and some cases, will defy this trend.

5.7 DETERMINE THE OVERALL TECHNOLOGY READINESS LEVEL FOR EACH OPPORTUNITY

For each opportunity being assessed, it is now important to be able to determine the Technology Readiness Level, which is an important metric to understand how far along the opportunity is, in general terms.

The concept of technology readiness levels was first developed at NASA in 1974 and officially established in 1989. Initially, there were seven levels defined, but in the 1990s, NASA transitioned to a nine-level scale, which has since been widely embraced.

For the purposes of this book, we shall use the definitions used by the European Union, which are more generic than the ones used by NASA, and applicable to a wider array of situations (Table 5.1).

Table 5.1 Technology Readiness Levels as defined by the EU.

Technology Readiness Level (TRL)	Description[1]
1	Basic principles observed
2	Technology concept formulated
3	Experimental proof of concept
4	Technology validated in lab
5	Technology validated in relevant environment (industrially relevant environment in the case of key enabling technologies)
6	Technology demonstrated in relevant environment (industrially relevant environment in the case of key enabling technologies)
7	System prototype demonstration in operational environment
8	System complete and qualified
9	Actual system proven in operational environment

While the concept of TRL typically applies to an individual technology, by definition, we are here expanding it to a sector or opportunity set, and averaging it, to be used as a proxy for how far ahead the technological state of art is, across the entire investing ecosystem.

This averaging can be achieved either mathematically by a careful census of the companies, technologies, and opportunities that are to be evaluated (which however brings up questions about whether to use weighted averages, and if so, how to weigh), or by using a qualitative approach and subject matter expertise, to assess what the TRL for the opportunity is.

It is important to note how, while TRLs are relatively quantitative in nature, they are still open to debate (as to what constitutes "demonstration in operational environment," for example) for individual technologies,

---

[1] https://ec.europa.eu/research/participants/data/ref/h2020/wp/2014_2015/annexes/h2020-wp1415-annex-g-trl_en.pdf

and the purpose of using them within the framework of transition finance investing is to provide the PM and investors with an easy way of addressing and understanding, at a glance, where the technology is for a specific opportunity.

5.8 DETERMINE THE INVESTMENT HORIZON FOR EACH OPPORTUNITY

The determination of the investment horizon refers to, in general, how long the duration of the investment in a specific transition finance opportunity would typically be. Considering that transition in finance opportunities are generally long-term by nature, it is unlikely that we would be looking at anything that has a horizon shorter than ~6/7 years, with multiple opportunities (such as "Northern Latitudes Farmland") stretching into significantly longer durations (20+ years).

Within the same opportunity, however, it is possible to have varying investment horizons and opportunistic exits, so, as for all of these initial KPI and metrics, we must not forget that we are always looking at them and making a determination at overall average level.

5.9 DETERMINE THE INVESTMENT MATURITY FOR EACH OPPORTUNITY

The determination of the investment maturity refers to, in general, the allocation of the average state of maturity for investments in the specific opportunity, in terms of readiness to invest. As in the case of TRL averaging, this

Table 5.2 Maturity for investment as used for transition finance investing opportunity grading.

Maturity for Investment	Description
In development	The opportunity set is in early stages, there are likely to be VC openings and/or PE ones, but the timing is 12/36 months away.
Pilot is ongoing	Pilot programs are ongoing within the opportunity set, allowing for investment within 6/18 months horizon.
Ready	Investment opportunities are ready for investment as of today.
Mature	Investments have already been made in the space in the last 12/36 months and others are available.
Probably late	Investments have been made in the last 5 years, and the most interesting plays are probably off the table.

is an overall value for the opportunity as a whole, and a value of "Probably late" (Table 5.2) doesn't, per se, mean that there are no good investments to be made within the specific opportunity (it simply implies that these investments will be fewer and far between, when compared to a similar opportunity where the investment maturity is "Ready").

5.10 DETERMINE THE CROWDEDNESS FOR EACH OPPORTUNITY

The determination of crowdedness, as shown in Table 5.3, of the opportunity allows the PM and the investment team to assess how popular the opportunity is within the investor community.

Table 5.3 Investment crowdedness as used for transition finance investing opportunity grading.

Crowdedness	Description
Not crowded yet	The opportunity has not yet become known to many investors, the number of VC deals is small, and there aren't any significant PE deals to be found. No companies have gone public doing exclusively what the opportunity focuses on.
Somewhat crowded	The Opportunity has started to gain acceptance and popularity amongst investors. There are a good number of VC deals, as well as PE deals. There still aren't any publicly traded companies that have IPO'd doing exclusively what the opportunity focuses on.
Likely crowded	The opportunity is well known, there are multiple VC and PE deals, and some companies have started IPO processes already.
Crowded	The opportunity is mainstream. VC and PE deals are commonplace and have a long track history. Public companies exist that focus exclusively on the opportunity, and have been publicly traded for a few years.
Unclear	There is insufficient data on existing deals to be able to make a determination. The opportunity is definitely not mainstream, but more research is required.

The crowdedness value can be assessed empirically, based on the PM and investment teams' knowledge of the VC/PE market space, or in a quantitative manner, where information on the number of deals is searched for algorithmically, and quantitative thresholds are set up for each of the different thresholds of crowdedness.

One option is that of using Google NGrams, to analyze the frequency of certain words and infer how popular certain investment ideas are,[2] or counting the number of Google page hits for a specific search term (for example, a search for "Geothermal capital raising announced" under Google News, returns ~ 70 hits as of May 2024).

---

[2] https://books.google.com/ngrams/

5.11 IDENTIFY THE ROOT PROBLEM FOR EACH OPPORTUNITY

The next step in the process is the identification of the root problem (Table 5.4) that creates the opportunity. This process is based on an analytical review of the opportunity, to clearly and concisely identify what the immediate root cause is, and explicitly naming it. The root problem should be Specific, Objective, Timebound, Relevant, and Measurable (STORM). It is worth noting that the same root problem can drive multiple opportunities. In the 5 W (*what, where, when, why,* and *who*) questions, this is the underlying "why?" driver for the opportunity that is being analyzed.

A few examples might be useful to show the level of detail that is required.

Table 5.4 Root problem examples for geothermal, HVAC manufacturers and installers, and Northern Latitudes Farmland.

Opportunity	Root Problem
Geothermal	Transition scenarios require moving away from fossil fuels in all but current policies. One of the main mechanisms that the transition scenarios all include is a carbon tax (aka carbon price).
HVAC Manufacturers and Installers	Climate change is steadily warming the planet and increasing temperatures in inhabited zones.
Northern Latitudes Farmland	Climate change is shifting hardiness zones toward the north, in the northern hemisphere (the southern hemisphere, due to geographical constraints, has a much minor impact, as there are limited landmasses in southern latitudes).

5.12 IDENTIFY WHAT THE ROOT PROBLEM CAUSES FOR EACH OPPORTUNITY

The root problem by itself does not drive the specific opportunity, and we have indeed noted that it can be common to have multiple opportunities, and the next step that needs to be taken is to answer the "so what?" question that the root problem brings up.

This is achieved by identifying the effects of the root problem (Table 5.5), within the confines of the specific opportunity, and spelling them out using the same framework (STORM) used for the root problem itself.

Let's look at how this pans out for our three sample cases:

Table 5.5 Root problem effect examples for geothermal, HVAC manufacturers and installers, and Northern Latitudes Farmland.

Opportunity	Root Problem Effects
Geothermal	Energy sources that do not emit CO_2, such as geothermal energy power, will benefit from an overall higher cost of energy, without having to be burdened by the carbon tax, and will have increased profitability.
HVAC Manufacturers and Installers	Demand for AC units will increase over time, as it will become critical in areas where it is currently in use, and necessary in areas where it isn't widespread now.
Northern Latitudes Farmland	Arable land is shifting northward, expanding the wheat belt into higher and higher latitudes. Scientists project it could go from about 55°N in 2023 to as much as 65°N – the latitude of Fairbanks, Alaska – by 2050.[3]

---

[3] https://www.sciencedirect.com/science/article/abs/pii/S0167880908000194
    Rodomiro Ortiz *et al.* (2008). *Climate change: Can wheat beat the heat?* Agriculture, Ecosystems & Environment, Volume 126, Issues 1–2, pp. 46-58, ISSN 0167-8809, https://doi.org/10.1016/j.agee.2008.01.019

Note that these effects have to be directly related to the root problem and measurable in direct financial terms, so that they can relate to investment strategies directly.

5.13 IDENTIFY WHAT NEEDS TO HAPPEN TO FIX THE ISSUE FOR EACH OPPORTUNITY

The next step in the process is to highlight what needs to happen to fix the issue that we have highlighted as the effect of the root problem. As before, this has to follow the STORM framework and be as clear, concise, and understandable as possible (i.e., avoid using acronyms, industry-speak, and assumptions).

Reverting to our three examples, the fixes are shown in Table 5.6.

Table 5.6 Fix examples for geothermal, HVAC manufacturers and installers, and Northern Latitudes Farmland.

Opportunity	What needs to happen to fix the issue?
Geothermal	Market leaders need to scale up to commercially viable sizes, and new technologies need to progress beyond proof-of-concept phase into full-scale implementation.
HVAC Manufacturers and Installers	To meet the increased requirements due to a warmer planet, the output of HVAC manufacturers and the number of installers globally needs to increase over time.
Northern Latitudes Farmland	The shift in hardiness zones is good news for perennial cash crops in the United States and northern latitudes in general and presents a long-term investment opportunity.

Examples of How to Build an Investment Portfolio

Table 5.7 Fix timing examples for geothermal, HVAC manufacturers and installers, and Northern Latitudes Farmland.

Opportunity	How soon does the fix need to happen?
Geothermal	All scenarios for Net Zero 2050 or disorderly transitions include significant amounts of alternative power between 2030 and 2050.
HVAC Manufacturers and Installers	The warming is already an ongoing concern (2 °C have already happened) and is continuing, therefore the investment opportunity is already active.
Northern Latitudes Farmland	This is an ongoing, long-term trend, which has already started and will likely accelerate in the coming years and decades.

5.14 IDENTIFY HOW SOON THE FIX NEEDS TO HAPPEN FOR EACH OPPORTUNITY

Now that the fix has been identified (which is the core of the opportunity, answering the "what?" question), we need to shift our attention to the "when?" question and provide an estimate on how soon the fix needs to happen.

The timing for our three examples is shown in Table 5.7.

5.15 IDENTIFY THE INVESTMENT OPPORTUNITY FOR EACH OPPORTUNITY

The next step in the process is the clear and concise explanation of what the investment opportunity exactly is. This needs to be a logical, consequential statement that flows from the previous steps, and cannot allow for unsubstantiated claims or unclear or fuzzy statements. If the process has

Table 5.8 Investment opportunity definition examples for geothermal, HVAC manufacturers and installers, and Northern Latitudes Farmland.

Opportunity	What is the investment opportunity?
Geothermal	Identify and invest in new companies (in the VC space) or emerging players (in the PE space) to gain a foothold in this new market.
HVAC Manufacturers and Installers	Invest in HVAC manufacturers (public strategy) and HVAC installers (growth fund), to front-run the increase in demand and prices that the scenarios are predicting.
Northern Latitudes Farmland	Acquire land in northern latitudes that is currently underpriced as it is not fully usable yet and hold it long-term as it becomes more productive and valuable over time, with the increasing temperature and northward shift of the hardiness zones.

been followed properly, this step should automatically generate itself from the previous three.

Table 5.8 shows what the investment opportunity looks like for our usual three examples.

5.16 IDENTIFY WHAT THE BENEFIT OF THE INVESTMENT IS FOR EACH OPPORTUNITY

The following step tells us what the benefit of investing in the specific opportunity, as identified, would be for the investment group. Once again, this needs to be an objective statement tied to financial returns, as opposed to a vague and hard-to-evaluate one (i.e., it has to be something that can be converted to measurable returns).

Going back to our example, the identified benefits are shown in Table 5.9:

Table 5.9 Investment benefit examples for geothermal, HVAC manufacturers and installers, and Northern Latitudes Farmland.

Opportunity	What is the benefit?
Geothermal	Acquisition of a leading position in a new and growing energy generation field, with increasing energy prices and margins.
HVAC Manufacturers and Installers	Ownership of a steady and increasing revenue flow linked to the increasing usage of HVAC, and an increasingly valuable set of assets.
Northern Latitudes Farmland	Ownership of productive land will come at a premium in climate transition scenarios, given the expected desertification and loss of productivity of currently high-yield areas.

Figure 5.9 The process for market size identification.

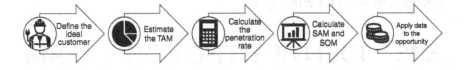

5.17 IDENTIFY THE POTENTIAL MARKET SIZE FOR EACH OPPORTUNITY

This stage of the process (Figure 5.9) is one that requires a significant amount of research, and is tied both to the scenario that is being used and the type of opportunities that have been identified and highlighted (Figure 5.10).

Instead of reviewing the usual three examples, we shall refer our readers to section 12.13 where the example of geothermal is presented in detail

Figure 5.10 The nested markets.

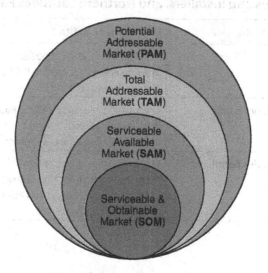

as well as section 13.13 (Northern Latitudes Farmland) and section 14.13 (Energy Efficiency for Buildings).

5.18 IDENTIFY THE LONG-TERM INVESTMENT VISION FOR EACH OPPORTUNITY

At this step of the process, it is necessary to identify what long-term investment vision (Figure 5.11) is being proposed for the individual opportunity.

These typically can be any of the following (or a combination):

1. Buy and hold
2. Buy, grow, and exit
3. Buy and lease
4. Buy and operate

Examples of How to Build an Investment Portfolio

Figure 5.11 An idealized vision of long-term investment vision identification.

Generated with AI using Perchance

5.19 IDENTIFY THE TRIGGER EVENT FOR EACH OPPORTUNITY

Transition finance investing is a type of investing where growth occurs as a result of climate drivers, which can be seen as the activation of specific trigger events (Figure 5.12). For a comprehensive review of the investment triggers, please refer to Chapter 6.

During this phase of the process, the investment trigger (or triggers) is identified, clearly specified and described, and a determination is made of whether it has already been activated, or the most likely, scenario-driven date for the activation (often the activation is dependent on some specific externality).

It is very important that the trigger also follow the STORM framework, as this is one of the key aspects investors will be inquiring about, since it is a major driver for the investment timing.

5.20 IDENTIFY THE PRIMARY FUND IN WHICH EACH OPPORTUNITY BELONGS

At this stage the opportunity needs to be allocated to a primary fund (one of the four funds that has been presented in section 4.9 and appears in Figure 5.13) for the purposes of initial allocation. The fact that an opportunity is primarily in one fund (for example in the Infrastructure Fund) does not disqualify it from also being a secondary opportunity in other funds (for example in the Growth Fund), and it is common to have opportunities that appear in multiple funds.

Figure 5.12 A conceptualization of the long-lasting effects of trigger events.

Generated with AI using Perchance

Figure 5.13 The four funds in transition finance investing.

As a rule of thumb, the determination for primary fund identification should be based on which fund the majority/plurality of the investments in the opportunity would fall under.

5.21 IDENTIFY THE PRIMARY STRATEGY IN WHICH EACH OPPORTUNITY BELONGS

A similar approach is used for the primary strategy identification (Figure 5.14) for the opportunity (VC, PE, credit), with the same considerations that we have used in the previous section.

The nature of the fund that is performing the analysis will also factor into this allocation, as is to be expected (i.e., a private equity fund performing a transition finance investing portfolio build-out will not be looking at primarily VC opportunities, and vice versa).

Figure 5.14 The three strategies for transition finance investing.

5.22 SELECT THE INVESTMENT THESES THAT ALIGN WITH YOUR INDIVIDUAL RISK APPETITE, INVESTMENT HORIZON, AND AREA OF EXPERTISE

Once the systematic review and categorization of the opportunities has been performed (and note how this is an exercise that has to be kept up to date on a regular basis for the reasons that we have covered in other portions of this book), it is time to shift to a fund-specific review, and short-list from the universe of potential investment opportunities, to the ones that match the risk appetite (Figure 5.15), investment horizon, and specific area of expertise for the individual investing team, PM, and firm.

This is a highly strategic process that, while still systematic and analytic in nature, needs to be specifically tailored to the individual investing team performing it, their track records, sizes, target AUM, and areas of expertise and focus.

Figure 5.15 The risk pyramid.

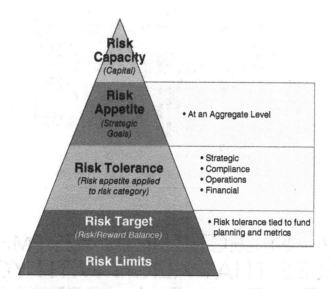

Given the vast nature of the opportunity set, and the long time horizons involved, it is recommended that the investment teams take sufficient time to grow from existing areas of expertise into adjacent and complementary ones, in an organic way, as opposed to immediately trying to tackle each and every opportunity at the same time.

5.23 DEEP DIVE IN INVESTMENT THESES OF INTEREST TO IDENTIFY TARGETS AND REFINE STRATEGIES

Once a subset of investment opportunities that align with the interests of the fund have been identified, it is time to perform a deep-dive analysis on each one of them, for the purpose of identification of potential targets and refinement of strategies (Figure 5.16).

Figure 5.16 The process of deep diving into investment theses.

The deep dives are the part of transition finance investment that requires the most amount of subject matter expertise, and the investment team must not hold back from reaching out to external SMEs as needed, as, often, the insider knowledge of some of the opportunities being pursued only comes after decades of work in the field.

In addition to gained experience and the teams own know-how, a significant amount of information and data can, and should, be obtained from online think-tanks, research, academia, and NGOs dedicated to specific themes being investigated.

As an example, Table 5.10 contains a series of useful resources that can be beneficial for a deep dive into geothermal energy (some of which, coupled with the author's own expertise, were used to write Chapter 12).

5.24 BUILD YOUR PORTFOLIO BASED ON IDENTIFIED TARGETS

Once the deep dives have been completed, and the potential investment targets have been identified, the build-out of an investment portfolio in transition finance isn't fundamentally different from any other comparable

Table 5.10 Deep dive source examples for geothermal.

Source	Description
https://www.thinkgeoenergy.com/	**ThinkGeoEnergy** provides business news about development, technology, finance, and related topics, along with market analysis and events for the geothermal energy market. Since 2008, it has focused on geothermal power and hydrothermal resources. It also covers new topics like deep geothermal heat exchange systems and mineral extraction from geothermal brine.
https://connect.spe.org/gtts/home	The **Society of Petroleum Engineers (SPE)** is a not-for-profit professional group with over 140,600 members across 144 countries focused on oil and gas exploration and production. The **Society of Petroleum Engineers Geothermal Technical Section** serves members interested in geothermal energy and its ability to change electric power generation and direct heating and cooling worldwide. The geothermal and oil and gas industries have exchanged knowledge to improve drilling, reduce costs, and innovate reservoir monitoring.
https://www.geode.energy/	**GEODE** focuses on geothermal innovation by uniting experts from the oil and gas and geothermal fields to enhance geothermal technology. This unique collaboration aims to meet growing energy demand and promote the use of geothermal resources for a sustainable energy future.
http://www.geothermal.org/	**Geothermal Rising (GR)** is the largest and oldest geothermal membership organization globally. It aims to build community and support the geothermal industry by covering various technologies and applications. GR is a nonprofit that focuses on education, community organization, and research for the international geothermal community, providing outreach and professional development services.

Examples of How to Build an Investment Portfolio

Source	Description
https://www.catf.us/superhot-rock/	The **Clean Air Task Force (CATF)** aims to protect against severe climate change effects by promoting the quick global growth and use of low-carbon energy and climate technologies through research, public advocacy, and private sector partnerships. CATF consists of climate and energy specialists with extensive experience, including scientists, engineers, MBAs, policy experts, lawyers, and communication professionals who create impact through technology innovation, policy advocacy, and thought leadership.
https://www.hotrockhero.org/	**Hotrock Energy Research Organization (HERO)** aims to lessen the environmental impact of power generation by focusing on Enhanced Geothermal Systems and other geothermal technologies. HERO educates the public on the significance of this research for energy supply and climate change. Established to promote EGS, HERO collaborates with experts to conduct research in areas with high geothermal potential.
https://projectinnerspace.org/	**Project Inner Space** is divided into two phases. Phase I, starting in fall 2022, aims to publish an interactive global geothermal resources map in 2025, created by experts with funding from Project InnerSpace. Phase II focuses on deploying teams to build new geothermal projects and showcasing their potential to reduce emissions in hard-to-decarbonize sectors.
https://www.nrel.gov/geothermal/	The **National Renewable Energy Laboratory (NREL)** supports the US Department of Energy (DOE) Geothermal Technologies Office (GTO) in geothermal energy development and planning. NREL releases various publications on geothermal energy, including journal articles, conference papers, and technical reports.

(Continued)

Table 5.10 (Continued)

Source	Description
https://www.catf.us/superhot-rock/	The **Clean Air Task Force** is an NGO aimed at achieving zero emissions and affordable energy solutions. They envision meeting global energy needs sustainably. A key focus is superhot rock geothermal energy, which is underappreciated in the decarbonization discussion. This energy source can provide reliable, zero-carbon power and produce hydrogen for fuel.
https://www.lovegeothermal.org/	The **International Geothermal Association (IGA)** focuses on promoting sustainable geothermal resource use globally. Their mission includes facilitating the global energy transition and tackling climate change through various strategies. They emphasize training and building a skilled workforce in geothermal energy. The IGA also serves as a platform for knowledge sharing and outreach to increase awareness and adoption of geothermal energy. They set high operational standards and advocate for geothermal energy as a clean, renewable resource while seeking to attract investment and create favorable financial models for the sector.
https://www.energy.gov/eere/geothermal/geovision	The **Geothermal Technologies Office (GTO)** started the GeoVision analysis to explore how geothermal energy can support the United States' energy future. It focuses on increasing access to geothermal resources, reducing costs, and enhancing education about geothermal energy while using detailed models to assess deployment potential and barriers.

Figure 5.17 An idealized diversified portfolio.

Generated with AI using Perchance

VC, PE, or private credit portfolio of similar scope and size, and falls back into the true and tested standard operating procedures that are common across the industry (Figure 5.17).

As such, we shall end this chapter here, as the focus of this book is not how to manage a portfolio once the target investments have been identified, which we assume our readers are well familiar with.

CHAPTER SIX

INVESTMENT TRIGGER EVENTS

What events set off the investments from sleepers to winners

6.1 WHAT IS AN INVESTMENT TRIGGER?

In transition finance investing, a trigger event is defined as an event, or sequence of events, that leads to an investment thesis shifting from a dormant state to an active one. This trigger event needs to have a direct, measurable causal relationship with the investment opportunity itself, and follow the STORM framework (Specific, Timebound, Objective, Relevant, and Measurable).

Triggers typically take the logical construct of *A leads to B which causes C*, and are generally specific to the investment opportunity, but can be shared across various similar opportunities, if the same event sets off multiple consequences.

A good example of a "single-trigger, multiple opportunities" is the *merger of the Voluntary Carbon Markets with the Compliance Markets*, which is one of the trigger events for many different transition finance opportunities tied to the explosive growth of the Carbon Dioxide Removal markets that this event will launch.

To clarify, activation of this trigger would set off the following opportunities (and several others):

- MMRV (Measurement, Monitoring, Reporting, and Validation) of Voluntary Carbon Credits
- VCM satellite monitoring
- BECCS
- Biochar
- Direct Air Capture
- Ocean-based CDR
- VCM End-to-End risk transfer solutions
- VCM exchanges
- VCM insurance products
- CCUS

For each opportunity, it is important to clarify how the trigger directly causes the opportunity to move from dormant to active, in a way that is clearly understandable.

For example, in the case of *MMRV (Measurement, Monitoring, Reporting, and Validation) of Voluntary Carbon Credits* the merging of the VCM and compliance carbon markets will cause an increase in the volume and demand for carbon removal, which will require robust, reliable, auditable, transparent and traceable MMRV solutions, causing the market for companies and technologies in this space to rapidly grow.

6.2 HOW DO WE IDENTIFY AN INVESTMENT TRIGGER?

The identification of the investment trigger for each opportunity derives from analytical review of the root problem, root problem effect, and root problem fix that have been identified for the investment opportunity. It has to be a logical consequence of these three prior steps, and has to be complemented by the insights that are gained by the scenario analysis and model results analysis, coupled with expert review based on SME opinion.

The identification of the trigger is a key aspect of the process, and requires a careful review and challenge process by the investment team, as it is critical for the success of the investment opportunity (after all, an incorrect trigger identification will lead to incorrect timing on a potentially valid opportunity).

It is also important to note that, in many instances, triggers are not single events, but the combination of multiple factors, with different timings and characteristics, and these should be identified and clearly spelled out as separate, but concurrently acting triggers, some of which might have already been activated, while others might be in the process of being activated, and others yet still to be activated.

The PM and the investment team need to ensure that clarity is made, in the case of multiple triggers, on which triggers are *foundational* (i.e., the opportunity will not proceed without these triggers being activated), which are *milestones* (i.e., the opportunity will not transition to a larger scale until they are activated) and which are *accelerators* (i.e., they speed up the process, but do not affect the achievement of an overall end level, except that by how fast that level is attained).

6.3 WHAT IS THE LIKELIHOOD AND TIMING OF A TRIGGER AND WHAT FACTORS AFFECT IT?

The determination of likelihood and timing of a trigger is opportunity-specific, and is driven by the following factors:

- Nature of the root cause, root cause consequences, and root cause fix
- Climate scenario being analyzed
- Geopolitical conditions and considerations
- Pace of technological innovation
- Subject matter expertise

Given this process often deals with taking a stance on when a specific event is likely to take place in the future, there is, by definition, a degree of arbitrary factors that come into play, and the determination of the timing and likelihood can only be taken as an estimate of future events, based on current knowledge and best practices, and liable to change if conditions or models were to be modified.

The situation is different for triggers that have already occurred (for example, those tied to specific levels of warming, which might have already happened), in which case the determination becomes quantitative and objective, and no longer subject to uncertainty and debate.

CHAPTER SEVEN
ABOUT HYDROGEN

Why hydrogen is not included as an opportunity in any of the funds

Within the transition finance and ESG community there has been a significant amount of time, effort, and capital dedicated to hydrogen-linked industries and investments. It is the view of the author, which will be explained in this chapter, that the role of hydrogen in transition finance has been very much overestimated, and the drawbacks that it has have been underestimated and dismissed without a solid reason to do so.

The key reason for this issue is the fact that hydrogen has been proposed as a potentially correct answer to a question that is posed incorrectly.

This question is as follows: "*Given burning fossil fuels is generating GHG emissions that are causing global warming, what could we burn instead of fossil fuels that doesn't generate GHG?*" The answer to this question, as simply, and naively, stated, could very well be "hydrogen," as it burns with only water as a reaction product, and is highly energetic.

Unfortunately, the question is more complicated and requires shifting the frame of reference from "*What do we burn instead of oil?*" to "*What alternative energy sources could we practically use to replace fossil fuels with that would allow us to generate the energy that mankind needs, without the GHG emissions?"*

Once the question is reformulated, without the constraint of having to burn something, the informed response to the question will, invariably, never be *"hydrogen"* again.

It's worthy to note how the knee-jerk reaction of thinking of burning the source of energy, which is an intrinsically inefficient way of transforming energy to anything but heat, is a clear manifestation of Abraham Kaplan's famous Law of the Instrument[1] which states: "it is tempting, if the only tool you have is a hammer, to treat everything as if it were a nail."

This change in answer from *"hydrogen"* to *"anything but hydrogen"* is due to the plethora of practical problems and intrinsic dangers linked to H_2 (which we will review in this chapter), and the immensely more effective, safe, and cheaper alternatives that are currently available (nuclear power, geothermal, wave and tidal, wind and solar, biomass and biofuels, and for the forward-looking entrepreneurial types among our readers, ocean thermal energy conversion, to name just a few of the better options).

Unfortunately, because of the built-up expectations around hydrogen, the riskiness and aleatory nature of investments in hydrogen are systematically downplayed and underestimated from what the chemical and physical properties of the hydrogen molecule would require them to be.

This section of the book is heavily indebted to Michael Barnard,[2] chief strategist, TFIE Strategy Inc., and his article, "The life story of a committed hydrogen for energy worker unfolds" published on *Cleantechnica* in February 2024.[3]

---

[1] https://en.wikipedia.org/wiki/Law_of_the_instrument

[2] https://www.linkedin.com/in/michael-barnard-42446/

[3] https://cleantechnica.com/2024/02/12/the-life-story-of-a-committed-hydrogen-for-energy-worker-unfolds/

7.1 THE PHYSICS AND CHEMISTRY OF HYDROGEN AND THE EFFECT ON WHAT ROLE IT MIGHT PLAY

While generating energy from water and converting it back is a simple experiment students do in basic chemistry, turning this easy reaction into an industrial, eco-friendly process faces challenges due to the properties of the H_2 molecule.

The first problem that needs to be addressed is the disconnect between the energy density of hydrogen by mass (which is indeed very high at a molecule level) and the energy density by volume which is, unfortunately, very low, due to the fact that hydrogen is the lightest element in the periodic table, and follows the standard ideal gas law ($PV = nRT$)[4] which tells us that one mole of an ideal gas will always, at standard temperature and pressure, occupy 22.4 liters of volume (and one mole of H_2 only weighs 2 grams).

Table 7.1 compares 1 kg of hydrogen and 1 kg of gasoline in terms of volume, energy content, and energy density. Hydrogen contains *three times more energy*, with 33.3 KW per kilogram, while gasoline has 13.3 KW. However, hydrogen takes up about 11,000 liters, compared to gasoline's 1.35 liters, making it *over 8,100 times larger in volume*.

Hydrogen has a significant advantage in energy per mass, but this is greatly reduced by its much higher volume, resulting in a much lower energy density by volume compared to gasoline.

The very low energy density of hydrogen makes it impractical to use in its natural form. If released into the atmosphere, hydrogen escapes quickly

---

[4] https://en.wikipedia.org/wiki/Ideal_gas_law

Table 7.1 Hydrogen versus gasoline energy content and energy density.

Product	Volume occupied at room temperature and pressure by 1 kg	Energy content for 1 kg	Energy density by unit of volume (W/l)
Gasoline	~1.35 liters	13,000 W	~9,600 W/l
Hydrogen	11,000 liters	33,300 W	3.0 W/l

to higher altitudes and is so light that free hydrogen molecules can reach escape velocity and drift into space, causing earth to lose a significant amount of hydrogen, even while gravity retaining other gases (the gravitational pull is sufficient to retain all other gases except helium).[5]

In addition to hydrogen's atmosphere-escaping capabilities, we also have to deal with issues that derive from its diminutive size, given the physical nature of the atom and molecule (the hydrogen atom is made of one proton and one electron, and is the smallest atom in the periodic table, as the molecule H_2 is simply two H atoms covalently bonded).

The tiny size of the molecule (a radius of about 120 picometers, compared to 140 picometers for water, which is one of the smaller molecules, and 208 picometers for methane) and the lack of polarity adds complexity with the practical aspects of dealing with it, as most containers, which are airtight for most standard molecules, do no succeed in containing hydrogen.

The small size and properties of hydrogen create challenges for its storage and transportation. Being a gas at room temperature and pressure makes hydrogen very energy diffuse. To store and transport it, either the temperature must be lowered to about 20 Kelvin (−253 °C) or it must be kept under high pressure and low temperature. Keeping hydrogen liquid requires expensive containers with very tight tolerances, which cost far

---

[5] https://en.wikipedia.org/wiki/Atmospheric_escape

more than those for fossil fuels, and it also needs a continuous energy supply to maintain the extremely cold temperatures.

The technology needed to compress hydrogen for storage is crucial for using it as an energy source, but it is expensive. As of the end of 2024, a compressor for 300 atmospheres costs about $10,000. While compression allows more hydrogen to be stored in a small space, a cubic meter still weighs in at around 20 kg, compared to about 830 kg for gasoline. Higher pressure increases storage but also raises compressor costs, with a 700 ATM unit costing around $25,000 and coming with increased maintenance needs.

Additional cooling is necessary to liquefy hydrogen, thus achieving the target high energy density greater than gasoline, but this process requires using about one-third of the hydrogen's energy. Once hydrogen is in liquid form, it demands advanced insulation technology to stop it from absorbing heat and evaporating, which can be dangerous due to fire and explosion risks. This insulation, which is similar to old-fashioned thermos flasks, is expensive and requires precise tolerances in manufacture. Insulation is a stopgap solution, as it only slows down heat flow to enable storage and transportation but doesn't prevent it altogether. Consequently, methods to capture venting hydrogen are mandatory (were it only for explosion prevention), adding even more costs and complications.

Alternative storage solutions for hydrogen that use *reversible bonds between hydrogen molecules and organic compounds* to lower storage pressure and temperature exist. These can reduce the necessary pressure to ~50 ATM at room temperature, which would be, in principle, cost-effective. However, energy is needed to release the hydrogen from the storage, which, again, consumes about one-third of the energy from the stored molecules. This energy is initially released when hydrogen bonds to the organic compound, but recovering it involves extra machinery and costs, and can lead to process inefficiencies and risks of failure.

Similar challenges occur when trying to use *metal hydrides to bond the hydrogen* such as lithium aluminum hydride and sodium borohydride, which produce significant heat during hydrogen bonding reactions. They also need heat provided to them to release the hydrogen (unsurprisingly, as the reaction must obey the laws of thermodynamics), and the nature of the mass balance also increases cost and weight, as metals constitute 98 to 99% of the system's mass. Additionally, the actual storing and releasing of hydrogen take a long time (hours), raising safety concerns for logistics and distribution.

7.2 THE PROBLEMS WITH MANUFACTURING HYDROGEN IN VOLUMES

Setting aside the problems of storing hydrogen, the situation is not better when considering its production for practical use, particularly regarding cost and environmental impact. Most hydrogen available for laboratory or industrial use is made from fossil fuels, mainly natural gas, through the steam reformation reaction, which is *not "clean" by any stretch of the imagination*. This process releases one molecule of CO_2 for every four molecules of hydrogen produced, and it also requires energy, usually sourced from burning fossil fuels.

The reaction, in fact, is very simple, albeit in two consecutive stages, and the balance of species is immediately evident, as is the need for energy in the form of heat:

Steam-methane reforming reaction

$$CH_4 + H_2O \text{ (+heat)} \rightarrow CO + 3H_2$$

Water-gas shift reaction

$$CO + H_2O \rightarrow CO_2 + H_2 \text{ (+small amount of heat)}$$

The process of producing hydrogen from methane leads to 10–12 kg of CO_2 emissions for every kilogram of hydrogen made, considering methane leaks, energy needs, and direct emissions. As of this writing, the hydrogen manufacturing process globally results in 100 to 120 megatons of CO_2 being released into the atmosphere each year just to meet current industrial use of the molecule.

One way to reduce GHG emissions is by capturing CO_2 and leaked methane from the hydrogen production reaction, a similar approach as used in various industrial processes. This recovery is complicated because methane must be captured at the burner and CO_2 at the reaction exit, requiring different technologies and increasing energy consumption.

Additionally, energy needs for GHG capture often lead to more emissions from energy production. The best current sorbents for CO_2 capture achieve about 85% efficiency,[6] which can rise to 98% or more with an extra capture stage; that, however, demands more energy and introduces more maintenance challenges.

Capturing CO_2 from the H_2 production process becomes harder and less practical once we shift to thinking about *what to do with the captured CO_2*. Most current CCUS processes reuse carbon dioxide by injecting it underground to aid oil extraction at well sites. This approach cannot be used for CO_2 captured from hydrogen production, which seeks carbon neutrality and is not done at active well pumping stations.

One option is to inject CO_2 into spent wells worldwide. This requires transporting the gas from hydrogen production plants to various abandoned wells, which are usually far apart. The EU estimates that nearly

---

[6] https://www.frontiersin.org/journals/energy-research/articles/10.3389/fenrg.2023.1167043/full

20,000 kilometers of pipelines are needed for this, which is about half the earth's circumference and would be prohibitively expensive.

Besides cost, a large network of CO_2 pipelines poses serious safety risks for humans, animals, and plants. Due to CO_2's higher density compared to nitrogen and oxygen, any leaks could create dangerous "surface lakes" of carbon dioxide that could be deadly for trapped living beings (as an example, a natural CO_2 eruptive event in Lake Nyos[7] in Cameroon, in 1986, killed over 1,700 people living in a village nearby and at least 3,500 livestock).[8]

Large distance CO_2 pipelines are, therefore, not safe nor practical for general use. They could only work in rare cases where they avoid populated areas, and would require extra safety measures such as underground installation, which raises infrastructure costs significantly and reduces use cases dramatically.

7.3 THE PITFALLS OF PRODUCING HYDROGEN BY ELECTROLYSIS

Given the challenges of producing hydrogen from methane as a clean fuel, we should consider other methods that appear viable and clean. The primary method that springs to mind is producing hydrogen from water through electrolytic reactions. This process, unfortunately, still needs all the hydrogen storage and transportation equipment that alternate manufacturing process have, uses a lot of electricity, and requires substantial

---

[7] https://en.wikipedia.org/wiki/Lake_Nyos_disaster
[8] https://blog.newspapers.com/lake-nyos-disaster-august-21-1986/

equipment for managing water, water vapor, and power to meet industrial needs.

Producing one ton of hydrogen through electrolysis needs about 55 MWh of energy.[9] As of December 31, 2024, electricity costs in New York City (as an example) are $44.6 per MWh, making the energy cost around $2,500. When adding costs like equipment and plant operation, the total cost per ton can exceed several thousand dollars, going well beyond the much-publicized target price of $10/kg that is needed now for H_2 to be commercially viable and three orders of magnitude higher than the aspirational $1/kg price that the DOE is targeting[10] for 2031.

The carbon credits cost to offset the electricity needed to power the electrolysis further burden this process by requiring CO_2 offsets of between 11 and 14 tons for each ton of H_2 made through electrolysis. This is *higher than the CO_2 generated from directly producing H_2 from CH_4*, as previously analyzed.

This analysis remains largely the same even considering the use of PEM[11] electrolyzers, which can operate intermittently when zero emissions electricity is available but are a technology that costs twice as much as alkaline electrolyzers, which, on the other hand, must run continuously.

One way of reducing the CO_2 offset cost is to use electricity produced from purely renewable sources, and only when there is excess production. Currently, excess renewable energy from wind and solar is available only about 15% of the time, and *this setup would end up increasing even more the costs per kg for the clean energy hydrolyzer setup* compared to a 24/7 system that uses whatever electricity is available from the grid (and offsets the emissions via carbon removal credits).

---

[9] https://en.wikipedia.org/wiki/Hydrogen_production
[10] https://www.energy.gov/topics/hydrogen-shot
[11] https://en.wikipedia.org/wiki/Proton_exchange_membrane_electrolysis

7.4 THE FALSE PROMISE OF PRODUCING HYDROGEN BY PYROLYSIS

H_2 can be produced from CH_4 through pyrolysis,[12] where pure methane is heated until it loses four H atoms, forming two H_2 molecules. This reaction also produces pure carbon, which can be sold for use in various industrial processes.

$$CH_4 + Heat \rightarrow 2H_2 + C$$

The mass balance of the process shows that it produces way more carbon than hydrogen. Specifically, it generates three times more carbon by weight than hydrogen. If this process were scaled up, it could quickly cover the demand for the entire commercial market for carbon, which is currently 14 megatons (the global demand for carbon would be completely met by producing just ~3% of the current global hydrogen market if we were to switch to CH_4 pyrolysis, and the remainder would be a waste product with costly disposal issues).

The carbon produced, as it comes from fossil fuels, cannot be seen as "captured" (as there is no link to removal from the atmosphere) and cannot generate carbon credits, meaning it must be treated as waste and disposed of, increasing costs.

Using natural methane from landfills or similar sources might allow for claims of carbon sequestration. However, collecting and concentrating this spread-out methane presents significant economic challenges that make it unfeasible on a commercially viable scale (and would also compete with the alternative use of this biogenic methane feedstock to produce bioethanol, which has dramatically less issues to transport, store, and use, when compared to H_2).

---

[12] https://en.wikipedia.org/wiki/Pyrolysis#Methane_pyrolysis_for_hydrogen

7.5 THE MIRAGE OF NATURALLY OCCURRING HYDROGEN

In recent years, naturally occurring hydrogen deposits, known as "white hydrogen"[13] have gained attention as a clean energy source to replace fossil fuels. These natural H_2 deposits have been discovered in various locations, including a successful operation in Mali that generates electricity for one local village, and potential commercial deposits in Albania and France. However, despite the initial promise, the actual scale of hydrogen needed for an energy transition compared with the estimated available deposits worldwide dim the prospects of this source being commercially viable and scalable.

The largest identified deposit is in France and estimated to contain around 45 megatons of hydrogen. This amount could cover about 50% of current hydrogen consumption **for one year** at 2024 usage rates and highlights that, without significantly larger undiscovered resources that are not considered likely, this type of deposit will be of limited importance in the energy ecosystem of the future.

7.6 THE DECEITFUL IDEA OF PRODUCING HYDROGEN IN CHEAP LOCATIONS AND SHIPPING IT TO POINTS OF USAGE

An approach to overcome the challenges of using hydrogen as an energy source suggests producing it in areas with low population and low-cost clean energy, like deserts, for cheap green hydrogen. However,

---

[13] https://en.wikipedia.org/wiki/Natural_hydrogen

this idea faces serious issues, as about 85% of hydrogen needs to be made where it is used because of high transportation costs and losses, and any hydrogen produced in remote locations would be burdened by materially relevant higher costs and production losses of over 30% in transport.

Hydrogen Pipelines

An alternative way to transport hydrogen is through existing pipelines that connect oil and gas sites. As of 2025, there are several thousand kilometers of hydrogen pipelines around the world, used for cleaning crude oil and separating it into various products, which is a major current use for hydrogen. Hydrogen, however, presents unique challenges in transport. Existing natural gas pipelines cannot be used long term for hydrogen because the metal the pipelines are made of becomes brittle when exposed to hydrogen under pressure, leading to failures in the system and costly (and dangerous) leaks.

Custom pipelines for hydrogen transportation need tight-tolerance materials, high-pressure compressors that are more expensive and power-hungry than methane ones, glass-based coatings, and special gaskets and seals. Additionally, once all things are considered, they usually transport less energy per pipe diameter than standard CH_4 pipelines.

If hydrogen were piped to homes, the current gas distribution grid couldn't be reused. New high-safety networks must be made at high cost to minimize hydrogen leaks, which are both a safety concern and would accelerate global warming. (Hydrogen is actually a very potent GHG in its own right,[14] which adds concerns over using it in diffuse scenarios.)

---

[14] Sand, M., Skeie, R.B., Sandstad, M. et al. (2023). A multi-model assessment of the Global Warming Potential of hydrogen. Commun Earth Environ 4, 203. https://doi.org/10.1038/s43247-023-00857-8

Hydrogen Transport via Trucks

Transportation via trucks is not a feasible option because the maximum compression achievable with a tractor trailer is about 180 atmospheres. At this pressure, a truck full of hydrogen carries only 1/15th to 1/20th of the energy of an equivalent truck carrying diesel fuel.

Attempting to solve the truck and shipping transportation issues by raising pressure to at least 700 ATM and lowering temperatures to very cold levels is riddled by problems such as tight tolerances, costly materials, high failure rates, and high repair costs, as we have seen earlier. Additionally, it would exacerbate the already relevant explosion risks from moving highly pressurized combustible materials at over 60 mph on infrastructure shared by the rest of mankind, where road accidents are a frequent occurrence.

Shipping Hydrogen

Transportation via ships has serious systemic issues, particularly with tankers having to carry 700 atmosphere liquid hydrogen, which is an extremely hazardous substance. Currently, LNG tankers are the costliest and least preferred method for global energy transport, used only when no better options exist. Liquefied hydrogen tankers would be 5 to 10 times more expensive, making them completely impractical as a realistic solution.

7.7 TRANSPORTING HYDROGEN AS AMMONIA IS NOT A GOOD IDEA

A possible solution that has been proposed to the challenges of hydrogen as a gas is converting it into ammonia (NH_4) by bonding it with nitrogen. Ammonia is already a significant chemical used in fertilizers and other processes, but it is a very dangerous substance (it is corrosive, toxic, flammable, and explosive in closed spaces) and needs careful handling throughout its supply chain. The production costs of ammonia, primarily produced through the Haber Bosch reaction, suggest that using ammonia to transport hydrogen would double the cost per ton of the hydrogen being transported. Additionally, when including liquefaction, transportation, and re-extraction costs, the overall expense could be 10 times higher than the alternative option of using coal as a source of energy and multiple times more expensive than natural gas.

7.8 HYDROGEN IN GROUND TRANSPORTATION

If the technological and transportation challenges were somehow resolved, the next question is what to do with the hydrogen produced and transported to its use location, and how the costs and efficiency compare to alternative options (both fossil fuel and zero emissions). We will start by looking at the use of hydrogen for ground transportation, which has seen the most testing and real-world trials in recent decades.

Currently, dirty hydrogen made from natural gas without carbon capture is sold at hydrogen refueling stations in Europe and California for $15 to $36 per kg. This is much higher than the expected cost of $1 to $2 per kg due to inefficiencies in transportation, storage, and distribution.

Hydrogen Fuel Cell Transportation

The first use case for hydrogen in ground transportation is in fuel cells, which convert hydrogen into electricity through chemical reactions.

Fuel cells were invented in 1838 by Sir William Grove[15] and have seen widespread use in specific applications like rocketry and satellites.

The main reason fuel cells are not widely used and have few applications is their high cost. They need precious metals like platinum and palladium, as well as advanced membranes that last only 1.5 to 3 years. Fuel cells are very sensitive to contamination, demanding only pure hydrogen and dry air to avoid breakdown. Any contaminants, even in small amounts, can damage the cells, which makes special hydrogen necessary. This feedstock differs from the standard hydrogen product that is generated from natural gas, which, if used, would destroy the fuel cells. Additionally, and for the same reason, hydrogen fuel cell vehicles must also use expensive air purification filters to avoid contamination from pollutants emitted from other traditional ICE vehicles with which they share the road, along with the usual costly components for hydrogen compression and management (sensors, dehumidification and thermal management of the water produced by the fuel cell, high-pressure tanks, and tight tolerance valves) that increase maintenance and operating costs.

Since vehicles are moving platforms, their components must also be toughened compared to stationary applications, due to vibrations and shocks, which increases costs and reduces life expectancy. Using fuel cells for transportation adds more challenges, as the water produced needs disposal and can freeze in low temperatures, leading to issues, which were obvious during the 2010 Winter Olympics where the fleet of hydrogen fuel cell buses put into service in Whistler[16] ended up being scrapped after just three years of use.[17]

---

[15] https://en.wikipedia.org/wiki/Fuel_cell

[16] https://nationalpost.com/opinion/brian-hutchinson-whistlers-hydrogen-bus-boondoggle

[17] https://www.cbc.ca/news/canada/british-columbia/bc-transit-s-90m-hydrogen-bus-fleet-to-be-sold-off-converted-to-diesel-1.2861060

An additional problem is the intrinsically low efficiency of fuel cells in energy conversion, which is about 60%, that causes the cost per kg of effective power to nearly double. Furthermore, fuel cells can also only provide limited peak power output, which makes vehicles struggle when extra power is needed, like starting heavy loads or driving uphill. This issue is often solved by coupling fuel cells to traditional batteries, creating hybrids, but this reduces range and efficiency and adds extra costs and maintenance needs.

Hydrogen Internal Combustion Engine Transportation

Given the challenges of using fuel cells for transportation, many manufacturers have been, and still are, experimenting with burning hydrogen in traditional internal combustion engines instead of gasoline, diesel, or natural gas. This approach has advantages over the fuel cell method, as hydrogen does not need extensive purification, and the technology is well established since the 19th century. Hydrogen is also a gas at normal temperature and pressure, making it easier to feed into the engine.

The negative aspects of this use case become clear when we look at the energy efficiency of ICE vehicles, which is around 30%. This low efficiency increases hydrogen costs, as less than a third of the stored energy is converted to kinetic energy (half as much as the fuel cell option).

Even if we overlook extra costs from poor efficiency, there are chemistry issues from burning hydrogen with air at high temperatures inside ICEs. This reaction leads to incomplete combustion and produces nitrous oxides (N_2O and NO_2), which are harmful greenhouse gases and pollutants (the former is one of the most powerful GHG known to man[18] at ~270

---

[18] https://research.noaa.gov/nitrous-oxide-emissions-grew-40-percent-from-1980-to-2020-accelerating-climate-change/

times worse than CO_2 as well as depleting the ozone layer, and the latter is a major pollutant with well-documented ill effects on humans and animals).[19]

Using a very air-rich mixture can reduce nitrous oxide emissions via complete combustion but decreases engine power output by ~50%. Larger engines or turbochargers can compensate for the lost power but add complexities and inefficiencies without providing major overall benefits.

Hydrogen as a Feedstock for Synthetic Fuels for Transportation

A proposed option for using hydrogen in ground transportation involves combining it with carbon to create synthetic fossil fuels for traditional uses, effectively recreating fossil fuels by chemical reactions.

This process involves hydrogenating carbon into hydrocarbons, which are our familiar and commonly used fuels. However, the challenge lies in sourcing the necessary feedstocks for the reaction. Currently, pure green carbon (the required reagent for this approach to be viable) costs between ~$100 and ~$1,200 per ton (generally obtained via direct air capture) and isn't produced in any quantity remotely close to what would be needed for the ground transportation market. The use of this process, assuming mankind solved, somehow, the issue of availability of sufficient carbon to make the fuels, would lead to gasoline prices that could be five times higher than today, making this approach not very attractive, as alternatives (such as electric vehicles) exist which are much more cost-efficient.

---

[19] https://www.epa.gov/no2-pollution/basic-information-about-no2

Hydrogen for Rail Transportation

Using hydrogen for rail transportation faces challenges like those in other sectors, along with the added difficulty of competing with electric trains, which are well established, cheaper, and more efficient. Studies show hydrogen usage would be at least three times more expensive[20] than electricity and increase risks due to transportation of explosive gases, posing significant danger of catastrophic outcomes in accidents.[21] It is easy to imagine the effects of a hydrogen-laden train accident, which would start with spillage of massive amounts of instantly freezing liquid, followed by an explosion of enormous proportions, and widespread destruction.

Hydrogen for Trucking Transportation

Using hydrogen for trucking faces similar unsurmountable challenges as railways and, within the space of zero emissions alternatives, competes with EV options such as the Tesla semi, which offers better safety and no hydrogen-related downsides.

Increased Risks Stemming from the Adoption of Hydrogen for Transportation in General

Widespread use of hydrogen in trucking and vehicular transportation in general would need many more vehicles to transport fuel than what is currently on the road (as we have seen previously), raising overall costs and materially increasing the risks of serious accidents, as hydrogen is much more dangerous than diesel or gasoline when transported.

---

[20] https://www.railjournal.com/fleet/baden-wurttemberg-rejects-hydrogen-as-diesel-alternative/

[21] https://www.hydrogeninsight.com/transport/no-more-hydrogen-trains-rail-company-that-launched-worlds-first-h2-line-last-year-opts-for-all-electric-future/2-1-1495801

7.9 HYDROGEN FOR HEATING AND STEAM GENERATION

A straightforward use case for hydrogen is in combustion furnaces to generate heat for direct heating or steam production. This method efficiently converts chemical energy to thermal energy, surpassing the energy efficiency of both fuel cells and hydrogen engines.

Pollution Due to Burning Hydrogen in Existing Furnaces

The analysis of this use case shows familiar issues due to hydrogen's chemical and physical nature. One problem is the production of nitrous oxides from H_2 combustion in air, as already seen in ICE.

High-velocity flames produce less nitrous oxides than slow flames, like those that are generated in current propane burners, and would seem a viable option to mitigate the production of nitrous oxides. Unfortunately, high-velocity flames need special hardware designed for high pressures and gas flow, which have tight tolerances and short life spans. This makes it hard to retrofit hydrogen into existing furnace systems, requiring nearly complete replacements. The increased costs and maintenance make this option, therefore, unappealing.

Safety Concerns of Using Hydrogen Burners in Residential Settings

Safety concerns exist regarding the wide range of air-to-hydrogen ratios that can cause explosions with hydrogen furnaces and how these would translate into risks in a residential setting where stringent controls aren't typically enacted (and where there isn't a constant presence of technicians on site to intervene if a malfunction is detected). A 2021[22] study by the UK Department for Business, Energy & Industrial Strategy[23] found that converting the heating systems in the UK from natural gas to hydrogen would result in a four-fold increase in explosion risk compared to current levels.

Cost Considerations for Hydrogen Burners

Even if safety issues are improved with added safety features, using hydrogen for heating remains much more expensive than natural gas. Current industrial hydrogen prices range from $3 to $10 per kg, leading to costs of $23 to $77 per gigajoule, compared to natural gas prices of $3 to $7 per gigajoule. This translates to H_2 being an alternative that increases heating costs by a factor of 10 times, which is hardly a viable option.

Competition from Alternative Zero-emissions Heating Options

It is difficult to believe that hydrogen could be widely adopted for heating, even with carbon taxes making natural gas less competitive. Using electricity for heating is a proven technology that is already adopted and used globally, that can be zero-emissions and has orders of magnitude fewer risks than hydrogen. Competition from electric heating becomes even stronger once we factor in the growing use of heat pumps, which are replacing natural gas heating, and improving energy efficiency in a material fashion.

---

[22] https://www.hy4heat.info/s/conclusions-inc-QRA.pdf
[23] https://www.hy4heat.info/

7.10 AMMONIA-FROM-HYDROGEN USES

One of the popularly advocated uses of hydrogen in transition finance is ammonia, as it avoids some strict requirements of using H_2 directly and could help shift the shipping industry to cleaner energy. Unfortunately, ammonia has significant safety concerns when the entire process is considered.

Usage of Ammonia in Shipping

Ammonia is not suitable for ground transportation or heating fuel due to its cost and dangers from its toxic and volatile nature. However, concerns are somewhat lessened for maritime transportation, which is a sector that struggles to find viable abatement options with current technologies.

The use of ammonia for shipping has significant safety risks related to its chemical properties. To transport enough ammonia (NH_4) on a ship for it to be useable as fuel, it must remain liquefied at or below −33 °C. While this is easier than the −250 °C needed for hydrogen, it still demands electricity for refrigeration. If the ship's engine fails, the refrigeration stops, leading to the ammonia warming up and converting into a toxic gas, which can be deadly to those on board and nearby. Imagine the scenario of an engine failure at sea, causing a stop in electricity generation, the ammonia getting warmed beyond liquefaction temperature, and the entire ship being engulfed in a cloud of poisonous gas which would kill any living being on board and in proximity of the vessel. To reduce this risk, ships can have multiple engines and backup systems, but this increases costs overall. Additionally, the intrinsically dangerous nature of ammonia as a fuel would be reflected in much higher insurance costs for ammonia ships compared to current heavy oil-fueled ones.

Loading ammonia on ships must also follow strict safety rules because it is a dangerous chemical. A leak can harm crew, workers, and the public. This limits the number of ships refueled at the same time and increases costs for ports, affecting fuel prices.

On the positive side, ammonia is produced from nitrogen and hydrogen without needing carbon, which eliminates sourcing issues. This results in a lower price, but still four to five times higher than current maritime fuel.

An ammonia accident in a populated area such as a port could cause thousands of victims, making safety and insurance costs high enough to prevent such ideas from being considered, or outright outlawed if they had managed to get to experimental stages and a serious incident had occurred.

7.11 HYDROGEN TO MAKE METHANOL FOR SHIPPING

In the race to zero-emissions shipping, there has been a fair amount of experimentation with methanol dual fuel vessels, with major shipping companies entering the fray and purchasing several of these ships.[24]

Usage of Hydrogen to Produce Methanol for Shipping

Methanol has a lot going for it, as it burns cleaner than hydrogen or diesel, is liquid at room temperature, and doesn't pose any of the extreme toxicity characteristics that ammonia has, and, therefore, is much better suited to use as a fuel on ships and other maritime applications.

---

[24] https://www.dnv.com/expert-story/maritime-impact/Methanol-as-fuel-heads-for-the-mainstream-in-shipping/

There have been proposals to use hydrogen to produce methanol for a new fleet of ships. The problem with this approach is, as we have seen before, linked to the requirement of carbon as a feedstock for the reaction, and is compounded by better alternative sources of methanol which compete for the market, such as bioethanol.

Simply put, using hydrogen for synthetic methanol is less economical and eco-friendly than producing bioethanol from fermentation of biofeeds, which is a promising and sustainable alternative and based on well-established reactions and pathways that mankind has been using for thousands of years most successfully.[25]

7.12 HYDROGEN FOR AIRPLANES

Another potential use for hydrogen is in aircraft, where a fair amount of R&D funding has been directed over the years. While it is technically possible to use hydrogen as fuel (as it is to fly an airplane using human power alone, by the way),[26] it remains impractical for widespread use due to chemical limitations.

Carrying Hydrogen in Aircraft for Direct Use

The first issue is that to carry hydrogen for an aircraft, it must be compressed and cooled to specific temperatures and pressures and fit inside the fuselage. This is difficult for aircraft needing to carry cargo or passengers,

---

[25] https://en.wikipedia.org/wiki/History_of_alcoholic_drinks
[26] https://en.wikipedia.org/wiki/MacCready_Gossamer_Albatross

as the fuselage is usually empty, while fuel is stored in the wings. This approach cannot be used for hydrogen, as the flat shape of wings cannot be used for pressure housing of any sort (pressure vessels need to be spherical or cylindrical, to avoid them exploding when pressurized). Housing the tanks in the fuselage would greatly reduce cargo capacity and increase transportation costs.

As we have seen for other use cases, hydrogen in containers has a high leakage rate, causing losses over time (which on an aircraft would reduce the potential range significantly). There is also a concern due to the need to handle venting of hydrogen inside an aircraft fuselage in flight, to prevent mid-air explosions. Implementing safety protocols to try to prevent a catastrophic event would require costly, unreliable technology, and lead to very high insurance costs (if any insurance company willing to underwrite such a policy were to be found in the first place).

Hydrogen and the Center of Mass for Aircraft

The idea of airplane usage includes a vital aspect related to the center of mass. Airlines often move passengers around to keep the aircraft balanced when not fully loaded, due to the criticality of maintaining a balance of weight while in flight (the fuel is held in the wings which are on the center of mass). With hydrogen, while the weight of tanks can be accounted for in construction, the changing weight of full and empty tanks poses a greater challenge, as they cannot be held in the wings and would have to be in the fuselage, and prone to massive swings in weight between takeoff (full) and landing (mostly empty). This is compounded by the need to segregate the tanks from the cargo and crew compartments on safety grounds, which would mean that the tanks will be in either the front or back of the aircraft (and the effect of changes in weight would be amplified).

Certification of a Hydrogen-Carrying Airplane

Once we consider all the issues that we have analyzed for putting compressed and incredibly cold hydrogen on an airplane, and couple them with the very high safety bar for certification of aircraft for carrying passengers, it rapidly becomes evident that it is virtually impossible to see such an airplane ever being allowed to fly commercially.

Using Hydrogen to Produce Kerosene for Aircraft

Synthetic kerosene, made from carbon feedstock and hydrogen, could offer hydrogen-based fuels for airlines. We have already seen the problems with the carbon feedstock in other scenarios where synthetic fuels are produced from hydrogen.

Even if these issues were to be brushed aside, synthetic kerosene produced from hydrogen would cost four to five times more than current jet fuel prices. Competing sustainable aviation fuels, particularly from biofuels, are already available, do not have the issues hydrogen faces, and are cheaper than hydrogen-produced kerosene, making them truly net-zero when assessed from start to finish, and a much more reasonable alternative.

7.13 HYDROGEN FOR GRID ENERGY STORAGE

A last possible use for hydrogen that has been proposed multiple times over the last 20 years is to utilize it to solve the energy storage problems associated with the discontinuous nature of alternative energy sources such as wind and solar.

Competing Technologies for Grid Energy Storage

The need for energy storage is well known and is currently being addressed by various technological options, depending on the type of energy to be stored (electricity or heat) and the duration of the storage (short term, medium term, or long term).

As of the end of 2024, the best way to store energy on a large scale is pumped hydro.[27] In this method, water is pumped uphill to reservoirs when energy is cheap, creating potential energy. When energy demand increases, the water is released to turn turbines and generate electricity. This technology is cost-effective but needs significant infrastructure and suitable geology, like hills or mountains.

For shorter and more expensive uses, often in residential or commercial real estate, battery storage is common. It is less efficient but not tied to specific location needs.

Thermal storage[28] has various options in different deployment stages and is quite efficient. This involves heating a medium with high thermal capacity when energy is available and using it to heat water or other materials when needed.

Redox flow energy storage systems, known as "flow batteries,"[29] store electrical energy in liquid electrolytes in external tanks. They are used for large-scale energy storage at competitive prices and have long life cycles.

With this ample, proven, and cost-competitive set of technologies for peak response and short-term storage available, and many others being developed as this book is being written, there seems to be a very limited

---

[27] https://en.wikipedia.org/wiki/Pumped-storage_hydroelectricity
[28] https://en.wikipedia.org/wiki/Thermal_energy_storage
[29] https://en.wikipedia.org/wiki/Flow_battery

space for storage systems based on hydrogen, due to the well-known cost and safety considerations we have seen for the prior use cases.

Hydrogen for Dark Doldrums Scenarios

One last option discussed for using hydrogen for power storage is the *Dunkelflaute*, a German term for times with little or no wind or sunlight, which makes generating energy from solar and wind difficult. This idea was proposed in the UK by Chris Llewellyn Smith and published by the Royal Society in 2023.[30]

In this scenario, there is a need to store energy for long periods to prepare for these "dark doldrums," which happen a few times a year. One suggestion is to produce large amounts of green hydrogen at low energy costs during off-peak times and store it in underground caves for later use. This approach involves non-trivial infrastructure costs, material risks, and, even in the most optimistic scenarios, would result in rare usage.

The problem with this method is that, even in *Dunkelflaute* situations, it's uncommon to need long-duration storage. Several alternative molecules, like bioethanol or biodiesel, could provide energy storage without the production, transportation, and usage problems that make hydrogen a poor technical choice. All of these alternatives would be cheaper, cleaner, and more energy efficient to use than hydrogen, effectively eliminating even this final possible usage.

---

[30] https://royalsociety.org/news/2023/09/electricity-storage-report/

CHAPTER EIGHT

OVERVIEW OF PRIMARILY GROWTH FUND INVESTMENT THESES

How to identify companies primed for rapid revenue or earnings growth in the transition finance space

8.1 WHICH OPPORTUNITIES ARE PRIMARILY GROWTH OPPORTUNITIES?

This fund includes companies primed for rapid revenue or earnings growth, outpacing either industry peers or the market overall.

The investment theses are varied, with a strong focus on the carbon markets space (VCM exchanges, VCM insurance, VCM E2E risk transfer, VCM MMRV) and the carbon dioxide removal technology itself (BECCS, biochar, DAC, ocean-based CDR). Additionally, there is a focus on growth sectors of transportation (electric airplanes), opportunistic responses to higher temperatures and economy transitions (energy efficiency for buildings, and workforce retraining and climate litigation), and modeling/compliance solutions (methane measure, novel modeling of hurricanes and tornado impacts, transition risk E2E modeling for financial institutions). The investment model is purchase and hold, or purchase, grow, and exit, depending on the area of focus.

An overall view of the primarily Growth Fund investment theses can be seen in Table 8.1.

Table 8.1 List of Growth Fund investment theses.

Investment Opportunity	Climate Driver	Investment Horizon	How Crowded Is the Space	Maturity for Investment
BECCS	Transition risk	Immediate to medium term	Not crowded yet	Ready
Biochar	Transition risk	Immediate to medium term	Not crowded yet	Ready
Energy efficiency for buildings	Transition risk	Immediate	Not crowded yet	Ready
DAC companies	Transition risk	Immediate to medium term	Crowded	Probably late

Overview of Primarily Growth Fund Investment Theses

Investment Opportunity	Climate Driver	Investment Horizon	How Crowded Is the Space	Maturity for Investment
Electric airplanes	Transition risk	Immediate to medium term	Likely crowded	Ready
Methane measure and VCM satellite monitoring	Transition risk	Immediate to medium term	Not crowded yet	In development
MMRV (Measurement, Monitoring, Reporting, and Validation) of Voluntary Carbon Credits	Transition risk	Immediate	Somewhat crowded	In development
Novel modeling for hurricane and tornado impacts	Acute Physical Risk	Immediate	Not crowded yet	In development
Ocean-based CDR	Transition risk	Medium term	Not crowded yet	In development
Transition and physical risk E2E model providers for financial institutions	Transition risk	Immediate to medium term	Not crowded yet	In development
VCM E2E risk transfer solutions	Transition risk	Immediate	Not crowded yet	In development
VCM exchanges	Transition risk	Immediate	Somewhat crowded	In development
VCM insurance products	Transition risk	Immediate	Somewhat crowded	In development
Workforce retraining companies	Transition risk	Immediate to medium term	Not crowded yet	In development
Climate litigation	Transition and Physical risk	Immediate	Not crowded yet	Ready
Vertical farming	Transition risk	Immediate	Somewhat crowded	In development

The total size of the current market for opportunities in the Growth Fund is US$ 365 billion as of 2024 (multiple sources, details in individual overview paragraphs), and is predicted to grow at a 7.41% CAGR to reach US$ 695 billion by 2032 (in a baseline, non-climate adjusted scenario).

Table 8.2 provides a view of the opportunities for which data is available, and the comparisons to the other funds, as well as to the overall totality of transition finance opportunities.

Table 8.2 Market projections for baseline scenario 2024–2032, for Growth Fund opportunities and comparison to aggregate values for all funds.

Market	2024 Size Estimate (US$ Billions)	CAGR (%)	Target Size (US$ Billions)	Target Year
BECCS	$ 1.90	4.97%	$ 2.80	2032
Energy Efficiency for Buildings	$ 331.00	6.41%	$ 544.00	2032
Electric Airplanes	$ 8.80	19.75%	$ 37.20	2032
Methane Measure and VCM Satellite Monitoring	$ 9.84	8.04%	$ 18.27	2032
Climate Modeling for Physical Risk and Transition Risk	$ 2.90	33.12%	$ 28.60	2032
Ocean-Based CDR	$ 0.56	19.84%	$ 2.40	2032
VCM Insurance	$ 2.10	6.21%	$ 3.40	2032
Vertical Farming	$ 8.50	27.40%	$ 59.00	2032
Total Growth Fund	**$ 365.60**	**8.37%**	**$ 695.67**	2032
Total Infrastructure Fund	$ 3,113.05	7.55%	$ 5,572.00	2032
Total Public Strategy Fund	$ 1,013.95	7.93%	$ 1,866.49	2032
Total Climate Alternatives Fund	$ 1,265.88	7.43%	$ 2,245.29	2032
TOTAL OVERALL FOR TRANSITION	**$5,758.48**	**7.64%**	**$10,379.45**	2032

Overview of Primarily Growth Fund Investment Theses

Figure 8.1 Market growth projections for transition finance Growth Fund opportunities, 2024–2032 baseline scenario.

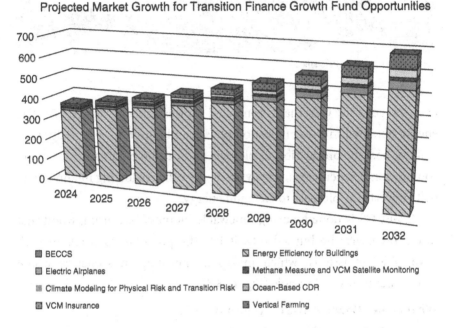

Figure 8.1 shows the data by year and opportunity, in graph form, and shows that the Energy Efficiency for Buildings space is, by far, the largest market (albeit not the one with the most growth).

8.2 BECCS: BIOENERGY WITH CARBON CAPTURE AND STORAGE

What is BECCS: By BECCS we refer to *Bioenergy with Carbon Capture and Storage*, which is the process of extracting energy from biomass (generally via combustion, partial, or complete) concurrent with the capture

Figure 8.2 Representative views of BECCS.

Generated with AI using Perchance

and storage of the CO_2 that is generated via this process (Figure 8.2). The energy obtained in the combustion phase can be used for electricity generation, heat, or production of biofuels and can be obtained from direct combustion, fermentation, pyrolysis, or any other oxidizing methodology that converts the biomass to CO_2 and energy.

If BECCS is done by using renewable biomass (i.e., using wood that would otherwise be burned/rot), it has the potential to result in negative GHG emissions, which makes it appealing in scenarios where carbon-neutrality is desirable (Figure 8.3).

What is the climate driver: Transition risk.

What is the root problem: Transition scenarios require very significant volumes of carbon removal in all but current policies.

What does this cause: Carbon removal technologies are required to meet the volumes of carbon postulated by the scenarios.

What needs to happen to fix the issue: CDR (Carbon Dioxide Removal) technologies need to scale up to produce the volumes of carbon removal required, the VCM markets need to merge with the compliance markets, and the certification/MMRV process needs to be standardized and auditable. Funding for credits needs to be established.

How soon does this need to happen: All scenarios for Net Zero 2050 or disorderly transitions include significant amounts (Gt) of carbon removal/avoidance credits by 2030.

Figure 8.3 Schematic cycle for BECCS.

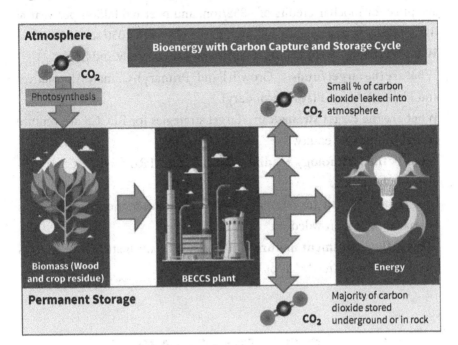

What is the opportunity: Identify and invest in new companies or emerging players in the BECCS ecosystem to gain a foothold in this new market.

What is the benefit: Access to a growing field with increasing carbon prices and profits, and growing markets, with equity valuations expected to grow significantly over time.

What is the market size: Estimates for the BECCS by the IPCC range up to 22 Gt/year, depending on the climate scenario that is chosen.[1] The value of such a market depends on the price of carbon at the year of reference,

---

[1] Smith, P. and Porter, J.R. (2018). Bioenergy in the IPCC Assessments. *GCB Bioenergy*, 10: 428–431. https://doi.org/10.1111/gcbb.12514

but would be equivalent to ~1.9 billion/year at the current (Q3 2024) average price for biochar credits of ~85$/ton, and over 6.6 billion per year at the $300/ton prices that are common in the Net Zero 2050 scenarios.

What is the long-term vision: Grow and exit, or grow and hold.

What are the target funds: Growth Fund (Primary), Climate Alternatives and Physical Assets Plays (Secondary).

What are the target strategies: Target strategies for BECCS are venture capital and private equity.

What is the technology readiness level: The TRL for BECCS is estimated to be TRL 8.

How crowded is the investment space: The crowdedness for BECCS is estimated at "not crowded yet" as of YE 2024.

What is the investment maturity: The investment maturity for BECCS is estimated to be "ready" as of YE 2024.

8.3 BIOCHAR

What is biochar: Biochar, as defined by the Carbon Standards International,[2] is "Biochar is a porous, carbonaceous material produced by pyrolysis of biomass and is applied so that the contained carbon remains stored as a carbon sink or replaces fossil carbon in industrial manufacturing." (Figure 8.4). For practical purposes, this translates into charcoal of different grades, particle size and quality, that might or might not be modified, and is intended for use in multiple applications, from

---

[2] WBC (2023): World Biochar Certificate – Guidelines for a Sustainable Production of Biochar and its Certification. Carbon Standards International, Frick, Switzerland (http://www.european-biochar.org), version 1.1 from 20th December 2024 https://www.carbon-standards.com/docs/transfer/4000036 EN.pdf

Figure 8.4   Representative views of biochar.

Generated with AI using Perchance

soil additives to filtration of various types. It typically is made up of the partially combusted remains of biomass that has undergone pyrolysis and is a form of charcoal (carbon and ashes). As per the case of BECCS, the production of biochar, if made from renewable feedstock, has the potential to be carbon neutral, or even carbon-negative, and holds great interest for climate transition scenarios that place value on Carbon Dioxide Removal methodologies.

Current uses of biochar are:

- Soil carbon sequestration tool
- Silage agent
- Litter additive
- Slurry treatment
- Manure composting
- Feed additive/supplement
- Water treatment in fish farming
- Carbon fertilizer
- Compost additive
- Substitute for peat in potting soil
- Plant protection
- Compensatory fertilizer for trace elements
- Insulation
- Air decontamination

- Decontamination in earth foundations
- Humidity regulation
- Soil additive for soil remediation, soil substrates, a barrier for preventing pesticides getting onto surface water, treating pond and lake water biogas production
- Biomass additive, biogas slurry treatment
- Active carbon filter, pre-rinsing additive, soil substrate for organic plant beds, composting toilets
- Micro-filters, macro-filters
- Exhaust filters – controlling emissions, room air filters
- Industrial materials – carbon filters, plastics
- Electronics – semiconductors, batteries
- Metallurgy – metal reduction
- Cosmetics – soaps, skin cream, therapeutic bath additives
- Paints and coloring – food colorants, industrial paints
- Energy production – pellets, substitute for lignite
- Medicines detoxification, carrier for active pharmaceutical ingredients, cataplasm or poultice for insect bites, abscesses, eczema
- Textiles fabric additive for functional underwear, thermal insulation for functional clothing, deodorant for shoe soles
- Wellness filling for mattresses, filling for pillows
- Food conservation

What is the climate driver: Transition risk.
What is the root problem: Transition scenarios require very significant volumes of carbon removal in all but current policies.
What does this cause: Carbon removal technologies are required to meet the volumes of carbon postulated by the scenarios.
What needs to happen to fix the issue: CDR (Carbon Dioxide Removal) technologies need to scale up to produce the volumes of carbon removal

required, the VCM markets need to merge with the compliance markets, and the certification/MMRV process needs to be standardized and auditable. Funding for credits needs to be established.

How soon does this need to happen: All scenarios for Net Zero 2050 or disorderly transitions include significant amounts (Gt) of carbon removal/avoidance credits by 2030.

What is the opportunity: Identify and invest in new companies or emerging players in the biochar ecosystem to gain a foothold in this new market.

What is the benefit: Access to a growing field with increasing carbon prices and profits, and growing markets, with equity valuations expected to grow significantly over time. Access to a growing commodities market for biochar that is additional to the carbon credit angle.

What is the market size: The biochar market was valued by Markets Research Future[3] at US$ 2.05 billion in 2023 and is expected to grow to US$ 3.99 billion by 2032, at a CAGR of 7.68%.

What is the long-term vision: Grow and exit or grow and hold.

What are the target funds: Growth Fund (Primary), Climate Alternatives and Physical Assets Plays (Secondary).

What are the target strategies: Target strategies for biochar are venture capital and private equity.

What is the technology readiness level: The TRL for biochar is estimated to be TRL 8.

How crowded is the investment space: The crowdedness for biochar is estimated at "not crowded yet" as of YE 2024.

What is the investment maturity: The investment maturity for biochar is estimated to be "ready" as of YE 2024.

---

[3] https://www.marketresearchfuture.com/reports/biochar-market-10808

PRINCIPLES OF TRANSITION FINANCE INVESTING

8.4 ENERGY EFFICIENCY FOR BUILDINGS

What is Energy Efficiency for Buildings: Energy Efficiency for Buildings covers all the energy-centered opportunities in the built environment (Figure 8.5). For more detailed analysis please refer to Chapter 14.

What is the climate driver: Transition risk.

What is the root problem: Transition scenarios require emissions reduction targets for GHG over time.

What does this cause: Existing buildings will face increasingly steep costs tied to their CO2 emissions used for heating/cooling. High-emissions buildings will lose value and might end up as stranded assets altogether.[4]

What needs to happen to fix the issue: Building owners will either have to offset (via VCM) or reduce their emissions (via conversion of buildings to improve efficiency) or face steep penalties (as is happening in France with high-emissions buildings not being allowed to be rented, as can be seen in detail in Chapter 14).

How soon does this need to happen: This is already an ongoing concern, with many countries pushing for increased energy efficiency in the real estate space, and imposing higher costs on the higher emitters.

Figure 8.5 Representative views of Energy Efficiency for Buildings.

Generated with AI using Perchance

---

[4] https://www.facilitiesnet.com/green/article/Buildings-Go-Net-Zero-Energy-Tackle-Climate-Change--18034

What is the opportunity: Identify and invest in companies or emerging players in the "Zero over Time" building conversion field (including solar panel installers) to gain a foothold in this new market.

What is the benefit: Ownership of a market position in a field that is set to grow sizably in all transition scenarios.

What is the market size: Focusing only on BEMS (Building Energy Management Systems), thermal insulation, and HVAC, the 2022 global market size is estimated at $331 billion, slated to grow 5.1% annually to reach $544 billion by 2032 [*sources provided in Chapter 14*].

What is the long-term vision: Buy and hold, buy-grow-exit.

What are the target funds: Growth Fund (Primary), Public Strategies Fund (Secondary).

What are the target strategies: Target strategies for Energy Efficiency for Buildings are venture capital, private equity, and private credit.

What is the Technology Readiness Level: The TRL for Energy Efficiency for Buildings is estimated to be TRL 9.

How crowded is the investment space: The crowdedness for Energy Efficiency for buildings is estimated at "not crowded yet" as of YE 2024.

What is the investment maturity: The investment maturity for Energy Efficiency for Buildings is estimated to be "ready" as of YE 2024.

8.5 DAC (DIRECT AIR CAPTURE)

What is DAC: Direct Air Capture is a technology-driven methodology used to capture CO_2 molecules directly from the air, via the use of different techniques (Figure 8.6). The end product can be either gaseous CO_2 or mineralized CO_2.

What is the climate driver: Transition risk.

Figure 8.6 Representative views of Direct Air Capture.

Generated with AI using Perchance

What is the root problem: Transition scenarios require very significant volumes of carbon removal in all but current policies.

What does this cause: Carbon removal technologies are required to meet the volumes of carbon postulated by the scenarios.

What needs to happen to fix the issue: CDR (Carbon Dioxide Removal) technologies need to scale up to produce the volumes of carbon removal required, the VCM markets need to merge with the compliance markets, and the certification/MMRV process needs to be standardized and auditable. Funding for credits needs to be established.

How soon does this need to happen: All scenarios for Net Zero 2050 or disorderly transitions include significant amounts (Gt) of carbon removal/avoidance credits by 2030.

What is the opportunity: Identify and invest in new companies or emerging players in the DAC ecosystem to gain a foothold in this new market.

What is the benefit: Access to a growing field with increasing carbon prices and profits, and growing markets, with equity valuations expected to grow significantly over time.

What is the market size: The global direct air capture market size was estimated at US$ 61.0 million in 2023 and expected to grow explosively at a CAGR of 61.0% from 2024 to 2030.[5]

What is the long-term vision: Grow and exit or grow and hold.

---

[5] https://www.grandviewresearch.com/industry-analysis/direct-air-capture-market-report

What are the target funds: Growth Fund (Primary), Infrastructure Fund (Secondary).

What are the target strategies: Target strategies for DAC are venture capital and private equity.

What is the Technology Readiness Level: The TRL for DAC is estimated to be TRL 7.

How crowded is the investment space: The crowdedness for DAC is estimated at "crowded" as of YE 2024.

What is the investment maturity: The investment maturity for DAC is estimated to be "probably late" as of YE 2024.

8.6 ELECTRIC AIRPLANES

What are electric airplanes: By electric airplanes we refer to aircraft that use electric engines powered by batteries, supercapacitors, or other kinds of electron storage devices (Figure 8.7). These are typically short-distance, low-speed airplanes, used for local travel (as opposed to intercontinental travel).

What is the climate driver: Transition risk.

What is the root problem: Transition scenarios require moving away from fossil fuels in all but current policies. One of the main mechanisms that the transition scenarios all include is a carbon tax (aka, carbon price).

Figure 8.7 Representative views of electric airplanes.

What does this cause: Sectors, such as aviation, which have high emissions that are hard to abate, will face constantly increasing taxation which will affect their cost structures in dramatic ways.

What needs to happen to fix the issue: Airplanes that rely on alternative energy sources need to be developed and certified. This is hard for long-haul flights, where range and speed make electric airplanes not a viable option, but doable for short-haul routes.

How soon does this need to happen: All scenarios for Net Zero 2050 or disorderly transitions include very significant amounts of emission reduction/offsetting in the airlines sector by 2030.

What is the opportunity: Identify and invest in new companies (such as Aura Aero)[6] or emerging players (such as EcoPulse,[7] Diamond Aircraft,[8] or Pipistrel aircraft)[9] to gain a foothold in this new market.

What is the benefit: Ownership of a steady and increasing revenue flow linked to the increasing volumes of electric planes required in transition scenarios.

What is the market size: While the forward-looking view for this market is scenario-dependent, current market research by Markets & Markets[10] estimates that the market was US$ 8.8 billion in 2022, is expected to reach US$ 37.2 billion by 2030, growing at a very strong CAGR of 19.8%.

What is the long-term vision: Purchase and hold, or purchase, grow, and exit.

What are the target funds: Growth Fund.

What are the target strategies: Target strategies for electric airplanes are venture capital, private equity, and private credit.

---

[6] https://aura-aero.com
[7] https://www.daher.com/en/ecopulse
[8] https://www.diamondaircraft.com/en
[9] https://www.pipistrel-aircraft.com
[10] https://www.marketsandmarkets.com/Market-Reports/electric-aircraft-market-52646445.html

What is the Technology Readiness Level: The TRL for electric airplanes is estimated to be TRL 9.

How crowded is the investment space: The crowdedness for Electric Airplanes is estimated at "likely crowded" as of YE 2024.

What is the investment maturity: The investment maturity for electric airplanes is estimated to be "probably late" as of YE 2024.

8.7 METHANE MEASURE AND VCM SATELLITE MONITORING

What is methane measure and VCM satellite monitoring: By methane measure, we cover technologies that allow direct measure of methane leaks at source point (either by satellite or via sensors), while the VCM satellite monitoring refers to the usage of satellites (typically the same being used for methane monitoring) for third-party independent verification of forestry status and carbon sequestration (Figure 8.8).

What is the climate driver: Transition risk.

What is the root problem: Transition scenarios require emissions reduction targets for GHG over time. Methane is between 20/400 times worse than CO_2 as a GHG and is much less monitored globally. Additionally, forestation/reforestation monitoring is hard to do.

Figure 8.8 Representative views of methane measure and VCM satellite monitoring.

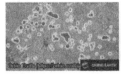

What does this cause: Methane is responsible for around 30% of the rise in global temperatures since the industrial revolution, and rapid and sustained reductions in methane emissions are key to limit near-term warming and improve air quality.[11] Forestation VCM credits are hard/costly to monitor from ground-based operations.

What needs to happen to fix the issue: Tracking of methane at sources will become increasingly key, and companies will provide more frequent and granular methane insights on specific sites/emitters. For the forestry credits, satellite monitoring will be key.

How soon does this need to happen: This is already an ongoing phenomenon, with methane being included in emissions calculations, and several players in the field working on providing actionable insights. For forestry monitoring, this is also an ongoing concern.

What is the opportunity: Identify and invest in companies or emerging players in methane measure arena (such as Orbio.earth[12] and Signal Climate Analytics)[13] and satellite imagery analytics to gain a foothold in this new market.

What is the benefit: Ownership of a market position in a field that is set to grow in all transition scenarios.

What is the market size: As in prior cases, the market projections are scenario-dependent. As a data point, the methane sensor market, according to Knowledge Sourcing,[14] will grow 10.36% annually, reaching US$ 719 million by 2030 from the current US$ 440 million. The global satellite earth observation market, according to StraitsResearch,[15] was valued at US$ 9.4 billion in 2024 and is projected to grow to US$ 17.2 billion by 2033, with a CAGR of 6.92% from 2025 to 2033.

---

[11] https://www.iea.org/reports/global-methane-tracker-2022/methane-and-climate-change
[12] https://www.orbio.earth
[13] https://signalclimateanalytics.com
[14] https://www.knowledge-sourcing.com/report/methane-sensors-market
[15] https://straitsresearch.com/report/satellite-earth-observation-market

What is the long-term vision: Buy and hold, buy-grow-exit.

What are the target funds: Growth Fund.

What are the target strategies: Target strategies for methane measure and VCM satellite monitoring are venture capital and private equity.

What is the Technology Readiness Level: The TRL for methane measure and VCM satellite monitoring is estimated to be TRL 7.

How crowded is the investment space: The crowdedness for methane measure and VCM satellite monitoring is estimated at "not crowded yet" as of YE 2024.

What is the investment Maturity: The Investment Maturity for Methane Measure and VCM satellite monitoring is estimated to be "in development" as of YE 2024.

8.8 MMRV (MEASUREMENT, MONITORING, REPORTING, AND VALIDATION) OF VOLUNTARY CARBON CREDITS

What is MMRV for the Voluntary Carbon Markets: MMRV means Measurement, Monitoring, Reporting, and Verification for the VCMs, and encompasses all the necessary steps that are required to ensure the integrity and trustworthiness of the markets and credits being traded (Figure 8.9).

What is the climate driver: Transition risk.

Figure 8.9 Representative views of MMRV of VCM.

What is the root problem: For the VCM to operate, it is necessary to have reliable MMRV to prove that an activity has avoided or removed harmful GHG emissions so that actions can be converted into credits with monetary value.[16]

What does this cause: Unreliable MMRV (such as happened with Verra in the notorious South Pole scandal)[17] reduces credibility of the VCM and prevents adoption.

What needs to happen to fix the issue: Robust, reliable, auditable, transparent, and traceable MMRV solutions need to be developed and implemented in the VCM markets.

How soon does this need to happen: All scenarios for Net Zero 2050 or disorderly transitions include significant amounts (Gt) of carbon removal/avoidance credits by 2030, which postulate a functioning VCM infrastructure.

What is the opportunity: Identify and invest in new companies or emerging players in the VCM MMRV ecosystem to gain a foothold in this new market.

What is the benefit: Access to a growing field with increasing carbon prices and profits, and growing markets, with equity valuations expected to grow significantly over time.

What is the market size: Scenario-dependent. As a baseline, the global Carbon Dioxide Removals market was valued at US$ 3.4 billion in 2024 by BCC Research[18] and is expected to grow to US$ 25.0 billion by 2029, at a very strong CAGR of 49.0%.

What is the long-term vision: Grow and exit.

What are the target funds: Growth Strategy.

---

[16] https://www.worldbank.org/en/news/feature/2022/07/27/what-you-need-to-know-about-the-measurement-reporting-and-verification-mrv-of-carbon-credits

[17] https://www.newyorker.com/magazine/2023/10/23/the-great-cash-for-carbon-hustle

[18] https://www.bccresearch.com/market-research/environment/carbon-dioxide-removals-market.html

What are the target strategies: Venture capital, private equity.
What is the Technology Readiness Level: TRL 8.
How crowded is the investment space: Somewhat crowded.
What is the investment maturity: In development.

8.9 NOVEL MODELING FOR HURRICANE, TORNADO, AND WILDFIRE IMPACTS

What is novel modeling for hurricane and tornado impacts: By novel modeling for hurricane and tornado impacts we refer to the new modeling techniques, as well as the back-testing, validation, implementation, and maintenance, required to move away from historical modeling and toward predictive modeling to allow correct estimates of risk and damage functions deriving from climate change (Figure 8.10). The main users of these models are insurance companies and regulators.
What is the climate driver: Acute physical risk.

Figure 8.10 Representative views of novel modeling for hurricane, tornado, and wildfire impacts.

Generated with AI using Perchance

What is the root problem: Existing CAT models are old and predict hurricane paths based on historical pathways, which are inaccurate for climate change scenarios.

What does this cause: Incorrect modeling causes insurers to mis-price risk and either run risks of failure, or to exit potentially profitable markets.

What needs to happen to fix the issue: New, science-based modeling approaches capable of addressing the gaps in current modeling need to be implemented and sold to insurers and re-insurers.

How soon does this need to happen: The matter is urgent, several areas of the world are experiencing increasing physical risk, insurance companies are abandoning markets in response both to climate change, and inadequate models[19,20] being used to predict likelihood and strength of events.

What is the opportunity: Identify and invest in new companies (such as https://reask.earth/) or emerging players (such as https://www.karenclarkandco.com/) to gain a foothold in this new market.

What is the benefit: Improved models and loss functions allow insurers and re-insurers to properly measure risk, offer adequate coverage, and generate profit in a scenario of evolving climate risk.

What is the market size: Scenario-dependent. The overall market for climate risk consulting, according to Verdantix,[21] had a market value of US$ 2.0 billion in 2022, forecasted to grow to US$ 9.1 billion by 2028, with a very appealing CAGR of 29%.

What is the long-term vision: Grow and exit, or grow and hold.

What are the target funds: Growth Strategy.

What are the target strategies: Venture capital and private equity.

What is the Technology Readiness Level: TRL 8.

How crowded is the Investment space: Not crowded yet.

What is the investment maturity: In development.

---

[19] https://www.insurance.com/home-and-renters-insurance/home-insurers-leaving-florida

[20] https://www.nytimes.com/2025/01/08/climate/california-homeowners-insurance-fires.html

[21] https://www.verdantix.com/report/market-size-and-forecast-climate-risk-consulting-2022-2028-global

Overview of Primarily Growth Fund Investment Theses

8.10 OCEAN-BASED CDR

What is ocean-based Carbon Dioxide Removal: By ocean-based CDR we refer to the series of technological methods that utilize the ocean as a carbon sink to store carbon dioxide removed from the atmosphere (Figure 8.11). These include direct methods, such as Direct Ocean Capture,[22] and indirect ones, such as terrestrial biomass sinking,[23] seaweed cultivation and sinking,[24] ocean alkalinization,[25] ocean upselling,[26] ocean fertilization,[27] and BECCS (Bioenergy with Carbon Capture and Storage), where the storage part is done using the ocean.

What is the climate driver: Transition risk.

What is the root problem: Transition scenarios require very significant volumes of carbon removal in all but current policies.

What does this cause: Carbon removal technologies are required to meet the volumes of carbon postulated by the scenarios.

Figure 8.11 List of ocean-based CDR with potentials and characteristics.

Category of CDR	Tech/Nature Based	Column3	Size Potential (Gt/yr)	Permanence	Leakage Potential	Measurability	Overall Quality (1-100)	Cost Projection as of 2021	Rating equivalent
Removal	Nature	Ocean Fertilization	~2.5	Unknown	Medium	Very low	17	untested and probably not viable	CCC
Removal	Nature	Ocean Upwelling	1.5-3.3	Unknown	Medium	Very low	17	~$150	CCC
Removal	Tech	Ocean Alkalinization	~1.5	Unknown	Medium	Very low	17	$50-$200	CCC
Removal	Tech	Direct Ocean Capture	?	Long	Low	High	83	TBD	AA
Removal	Nature	BECCS	0.5-5.2	Long	Medium	Very high	83	$100-200S (target 2050, some sources state as low as $20)	AA
Removal	Nature	Seaweed Cultivation	~1	Long	Low	Very high	100	~$75	AAA
Removal	Nature	Biomass sinking	1-2	Long	Low	Very high	100	~$50 (dependent on price of timber and ballast)	AAA

---

[22] https://www.weforum.org/stories/2024/10/direct-ocean-capture-carbon-removal-technology

[23] https://illuminem.com/illuminemvoices/marine-biomass-carbon-removal-and-storage-sink-it-and-forget-it

[24] https://www.edf.org/sites/default/files/2022-10/Carbon%20Sequestration%20by%20Seaweed.pdf

[25] https://climate.law.columbia.edu/sites/default/files/content/docs/Webb%20et%20al_Removing%20CO2%20Through%20Ocean%20Alkalinity%20Enhancement%20_2021-09.pdf

[26] https://climate.law.columbia.edu/content/removing-carbon-dioxide-through-artificial-upwelling-and-downwelling-legal-challenges-and

[27] https://oceanacidification.noaa.gov/carbon-dioxide-removal

What needs to happen to fix the issue: CDR (Carbon Dioxide Removal) technologies need to scale up to produce the volumes of carbon removal required, the VCM markets need to merge with the compliance markets, and the certification/MMRV process needs to be standardized and auditable. Funding for credits needs to be established.

How soon does this need to happen: All scenarios for Net Zero 2050 or disorderly transitions include significant amounts (Gt) of carbon removal/avoidance credits by 2030.

What is the opportunity: Identify and invest in new companies or emerging players in the ocean-based CDR ecosystem to gain a foothold in this new market.

What is the benefit: Access to a growing field with increasing carbon prices and profits, and growing markets, with equity valuations expected to grow significantly over time.

What is the market size: As in many transition risk-driven opportunities, the market size for ocean CDR is highly scenario-dependent. Ocean-based CDR has a max size potential of between ~8 and ~15.5 Gt/year,[28] which is more than land-based CDR. For sizing purposes, according to Virtue Market Research,[29] the ocean carbon removal market was valued at US$ 564 million in 2023 and is expected to reach US$ 1,745 million by 2030, growing at a CAGR of 17.5% from 2024 to 2030.

What is the long-term vision: Grow and exit or grow and hold.

What are the target funds: Growth Strategy, Climate Alternatives and Physical Asset Plays Strategy.

What are the target strategies: Venture capital and private equity.

What is the Technology Readiness Level: TRL 7.

How crowded is the investment space: Not crowded yet.

What is the investment maturity: In development.

---

[28] Webb, Romany M. (2023). Ocean Carbon Dioxide Removal for Climate Mitigation - The Legal Framework. Sabin Center for Climate Change Law, Columbia Law School.

[29] https://virtuemarketresearch.com/report/ocean-carbon-removal-market

8.11 TRANSITION AND PHYSICAL RISK E2E MODEL PROVIDERS FOR FINANCIAL INSTITUTIONS

What are transition and physical risk E2E model providers for financial institutions: By transition and physical risk E2E modeling we refer to model frameworks that integrate all factors from climate models, all the way to climate premium assessments (Figure 8.12). The natural customers for these services are financial institutions, both for risk and for investment use, who, in the wake of the increasing complexity (and, therefore, cost) of modeling and the ever-growing amount of data required, find developing such models in-house evermore antieconomic.

What is the climate driver: Transition risk.

What is the root problem: Regulators around the world are increasing scrutiny on climate risk for financial institutions and transition finance is set to grow dramatically in the next several decades, requiring solid modeling for investment and risk management purposes.

What does this cause: Financial institutions need to build frameworks for the identification, measure, monitor, and control of climate risk and climate opportunity within their business. This requires the development and implementation of complex and costly E2E model frameworks that most institutions cannot afford to do in-house.

Figure 8.12 Characteristics of transition and physical risk E2E modeling for financial institutions.

What needs to happen to fix the issue: Third-party providers need to offer E2E turnkey solutions that meet regulatory, validation, and audit requirements for climate risk.

How soon does this need to happen: The matter is of a certain urgency, as financial regulators are addressing climate change through various actions, and have been doing so for several years. They are enhancing disclosure requirements for companies to provide clear climate-related information, incorporating climate risks into stress tests to evaluate financial stability, setting sustainability standards for green finance, using supervisory powers to tackle financial threats and protect investor rights related to climate risk, working on improving climate and emissions data quality, and strengthening the overall oversight against greenwashing. All these activities have direct bearing on, and require, a growing and increasingly complex set of models that need to be developed, implemented, run, and maintained on an ever more frequent basis. This requires large, dedicated teams of specialists (programmers, climate scientists, data scientists, regulatory experts, etc.) which, if done in-house, impose a growing financial and organizational burden on any institution. While the largest Tier I banks still have internal modeling teams (the author having headed the global climate modeling analytics team for Citibank, as an example), the smaller Tier II and Tier III banks cannot justify the cost of setting up and maintaining such infrastructure yet face increasing requirements to produce analytics and data related to physical and transition risk. For the buy-side the option of in-housing is even more remote, as this type of upfront fixed cost investment, which is used in select, initial, stages of the investment cycle, is almost impossible to justify.

What is the opportunity: Identify and invest in SAAS providers for modeling services in the transition/physical risk space that offer E2E solutions (inclusive of validation documentation, scenario customization, and full model transparency).

What is the benefit: Establish a leading position in a growing market, with side benefits of the models being usable and expandable to the buy-side.

What is the market size: The speed at which these models will be required is driven on one side by regulatory requirements, and on the other by the need to gain a competitive edge over other investors. While the risk (regulatory) side is based on compliance, and therefore on what governments and administrations decide to do on this subject (and hard to predict), the investment side is self-sustaining and independent of any expected regulation or guidelines being issued. As per the prior example of novel modeling for physical risk, we can use the overall market size for climate risk consulting as a yardstick to have a general idea of size. As we saw earlier, according to Verdantix[30] this market had a value of $2.0 billion in 2022 and is forecasted to grow to $9.1 billion by 2028, with a (quite impressive) CAGR of 29%.

What is the long-term vision: Grow and exit, or grow and hold.
What are the target funds: Growth Strategy.
What are the target strategies: Venture capital and private equity.
What is the Technology Readiness Level: TRL7.
How crowded is the investment space: Not crowded yet.
What is the investment maturity: In development.

8.12 VCM E2E RISK TRANSFER SOLUTIONS

What is Voluntary Carbon Markets End-to-End risk transfer solutions: By VCM E2E risk transfer solutions we refer to financial instruments and rails that allow the separation of project risk from financial risk in the carbon trading space, via the application of well-established financial markets instruments such as portfolio theory, collateralized

---

[30] https://www.verdantix.com/report/market-size-and-forecast-climate-risk-consulting-2022-2028-global

Figure 8.13 Flowchart for End-to-End Voluntary Carbon Markets risk transfer.

debt obligations, and collateralized loan obligations (and similar new VCM-specific instruments) (Figure 8.13).

What is the climate driver: Transition risk.

What is the root problem: Transition scenarios require very significant volumes of carbon removal in all but current policies.

What does this cause: Buyers of carbon offsets are exposed to project risk when buying VCM, and even after retiring them.

What needs to happen to fix the issue: End-to-End risk transfer solutions need to be provided to the VCM buyers, to decouple the project risk from the rest of the risks, so that the buyer can purchase a clean "project-risk-free" financial instrument.

How soon does this need to happen: All scenarios for Net Zero 2050 or disorderly transitions include significant amounts (Gt) of carbon removal/avoidance credits by 2030.

What is the opportunity: Identify and invest in new companies (such as Sankhya)[31] or emerging players in the VCM markets to gain a foothold in this new market.

What is the benefit: Access to a growing field with increasing carbon prices and profits, and growing markets, with equity valuations expected to grow significantly over time.

What is the market size: Scenario-dependent, as these instruments are directly tied to the size and acceptance of the VCM globally. At the

---

[31] https://www.sankhya.earth

moment of writing, this is a fairly novel concept, and no specific market research has been published on the potential size.
What is the long-term vision: Grow and exit or grow and hold.
What are the target funds: Growth Strategy.
What are the target strategies: Venture capital and private equity.
What is the Technology Readiness Level: TRL7.
How crowded is the investment space: Not crowded yet.
What is the investment maturity: In development.

8.13 VCM EXCHANGES

What are VCM exchanges: By VCM exchanges we refer to the analogous of stock exchanges, dedicated to trading Voluntary Carbon Markets, as exemplified in Figure 8.14. They can be either self-standing entities, or part of stock or commodities exchanges.
What is the climate driver: Transition risk.
What is the root problem: Transition scenarios require very significant volumes of carbon removal in all but current policies.
What does this cause: Functioning and widespread VCM market infrastructure needs to be in place.
What needs to happen to fix the issue: CDR (Carbon Dioxide Removal) technologies need to scale up to produce the volumes of carbon removal required, the VCM markets need to merge with the compliance markets, and the certification/MMRV process needs to be standardized and auditable. Funding for credits needs to be established.
How soon does this need to happen: All scenarios for Net Zero 2050 or disorderly transitions include significant amounts (Gt) of carbon removal/avoidance credits by 2030.
What is the opportunity: Identify and invest in new companies or emerging players in the VCM exchanges to gain a foothold in this new market.

Figure 8.14 Representational views of VCM exchanges.

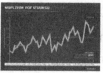

Generated with AI using Perchance

What is the benefit: Access to a growing field with increasing carbon prices and trading volumes, growing markets, and equity valuations expected to grow significantly over time.

What is the market size: As in many other cases, the market size is highly scenario-dependent. Given the novelty of the concept, and the in-flux nature of the VCM space in general, there are no known specific market studies that can be referred to at the moment.

What is the long-term vision: Grow and exit via acquisition by major stock exchange.

What are the target funds: Growth Strategy.

What are the target strategies: Private equity.

What is the Technology Readiness Level: TRL7.

How crowded is the investment space: Somewhat crowded.

What is the investment maturity: In development.

8.14 VCM INSURANCE PRODUCTS

What are Voluntary Carbon Markets insurance products: By VCM insurance we mean the provision of risk mitigation services, via insurance policies, for the buyers of voluntary carbon markets credits (Figure 8.15). These are typically project-related, and meant to reduce the risk, and increase the confidence, that investors have in the specific credits.

Figure 8.15 Interconnections for Voluntary Carbon Markets insurance products.

What is the climate driver: Transition risk.

What is the root problem: Transition scenarios require very significant volumes of carbon removal in all but current policies.

What does this cause: Carbon removal technologies and well-established and functioning carbon markets are required to meet the volumes of carbon postulated by the scenarios.

What needs to happen to fix the issue: CDR (Carbon Dioxide Removal) technologies need to scale up to produce the volumes of carbon removal required, the VCM markets need to merge with the compliance markets, and the certification/MMRV process needs to be standardized and auditable. Funding for credits needs to be established.

How soon does this need to happen: All scenarios for Net Zero 2050 or disorderly transitions include significant amounts (Gt) of carbon removal/avoidance credits by 2030.

What is the opportunity: Identify and invest in new companies or emerging players in the VCM insurance ecosystem to gain a foothold in this new market.

What is the benefit: Access to a growing field with increasing carbon prices, profits, and market size, with equity valuations expected to grow significantly over time.

What is the market size: Scenario-dependent. According to Bloomberg,[32] the size of the voluntary carbon market was just under $2 billion in 2022. A detailed research paper[33] by Kita and Oxbow Partners estimates that by 2030 the Gross Written Premium (GWP) for VCM insurance could be up to $1 billion annually and by 2050 could be up to $10–30 billion annually, underwritten across the industry.

What is the long-term vision: Grow and exit or grow and hold.

What are the target funds: Growth Strategy.

What are the target strategies: Venture capital and private equity.

What is the Technology Readiness Level: TRL8.

How crowded is the investment space: Somewhat crowded.

What is the investment maturity: In development.

8.15 WORKFORCE RETRAINING COMPANIES

What are workforce retraining companies: By workforce retraining companies we mean companies whose primary purpose is to upskill workers to meet the requirements of new industries, services, and sectors that

---

[32] https://www.bloomberg.com/news/articles/2024-05-24/carbon-offset-projects-face-trust-issues-wildfires-insurance-could-help?embedded-checkout=true

[33] https://www.kita.earth/s/Kita-Oxbow-Gross-Written-Carbon.pdf

Overview of Primarily Growth Fund Investment Theses

Figure 8.16 Notional representations of workforce retraining.

Generated with AI using Perchance

are growing due to transition finance opportunities (Figure 8.16). These companies would typically focus on workers with skillsets that are in diminished demand (such as internal combustion engine–related skills), and would be either funded directly by the trainees or by companies who need to hire skilled personnel in areas where the skillset is scarce.

What is the climate driver: Transition risk.

What is the root problem: Transition scenarios will result in many industries, sectors, and regions to experience reductions in force, while others will experience significant and stable growth over time.[34]

What does this cause: Large portions of the workforce will need to be retrained to acquire new skillsets and talents, to be eligible for hire into the growing sectors.[35]

What needs to happen to fix the issue: Institutions need to be set up to provide workforce retraining opportunities, to ensure that the market need is met.

How soon does this need to happen: This is starting to happen in certain sectors, with rising demand for solar photovoltaic installers, wind turbine technicians, and building retrofit specialists, and will accelerate over time, tied to the climate scenario of choice.

---

[34] https://www2.deloitte.com/content/dam/Deloitte/global/Documents/Energy-and-Resources/gx-eri-net-zero-workforce-ipc.pdf

[35] https://www.mckinsey.com/capabilities/sustainability/our-insights/the-economic-transformation-what-would-change-in-the-net-zero-transition

What is the opportunity: Identify and invest in companies or emerging players in the workforce upskilling/retraining space.
What is the benefit: Ownership of a leading market position in a field that is set to grow in all transition scenarios.
What is the market size: Once again, the market size is very much scenario dependent. As a short-term data point, however, we can point to the ResearchAndMarkets report on global corporate training[36] (which covers everything, not just retraining) which values the entire market at US$ 352 billion with an expected CAGR of 11.7% during 2025–2030, leading it to reach ~ US$ 613 billion by the end of the decade.
What is the long-term vision: Buy and hold, buy-grow-exit.
What are the target funds: Growth Strategy.
What are the target strategies: Venture capital and private equity.
What is the Technology Readiness Level: TRL7.
How crowded is the investment space: Not crowded yet.
What is the investment maturity: In development.

8.16 CLIMATE LITIGATION

What is climate litigation: By climate litigation we mean the legal strategy to hold governments, corporations, or individuals accountable for the climate change effects deriving from anthropogenic GHG emissions into the atmosphere (Figure 8.17). It can typically focus on future damages (which include greenwashing cases, failure to adapt cases, and failure to enforce climate standards cases) and past/current damages (this includes damage compensation to both acute and chronic physical risk effects, as well as pollution-related cases).

---

[36] https://www.researchandmarkets.com/report/corporate-training

Figure 8.17 Notional representations of climate litigation.

Generated with AI using Perchance

What is the climate driver: This is one of the rare cases of dual climate drivers, as future damages are driven by transition risk, while past/current damages are driven by physical risk.

What is the root problem: Climate change, driven by excess GHG emissions of anthropogenic origin, has impacts on multiple aspects of society and individuals.

What does this cause: Entities that believe they have suffered damages, or are likely to suffer damages, resulting from climate change are going to resort to legal channels to receive satisfaction.

What needs to happen to fix the issue: In this case there is no specific fix that needs to occur, as it is a phenomenon that will follow a trajectory as tobacco, talcum powder, and oxycontin litigation have in the past.

How soon does this need to happen: Climate litigation is on the rise. The Climate Change Laws of the World (CCLW)[37] database shows that there has been a sharp rise in the number of climate change-related lawsuits filed worldwide over time and 54% of the cases have had outcomes that were in favor of action on climate change.

What is the opportunity: Third-party litigation funding of climate liability cases, where funds are provided to a business, law firm, or individual to pursue a lawsuit, in return for a percentage of any compensation awarded.

---

[37] https://climate-laws.org

What is the benefit: Investment in an uncorrelated asset class with high returns and low volatility, as success in a lawsuit is dependent, in significant proportion, on legal and economic aspects of the case in point and has no linkage to the financial markets.

What is the market size: While it is hard to predict future litigiousness, and the responses of many different international courts and jurisdictions, as well as legislators, it is very clear how there has been a strong increase in litigation since the Sabin Center for Climate Law started tracking these cases in 1986.[38] The growth in the last 25 years has been roughly exponential, with over 70% of the over 2,600 cases on record having occurred in the last eight years, but there are no current market studies available that can be used for forward-projections. It is noteworthy to highlight how climate litigation is one of the few investment theses that is not overtly scenario-dependent, as the choice of scenario (for example, a Net Zero 2050 as opposed to a Current Policies one) is likely to influence the type of lawsuits, but not necessarily the overall number. In an aggressive decarbonization scenario, such as the Net Zero 2050, we would expect many lawsuits on failure to comply, greenwashing, and failure to adapt (i.e., the transition finance–driven cases), and a lesser amount of past/current damage ones, as the amount of physical risk effects would be mitigated compared to current policies. In the flipside scenario, we would see a much lower number of the transition finance–driven cases, as the scenario assumes that not much climate legislation and enforcement would happen, but the number of physical risk lawsuits would be vastly superior, due to the effects of an unmitigated emissions scenario, which would lead to much higher numbers of damage compensation and pollution cases being filed.

What is the long-term vision: The long-term vision for this investment is different than most other investments, as this is a purely financial play which has a defined scope, risk, and timeframe, and ends at a set date (the

---

[38] https://www.lse.ac.uk/granthaminstitute/wp-content/uploads/2024/06/Global-trends-in-climate-change-litigation-2024-snapshot.pdf

final sentencing/settlement date) while holding no residual value. As a result, it would have to be described as "hold to maturity" (although there could be secondary market transactions on interests in such a venture, at intermediate steps of the process).

What are the target funds: Given the nature of the investment, returns and risk profile, the closest fund for this strategy would be the Growth Fund.

What are the target strategies: Depending on the amount invested, this strategy can be suited for VC or PE investments (albeit the risk profile and potentially long timeframes might be on the high end of the spectrum for PE).

What is the Technology Readiness Level: TRL9.

How crowded is the investment space: "Not crowded yet," as of the writing of this book.

What is the investment maturity: Ready.

8.17 VERTICAL FARMING

What is vertical farming: By vertical farming we mean indoors-based crop growth in structured layers (typically stacked), by using artificial growing systems such as hydroponics, aquaponics, or other methods of soilless agriculture (Figure 8.18). It allows growing crops 365 days per year

Figure 8.18 Examples of vertical farming companies.

in a controlled environment, minimizing space, water, and fertilizer requirements and allowing maximum levels of recycling of nutrients and minerals to be achieved. For several crops, the yield per acre can be increased by a factor of 15–20 by installing vertical farms, as opposed to open air farming or greenhouses.

What is the climate driver: Vertical farming is another opportunity that has dual drivers, one being physical risk (both acute and chronic), as exposed farmland becomes increasingly subject to the vagaries of a changing climate, reduced precipitation (or flooding) and excessive heat. The other driver is transition risk, which is tied to the premium that low GHG-emitting food is expected to have in future years, coupled with the additional driver of growing populations and shrinking, or at best stable, acreage of productive cropland.

What is the root problem: Demand for agricultural produce is growing with the growing population, while the amount of farmland is not. Climate change is straining traditional agricultural hotspots in the world, with heat stress, water stress, and increased frequency of extreme weather events.

What does this cause: The production of agricultural produce is likely to be insufficient to feed a growing world over time, and will also be increasingly erratic, due to uncertain weather. As a result, food prices are likely to increase.

What needs to happen to fix the issue: Alternative ways to produce more farmland are required (i.e., vertical farms). These technologies need to be aligned with the scarcity of available land and water resources that is foreseen, as well as be highly efficient both energetically and from a waste perspective.

How soon does this need to happen: While vertical farms have been ongoing for quite a while, they have not yet been the success that proponents of the concept had predicted. This is due mainly to two initial misconceptions, the first one being the expectation that consumers would pay significant premia for vertically farmed produce over standard fare (this has turned out to be a fallacy, with the exclusion of some very niche applications for high-value-add use cases such as fine dining and similar). The second misconception was that it would have been sufficient to come up with a working setup, while not focusing on efficiency, automation, and cost optimization for the process. This misconception resulted in very large sums of money being invested in companies that did not have the technology to be profitable at any scale and resulted in well-publicized failures and bankruptcies. For vertical farming to be successful in the short, as well as the long, run, the focus needs to shift to companies that can prove core profitability at scale, with standard (i.e., not incentivized) economics, and compete with normal produce in the marketplace.

What is the opportunity: Identify and invest in companies or emerging players in the vertical farming space that show core profitability and intrinsic scalability.

What is the benefit: Ownership of a market position in a field that is set to grow sizably in all transition scenarios.

What is the market size: Once again, the market size for long-term views is very much scenario-dependent. As a current, short-term, data point, StraitsResearch estimates[39] that the global vertical farming market was US$ 8.5 billion in 2022 and expected to reach US$ 59 billion by 2031, growing at an impressive CAGR of 24.1% during the 2023–2031 period.

What is the long-term vision: Buy and hold, buy-grow-exit.

What are the target funds: Growth Strategy.

What are the target strategies: Venture capital and private equity.

What is the Technology Readiness Level: TRL9.

How crowded is the investment space: Not crowded yet.

What is the investment maturity: Ready.

---

[39] https://straitsresearch.com/report/vertical-farming-market

CHAPTER NINE

OVERVIEW OF PRIMARILY PUBLIC STRATEGY FUND INVESTMENT THESES

How to identify capital deployment opportunities in private credit and invest/coinvest in joint ventures with publicly traded companies

9.1 WHICH OPPORTUNITIES ARE PRIMARILY PUBLIC STRATEGY FUND OPPORTUNITIES?

The Public Strategy focuses on publicly traded companies, to lend capital as private credit and invest/coinvest in joint ventures. It also focuses on understanding the risks and identifying the opportunities of climate change in the transition finance space, as it applies to public companies.

The investment theses range from traditional plays such as various types of metals and mining securities, and the energy sector (nuclear reactor manufacturers), to more climate-specific ones, such as insurance companies with novel modeling approaches for coastal areas, HVAC manufacturers and installers, and cutting-edge transportation sector technology companies, such as EVs (cars and motorcycles), electric trucks, Mag-lev trains, and emissions-free shipping.

The investment model is purchase and hold, or purchase, grow, and exit, depending on the area of focus.

An overall view of the primarily Public Strategy Fund investment theses can be seen in Table 9.1.

The total size of the current market for opportunities in the Public Strategy Fund is US$ 1.013 trillion as of 2024 (multiple sources, details in individual overview paragraphs), and is predicted to grow at a 7.93% CAGR to reach US$ 1.866 trillion by 2032 (in a baseline, non-climate adjusted scenario).

Table 9.2 provides a view of the opportunities for which data is available, and the comparisons to the other funds, as well as to the overall totality of transition finance opportunities.

Figure 9.1 shows the data by year and opportunity, in graph form, and shows that there is no single dominating opportunity by market size, with Electric transportation, Insurers with novel climate models, Critical minerals mining, and Copper mining all being of comparable sizes by the end of the period.

Table 9.1 Primarily Public Strategy Fund opportunities.

Investment Opportunity	Climate Driver	Investment Horizon	How Crowded Is the Space	Maturity for Investment	TRL
Aluminum mines and smelters	Transition risk	Immediate	Likely crowded	Probably late	9
Copper mines	Transition risk	Immediate	Likely crowded	Probably late	9
Electric transportation (cars/trucks/trains/motorcycles)	Transition risk	Immediate	Crowded	Probably late	8
Insurance companies with novel modeling approaches for coastal areas	Climate risk - Physical acute risk	Medium term	Not crowded yet	In development	7
Nuclear reactor manufacturers	Transition risk	Immediate	Likely crowded	Probably late	9
Critical minerals mines	Transition risk	Immediate	Likely crowded	Probably late	9
Uranium mines	Transition risk	Immediate	Likely crowded	Probably late	9
HVAC manufacturers and installers	Transition risk	Immediate	Likely crowded	Mature	9
Sustainable steel	Transition risk	Medium term	Not crowded yet	In development	7
Emissions-free shipping	Transition risk	Medium term	Not crowded yet	In development	7

Table 9.2 Market projections for baseline scenario 2024–2032, for Public Strategy Fund opportunities and comparison to aggregate values for all funds.

Market	2024 Size Estimate (US$ Billions)	CAGR (%)	Target Size (US$ Billions)	Target Year
Aluminum mines and smelters	$ 229.00	7.32%	$ 403.00	2032
Copper mines	$ 436.80	6.53%	$ 724.40	2032
Electric transportation	$ 721.35	6.76%	$ 1,217.00	2032
Insurers with novel climate models	$ 740.00	2.19%	$ 880.00	2032
Nuclear reactor manufacturers	$ 34.40	3.50%	$ 45.30	2032
Critical minerals mining	$ 320.00	16.95%	$ 1,120.00	2032
Uranium	$ 8.50	7.62%	$ 15.30	2032
HVAC manufacturers and installers	$ 294.00	6.35%	$ 481.00	2032
Sustainable steel	$ 329.00	9.62%	$ 686.00	2032
Total Growth Fund	$ 365.60	8.37%	$ 695.67	2032
Total Infrastructure Fund	$ 3,113.05	7.55%	$ 5,572.00	2032
Total Public Strategy Fund	**$1,013.95**	**7.93%**	**$ 1,866.49**	2032
Total Climate Alternatives Fund	$ 1,265.88	7.43%	$ 2,245.29	2032
TOTAL OVERALL FOR TRANSITION	**$5,758.48**	**7.64%**	**$ 10,379.45**	**2032**

9.2 ALUMINUM MINES AND SMELTERS

What are aluminum mines and smelters: By aluminum mining and smelting we consider all the value chain of companies involved in the process that begins with prospecting for aluminum ore and ends with the finished aluminum ingot commodity (Figure 9.2).

Overview of Primarily Public Strategy Fund Investment Theses

Figure 9.1 Market growth projections for transition finance Public Strategy Fund opportunities, 2024–2032 baseline scenario.

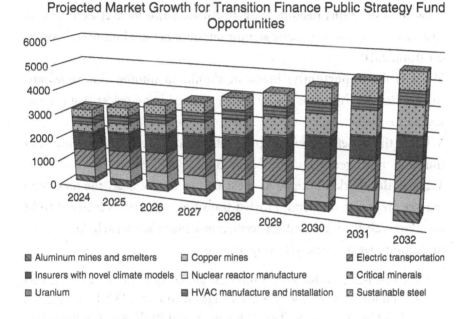

Figure 9.2 Representational images for aluminum mining and smelting.

Generated with AI using Perchance

What is the climate driver: Transition risk.

What is the root problem: Transition scenarios require electrification of transportation, households, and industry in all but current policies.

What does this cause: Many of the technologies (such as electric vehicles) need lightweight metals (Al) to meet energy efficiency requirements.

What needs to happen to fix the issue: To meet the increased aluminum requirements of the transition scenarios, the output of aluminum mining globally needs to increase over time.

How soon does this need to happen: All scenarios for Net Zero 2050 or disorderly transitions include significant amounts of aluminum between 2030 and 2050.

What is the opportunity: Invest in aluminum mining companies and prospecting, to front-run the increase in demand and prices that the scenarios are predicting.

What is the benefit: Ownership of a steady and increasing revenue flow linked to the increasing usage of aluminum.

What is the market size: As is most frequently the case, the long-term market projections depend on what transition scenario is believed to be the most realistic one. For short-term, non-climate-scenario linked market projections, we have the following insights:

> Fortune Business Insights[1] values the global aluminum market at US$ 229 billion in 2023 and expects it to grow to US$ 403 billion by 2032, with a CAGR of 6.2%. This is for the metal itself, and not the actual mining business.
>
> The mining of bauxite, the main aluminum ore, according to Allied Market Research,[2] was globally worth US$ 18.1 billion in 2022, and expected to reach US$ 26.9 billion by 2032, growing at a 4.1% CAGR from 2023 to 2032.
>
> The aluminum smelting market, according to Market Research Future,[3] was valued at US$ 94.5 billion in 2022 and is projected to reach US$ 167.3 billion by 2032, growing at a CAGR of 5.88% from 2024 to 2032.

---

[1] https://www.fortunebusinessinsights.com/industry-reports/aluminium-market-100233
[2] https://www.alliedmarketresearch.com/bauxite-mining-market
[3] https://www.marketresearchfuture.com/reports/aluminum-smelting-market-25896

Overview of Primarily Public Strategy Fund Investment Theses

What is the long-term vision: Purchase and hold.
What are the target funds: Public Strategy and Infrastructure Strategy.
What are the target strategies: Private equity and private credit.
What is the Technology Readiness Level: TRL9.
How crowded is the investment space: Likely crowded.
What is the investment maturity: Probably late.

9.3 COPPER MINES

What are copper mines: By copper mining we consider all the value chain of companies involved in the process that begins with prospecting for copper ore, and ends with the finished copper ingot commodity (Figure 9.3).
What is the climate driver: transition risk.
What is the root problem: Transition scenarios require electrification of transportation, households, and industry in all but current policies.
What does this cause: Demand for copper will increase dramatically, as it is the principal conductor used for electrification.
What needs to happen to fix the issue: To meet the increased requirements of the transition scenarios, the output of copper mining globally needs to increase over time.
How soon does this need to happen: All scenarios for Net Zero 2050 or disorderly transitions include significant amounts of copper between 2030 and 2050.

Figure 9.3   Representational images for copper mining.

   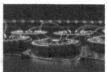

Generated with AI using Perchance

What is the opportunity: Invest in copper mining companies and prospecting, to front-run the increase in demand and prices that the scenarios are predicting.

What is the benefit: Ownership of a steady and increasing revenue flow linked to the increasing usage of copper.

What is the market size: As is most frequently the case, the long-term market projections depend on what transition scenario is believed to be the most realistic one. For short-term, non-climate-scenario linked market projections, we have the following insights:

Precedence Research[4] values the global copper market at US$ 318 billion in 2023, projected it at US$ 333 billion for 2024, and expected it to grow to around US$ 548 billion by 2034, with a CAGR of 5.11% from 2024 to 2034. Again, this is the market for the metal alone.

The mining of copper, according to market.us,[5] was globally worth US$ 8.8 billion in 2023, and projected to reach US$ 12 billion by 2033, expanding at a CAGR of 3.5%.

The copper smelting market, according to Market Research Future,[6] was valued at US$ 110.6 billion in 2022 and is projected to reach US$ 164.4 billion by 2032, growing at a CAGR of 4.04% from 2024 to 2032. Note that this includes smelting of recycled copper, in addition to the usual primary sources from mining.

What is the long-term vision: Purchase and hold.
What are the target funds: Public Strategy and Infrastructure Strategy.
What are the target strategies: Private equity and private credit.
What is the Technology Readiness Level: TRL9.
How crowded is the investment space: Likely crowded.
What is the investment maturity: Probably late.

---

[4] https://www.precedenceresearch.com/copper-market
[5] https://www.news.market.us/copper-mining-market-news
[6] https://www.marketresearchfuture.com/reports/copper-smelting-market-26251

9.4 ELECTRIC TRANSPORTATION (CARS/TRUCKS/TRAINS/MOTORCYCLES)

What is electric transportation (cars/trucks/trains/motorcycles): For the purposes of this opportunity, we define electric transportation (Figure 9.4) as the consolidation of all vehicles that meet the US Department of Energy's definition[7] of an electric vehicle, as follows:

> An EV is defined as a vehicle that can be powered by an electric motor that draws electricity from a battery and is capable of being charged from an external source. An EV includes both a vehicle that can only be powered by an electric motor that draws electricity from a battery (EV) and a vehicle that can be powered by an electric motor that draws electricity from a battery and by an internal combustion engine (plug-in hybrid electric vehicle).

What is the climate driver: Transition risk.

What is the root problem: Transition scenarios require moving away from fossil fuels in all but current policies. One of the main mechanisms that the transition scenarios all include is a carbon tax (aka, carbon price).

Figure 9.4 Representational images for electric transportation.

---

[7] https://afdc.energy.gov/laws/12660

What does this cause: Sectors, such as transportation, which have high emissions that are hard to abate, will face constantly increasing taxation which will affect their cost structures in dramatic ways.

What needs to happen to fix the issue: Transportation that relies on alternative energy sources needs to be developed and gain market share. This is an ongoing reality for autos, trains, and motorcycles (at different levels of maturity) and less mature for trucks.

How soon does this need to happen: All scenarios for Net Zero 2050 or disorderly transitions include very significant amounts of emission reduction/offsetting in the transportation sector by 2030.

What is the opportunity: Identify and invest in new companies (such as Ironlev)[8] or emerging players (as Zero Motorcycles)[9] in electric transportation to gain a foothold in this new market.

What is the benefit: Ownership of a steady and increasing revenue flow linked to the increasing volumes of electric transportation required in transition scenarios.

What is the market size: The long-term market projections, especially for electric transportation, depend heavily on what transition scenario is believed to be the most realistic one. For short-term, non-climate-scenario linked market projections, we have the following insights:

> For electric cars, MarketsAndMarkets[10] estimates the global market to be worth US$ 396 billion as of 2024 and projects it to grow to US$ 620 billion by 2030 at a CAGR of 7.7%.
>
> Looking at electric trucks, Grand View Research[11] values the global market at US$ 22.6 billion in 2023 and expects it to grow at a very robust 27.1% CAGR from 2024 to 2030, reaching ~ US$ 95 billion at the end of the forecast period.

---

[8] https://www.ironlev.com/transport
[9] https://zeromotorcycles.com
[10] https://www.marketsandmarkets.com/Market-Reports/electric-vehicle-market-209371461.html
[11] https://www.grandviewresearch.com/industry-analysis/electric-trucks-market

Overview of Primarily Public Strategy Fund Investment Theses

In the electric motorcycle space, ZionMarketResearch[12] valued the global motorcycle market at US$ 139.25 billion in 2023 and expects growth to US$ 192 billion by 2032, with a CAGR of 3.68% from 2024 to 2032.

The electric train market, according to Market Research Future,[13] was valued at US$ 163.5 billion US$ in 2022, and projected to grow to 310 billion US$ by 2032, at a CAGR of 6.6%.

What is the long-term vision: Purchase and hold, or purchase, grow, and exit.
What are the target funds: Public Strategy and Growth Strategy.
What are the target strategies: Venture capital, private equity, and private credit.
What is the Technology Readiness Level: TRL8.
How crowded is the investment space: Crowded.
What is the investment maturity: Probably late.

9.5 INSURANCE COMPANIES WITH NOVEL MODELING APPROACHES FOR COASTAL AREAS

What are insurance companies with novel modeling approaches for coastal areas: As we have seen the need for novel modeling methodologies for insurance companies to tackle physical risk (Figure 9.5), as highlighted in section 8.9, there is, as a counterpoise, the need for insurance companies that utilize such models for their pricing of policies.

---

[12] https://www.zionmarketresearch.com/report/electric-motorcycle-market
[13] https://www.marketresearchfuture.com/reports/electric-train-market-23153

Figure 9.5 Examples of novel modeling approaches for physical risk insurance companies.

What is the climate driver: Acute physical risk.

What is the root problem: Insurers and re-insurers rely on outdated CAT models for coastal areas.

What does this cause: Many insurers are exiting potentially profitable markets, or mispricing risk, putting re-insurers at risk of default, due to geographical concentration.

What needs to happen to fix the issue: Insurance companies need to update their models, or new players need to enter these markets, leveraging better modeling techniques.

How soon does this need to happen: The matter is urgent, several areas of the world are experiencing increasing physical risk, and insurance companies are abandoning markets due to inadequate models, while the increase of extreme events in concentrated areas is putting local re-insurers at significant risk (see the recent massive damage sustained by Acapulco in Mexico as a result of hurricane[14] Otis, as an example).

What is the opportunity: Identify and invest in smaller, nimbler insurers that are adapting faster to the new environment and using new models. Invest in new insurance players that are developing specific products for these markets and geographies.

---

[14] https://www.nesdis.noaa.gov/news/hurricane-otis-causes-catastrophic-damage-acapulco-mexico

What is the benefit: Market shares will be easy to obtain, as traditional players are abandoning the markets, the business model is well established, and, with good modeling, there are no bad risks, just bad pricing.[15]

What is the market size: The market size here is represented by the totality of the insurance market for real estate. According to Statista,[16] the property insurance market is expected to grow from US$ 0.74 trillion in 2025, at 4.43% CAGR until 2029, which would get it to US$ 0.88 trillion.

What is the long-term vision: Grow and exit or grow and hold.

What are the target funds: Public Strategy and Growth Strategy.

What are the target strategies: Private equity and private credit.

What is the Technology Readiness Level: TRL7.

How crowded is the investment space: Not crowded yet.

What is the investment maturity: In development.

9.6 NUCLEAR REACTOR MANUFACTURERS

What are nuclear reactor manufacturers: By nuclear reactor manufacturers we cover the value chain of technological products and services, including the reactors themselves, involved in the peaceful use of nuclear power for energy purposes (Figure 9.6).

What is the climate driver: Transition risk.

What is the root problem: Transition scenarios require moving away from fossil fuels in all but current policies.

---

[15] https://pdfcoffee.com/valueinvestorinsight-issue-284-pdf-free.html

[16] https://www.statista.com/outlook/fmo/insurances/non-life-insurances/property-insurance/worldwide

Figure 9.6 Representational images for nuclear reactor manufacturers.

Generated with AI using Perchance

What does this cause: Energy sources that do not emit CO_2, such as nuclear power, need to grow significantly in the near future.

What needs to happen to fix the issue: To meet the increased projected generation potential allocated to nuclear power, the number of nuclear reactors that are commissioned needs to increase dramatically.

How soon does this need to happen: All scenarios for Net Zero 2050 or disorderly transitions include significant amounts of nuclear power between 2030 and 2050.

What is the opportunity: Invest in companies that manufacture components and/or reactors (https://www.terrapower.com/ and https://www.newcleo.com/), as well as companies that operate them.

What is the benefit: Ownership of a steady and increasing revenue flow linked to the increasing usage of nuclear powerplants in transition scenarios.

What is the market size: This is linked to scenarios, and delayed due to the long time needed from decision to first power. To provide a frame of reference, according to StraitsResearch,[17] the global nuclear power market was valued at US$ 34.43 billion in 2023, expected to grow to US$ 45.31 billion by 2032 with a CAGR of 3.10% over the forecast.

What is the long-term vision: Grow and exit or grow and hold.

What are the target funds: Private equity, private credit.

---

[17] https://straitsresearch.com/report/nuclear-power-market

What are the target strategies: Public Strategy.
What is the Technology Readiness Level: TRL9.
How crowded is the investment space: Likely crowded.
What is the investment maturity: Probably late.

9.7 CRITICAL MINERAL MINES

What is critical mineral mining: By critical mineral, borrowing from the US Department of Energy,[18] we mean "any non-fuel mineral, element, substance, or material that [...] has a high risk of supply chain disruption; and [...] serves an essential function in one or more energy technologies, including technologies that produce, transmit, store, and conserve energy." It includes the well-known rare earths, lithium, vanadium, and cobalt. By mining we mean the entire value chain of companies involved in the process that begins with prospecting for critical mineral ores and ends with the finished ingot commodity, as notionally represented in figure 9.7.
What is the climate driver: Transition risk.
What is the root problem: Transition scenarios require electrification of transportation, households, and industry in all but current policies.
What does this cause: Demand for critical minerals will increase dramatically, as all these elements are critical to production of the new electric-based infrastructure that will be needed (as an example vanadium will be used for Direct Air Capture).[19]
What needs to happen to fix the issue: To meet the increased requirements of the transition scenarios, the output of ores needs to increase over time.

---

[18] https://www.energy.gov/cmm/what-are-critical-materials-and-critical-minerals
[19] https://pubs.rsc.org/en/content/articlehtml/2024/sc/d3sc05381d

Figure 9.7 Representational images for critical minerals mining.

  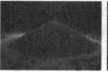 

Generated with AI using Perchance

How soon does this need to happen: All scenarios for Net Zero 2050 or disorderly transitions include significant amounts of these elements between 2030 and 2050.

What is the opportunity: Invest in critical mineral mining companies and prospecting, to front-run the increase in demand and prices that the scenarios are predicting.

What is the benefit: Ownership of a steady and increasing revenue flow linked to the increasing usage of transition-critical elements.

What is the market size: According to the International Energy Association,[20] "the market size for energy transition minerals doubled over the past five years, reaching US$ 320 billion in 2022" and "Critical minerals demand for clean energy is set to grow by up to three-and-a-half times over the period to 2030."

What is the long-term vision: Purchase and hold.

What are the target funds: Public Strategy and Infrastructure Strategy.

What are the target strategies: Private equity and private credit.

What is the Technology Readiness Level: TRL9.

How crowded is the investment space: Likely crowded.

What is the investment maturity: Probably late.

---

[20] https://www.iea.org/reports/critical-minerals-market-review-2023

Overview of Primarily Public Strategy Fund Investment Theses

9.8 URANIUM MINES: PROSPECTING AND PROCESSING

What are uranium mines: prospecting and processing: By uranium mining and smelting we consider all the value chain of companies involved in the process that begins with prospecting for uranium ore and ends with the finished uranium pellet commodity (Figure 9.8).

What is the climate driver: Transition risk.

What is the root problem: Transition scenarios require moving away from fossil fuels in all but current policies.

What does this cause: Energy sources that do not emit CO_2, such as nuclear power, need to grow significantly in the near future.

What needs to happen to fix the issue: To meet the increased projected generation potential allocated to nuclear power, the output of uranium ore needs to increase over time.

How soon does this need to happen: All scenarios for Net Zero 2050 or disorderly transitions include significant amounts of nuclear power between 2030 and 2050.

What is the opportunity: Invest in uranium mining companies, prospecting, and processing to front-run the increase in demand and prices that the scenarios are predicting.

Figure 9.8 Representational images for uranium mining: Prospecting and processing.

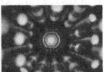

Generated with AI using Perchance

What is the benefit: Ownership of a steady and increasing revenue flow linked to the increasing usage of nuclear powerplants in transition scenarios.

What is the market size: According to VerifiedMarketResearch,[21] the global Uranium mining market was worth US$ 8.0 billion in 2023 and is expected to reach US$ 12.6 billion by 2030, with an 8.4% CAGR from 2024 to 2030.

What is the long-term vision: Purchase and hold.

What are the target funds: Public Strategy and Climate Alternatives and Physical Assets Plays.

What are the target strategies: Private equity and private credit.

What is the Technology Readiness Level: TRL9.

How crowded is the investment space: Likely crowded.

What is the investment maturity: Probably late.

9.9 HVAC MANUFACTURERS AND INSTALLERS

What are HVAC manufacturers and installers: By HVAC manufacturers and installers we cover the entire value chain from the design and development of HVAC systems to their installation, maintenance, end-of-life disposal (Figure 9.9).

What is the climate driver: Transition risk

What is the root problem: Climate change is steadily warming the planet and increasing temperatures in inhabited zones.

---

[21] https://www.verifiedmarketresearch.com/product/uranium-mining-market/

Overview of Primarily Public Strategy Fund Investment Theses

Figure 9.9 Representational images for HVAC manufacturing and installation.

Generated with AI using Perchance

What does this cause: Demand for AC units will increase over time, as it will become critical in areas where it is currently in use, and necessary in areas where it isn't widespread now.

What needs to happen to fix the issue: To meet the increased requirements due to a warmer planet, the output of HVAC manufacturers and the number of installers globally need to increase over time.

How soon does this need to happen: The warming is already an ongoing concern (2 °C have already happened) and is continuing.

What is the opportunity: Invest in HVAC manufacturers (Public Strategy) and HVAC installers (Growth Fund), to front-run the increase in demand and prices that the scenarios are predicting.

What is the benefit: Ownership of a steady and increasing revenue flow linked to the increasing usage of HVAC.

What is the market size: According to Global Markets Insights,[22] the estimated size of the global HVAC market in 2023 was US$ 294 billion and expected to grow at a CAGR of 5.6% in the period leading to 2032 to reach a projected value of the market at US$ 481 billion by 2032.

What is the long-term vision: Purchase and hold, or purchase, grow, and sell.

What are the target funds: Public Strategy and Growth Strategy.

---

[22] https://www.gminsights.com/industry-analysis/hvac-market

What are the target strategies: Venture capital, private equity, and private credit.
What is the Technology Readiness Level: TRL9.
How crowded is the investment space: Likely crowded.
What is the investment maturity: Mature.

9.10 SUSTAINABLE STEEL

What is sustainable steel: By sustainable steel, or green steel, we refer to steel made using eco-friendly methods to lessen climate impact (Figure 9.10).
What is the climate driver: Transition risk.
What is the root problem: Climate change due to GHG emissions is steadily warming the planet and increasing temperatures in inhabited zones. Steel production accounts for 7% of global GHG emissions. Steel usage and production are projected to increase in scenarios where the economy moves away from fossil fuels.
What does this cause: Demand for sustainable steel ("green steel") will grow stronger over time, as traditional steel will face increasingly high costs to offset carbon emissions.

Figure 9.10 Representational images for sustainable steel and examples of companies in the space.

What needs to happen to fix the issue: Lower-carbon emitting steel production processes need to come online, and scale up.

How soon does this need to happen: All scenarios for Net Zero 2050 or disorderly transitions include very significant amounts of emission reduction/offsetting in the steel sector from 2030 onwards.

What is the opportunity: Identify and invest in new companies (such as Electra,[23] Hybrit,[24] Stegra[25]) or emerging players (as SSAB,[26] JSW,[27] Iberdrola,[28] Boston Metal[29]) in sustainable steel to gain a foothold in this new market.

What is the benefit: Ownership of a steady and increasing revenue flow linked to the increasing usage of sustainable steel.

What is the market size: According to BIS Research,[30] the global sustainable steel market was valued at US$ 329 billion in 2023 and is projected to reach US$ 820 billion by 2034, growing at a strong CAGR of 8.52%.

What is the long-term vision: Purchase and hold, or purchase, grow, and sell.

What are the target funds: Public Strategy and Growth Strategy.

What are the target strategies: Private equity, private credit.

What is the Technology Readiness Level: TRL7.

How crowded is the investment space: Not crowded yet.

What is the investment maturity: In development.

---

[23] https://www.electra.earth
[24] https://www.hybritdevelopment.se/en
[25] https://stegra.com
[26] https://www.ssab.com/en
[27] https://www.jsw.in/sustainability/sustainable-steel
[28] https://www.iberdrola.com/sustainability/green-steel
[29] https://www.bostonmetal.com
[30] https://bisresearch.com/industry-report/sustainable-steel-market.html

9.11 EMISSIONS-FREE SHIPPING

What is emissions-free shipping: The concept of "green shipping" minimizes environmental impact by reducing carbon emissions and pollution (Figure 9.11). Under this definition we cover multiple technologies and services that are required to improve the efficiency of commercial shipping globally.

What is the climate driver: Transition risk.

What is the root problem: Transition scenarios require moving away from fossil fuels in all but current policies. One of the main mechanisms that the transition scenarios all include is a carbon tax (aka, carbon price).

What does this cause: Sectors, such as shipping, which have high emissions that are hard to abate, will face constantly increasing taxation which will affect their cost structures in dramatic ways.

What needs to happen to fix the issue: Shipping that relies on alternative energy sources needs to be developed and gain market share.

How soon does this need to happen: All scenarios for Net Zero 2050 or disorderly transitions include very significant amounts of emission reduction/offsetting in the transportation sector by 2030.

What is the opportunity: Identify and invest in new companies (such as Neoline,[31] and Nautilus[32]) or emerging/established players (as Yara

Figure 9.11 Examples of companies in the emissions-free shipping space.

[31] https://www.neoline.eu/en
[32] https://nautilus-project.eu

Birkeland/Kongsberg,[33] MAN Energy Solutions,[34] or Maersk[35]) in electric transportation to gain a foothold in this new market.

What is the benefit: Ownership of a steady and increasing revenue flow linked to the increasing volumes of emissions-free shipping required in transition scenarios.

What is the market size: Market studies are hard to find for this sector, as it is still nascent. The Global Maritime Forum,[36] however, states that "Projections show that shipping's demand for e-fuels could rapidly scale to over 500 million tonnes by 2040, rising to 600 million tonnes by 2050. Meeting such demand could require an additional 2TW of renewable energy generation capacity." They also estimate the that "maritime transition is a trillion-dollar market opportunity."

What is the long-term vision: Purchase and hold, or purchase, grow, and exit.

What are the target funds: Public Strategy and Growth Strategy.

What are the target strategies: Private equity, private credit.

What is the Technology Readiness Level: TRL7.

How crowded is the investment space: Not crowded yet.

What is the investment maturity: In development.

---

[33] https://www.yara.com/knowledge-grows/game-changer-for-the-environment
[34] https://www.man-es.com/discover/methanol-fueled-ships
[35] https://www.cnbc.com/2023/09/14/shipping-giant-maersk-unveils-first-vessel-operating-on-green-methanol.html
[36] https://globalmaritimeforum.org/press/decarbonisation-of-shipping-could-create-up-to-four-million-green-jobs

CHAPTER TEN

OVERVIEW OF PRIMARILY INFRASTRUCTURE STRATEGY FUND INVESTMENT THESES

How to identify climate-driven public assets and services that are essential for a functioning society, such as power, transport, water, and waste

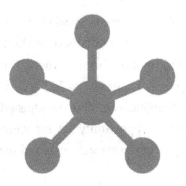

10.1 WHICH OPPORTUNITIES ARE PRIMARILY INFRASTRUCTURE STRATEGY FUND OPPORTUNITIES?

The Infrastructure Fund invests in climate-driven public assets and services that are essential for a functioning society, such as power, transport, water, and waste.

Climate change drivers are acting in unison with traditional drivers such as population growth, aging infrastructure, GDP growth in developing countries, and governmental subsidies to increase the attractiveness of the sector.

As shown in Table 10.1, the investment theses range from traditional infrastructure deals in the water space, hydroelectric power space, wind and solar power generation, and the electric grid upgrade space, to more transition-focused energy plays such as Carbon Capture Utilization and Storage (CCUS), energy storage, geothermal energy generation, Sustainable Aviation Fuel (SAF) and tidal power, as well as physical risk–driven plays such as tidal zone protection technology infrastructure.

The investment model is purchase and hold, or purchase, grow and exit, depending on the area of focus.

The total size of the current market for opportunities in the Infrastructure Strategy Fund is the largest of the four funds, with US$ 3.113 trillion as of 2024 (multiple sources, details in individual overview paragraphs), and is predicted to grow at a 7.55% CAGR to reach US$ 5.572 trillion by 2032 (in a baseline, non-climate adjusted scenario). This represents 54% of the entire opportunity set for which market studies are available, and is reflective of the greater costs and required investments in the infrastructure space.

Table 10.1 Primarily Infrastructure Strategy Fund opportunities.

Investment Opportunity	Climate Driver	Investment Horizon	How Crowded Is the Space	Maturity for Investment	TRL
CCUS (Carbon Capture, Utilization, and Storage) infrastructure	Transition risk	Immediate to medium term	Crowded	Probably late	9
Electric grid infrastructure upgrade	Transition risk	Immediate	Likely crowded	Probably late	9
Energy storage	Transition risk	Medium term	Not crowded yet	In development	6
Geothermal energy generation	Transition risk	Immediate	Not crowded yet	In development	7
Hydroelectric power generation	Transition risk	Immediate	Likely crowded	Probably late	9
Sustainable Aviation Fuel	Transition risk	Immediate to medium term	Crowded	Probably late	9
Biofuels and waste to energy	Transition risk	Immediate to medium term	Not crowded yet	In development	7
Tidal power generation	Transition risk	Immediate	Not crowded yet	In development	7
Water	Chronic physical risk	Immediate to medium term	Not crowded yet	Mature	9
Wind and solar power generation	Transition risk	Immediate	Crowded	Probably late	9
Sustainable concrete	Transition Risk	Immediate to medium term	Likely crowded	In development	8
Ocean thermal energy conversion	Transition Risk	Immediate to medium term	Not crowded yet	In development	6
Coastal tidal protection	Chronic physical risk	Immediate to medium term	Not crowded yet	Mature	8

Table 10.2 provides a view of the opportunities for which data is available, and the comparisons to the other funds, as well as to the overall totality of transition finance opportunities.

Figure 10.1 shows the data by year and opportunity, in graph form, and shows that there is no single dominating opportunity by market size, with energy storage, hydroelectric power, wind and solar power, and biofuels and waste to energy all being of comparable sizes by the end of the period.

Table 10.2 Market projections for baseline scenario 2024–2032 for Infrastructure Strategy Fund opportunities and comparison to aggregate values for all funds.

Market	2024 Size Estimate (US$ Billions)	CAGR (%)	Target Size (US$ Billions)	Target Year
CCUS infrastructure	$3.00	16.24%	$10.00	2032
Energy storage	$256.00	8.89%	$506.00	2032
Geothermal	$8.40	4.67%	$12.10	2032
Hydroelectric power	$227.00	7.80%	$414.00	2032
Biofuels and waste to energy	$166.50	7.99%	$307.90	2032
Tidal and wave power	$0.98	45.56%	$19.75	2032
Wind and solar power	$350.00	6.79%	$592.00	2032
Ocean thermal energy conversion	$0.20	23.75%	$1.10	2032
Coastal flooding protection	$1.87	8.68%	$3.64	2032
Total Growth Fund	$365.60	8.37%	$695.67	2032
Total Infrastructure Fund	**$3,113.05**	**7.55%**	**$5,572.00**	**2032**
Total Public Strategy Fund	$1,013.95	7.93%	$1,866.49	2032
Total Climate Alternatives Fund	$1,265.88	7.43%	$2,245.29	2032
TOTAL OVERALL FOR TRANSITION	**$5,758.48**	**7.64%**	**$10,379.45**	**2032**

Figure 10.1 Market growth projections for transition finance Infrastructure Strategy Fund opportunities, 2024–2032 baseline scenario.

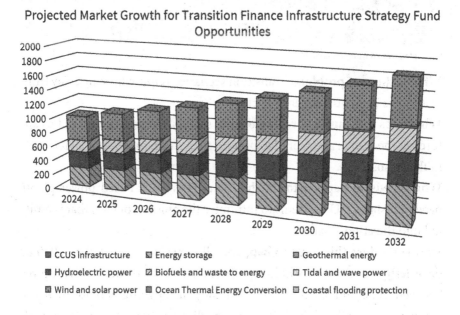

10.2 CCUS (CARBON CAPTURE, UTILIZATION, AND STORAGE) INFRASTRUCTURE

What is CCUS (Carbon Capture, Utilization, and Storage) infrastructure: By CCUS infrastructure we mean all the technology and infrastructure required to sustain Carbon Capture, Utilization, and Storage (CCUS), which captures CO_2 emissions at emissions point to store or reuse them, combating climate change (Figure 10.2).

What is the climate driver: Transition risk.

Figure 10.2 Representational views of CCUS infrastructure.

Generated with AI using Perchance

What is the root problem: Transition scenarios require moving away from fossil fuels in all but current policies.

What does this cause: For hard to abate sectors, emissions need to be captured at the source and stored to prevent them from increasing GHG levels in the atmosphere.

What needs to happen to fix the issue: Fossil-fuel-based power plants need to install CCUS systems to minimize the amount of CO_2 that is emitted into the atmosphere.

How soon does this need to happen: All scenarios for Net Zero 2050 or disorderly transitions include significant amounts of alternative power between 2030 and 2050. CCUS is already an ongoing activity in many countries and, in the United States, is subsidized by the federal government.

What is the opportunity: Invest in CCUS companies (such as 1point five,[1] SLB Capturi[2] Calix,[3] CarbonAmerica,[4] CarbonClean,[5] CarbonFree,[6] Carbon8,[7] Capsol,[8] NetPower,[9] and Svante[10]) to benefit from the market growth.

---

[1] https://www.1pointfive.com
[2] https://capturi.slb.com
[3] https://calix.global
[4] https://www.carbonamerica.com
[5] https://www.carbonclean.com
[6] https://carbonfree.cc
[7] https://www.carbon8.co.uk
[8] https://www.capsoltechnologies.com
[9] https://netpower.com
[10] https://www.svanteinc.com

What is the benefit: Ownership of a steady and increasing revenue flow linked to the increasing volume of CCUS in transition scenarios.

What is the market size: The market for CCUS, like all carbon markets, is strongly dependent on which transition scenario is expected to happen.

As a current, nonspecifically scenario-aligned projection, we can look at the views expressed by AlliedMarketResearch,[11] according to whom the CCUS market was worth US$ 3.0 billion in 2022 and is expected to grow to US$ 10.3 billion by 2032, with a strong CAGR of 13.3%.

What is the long-term vision: Purchase and hold, or purchase, grow, and exit.

What are the target funds: Infrastructure Strategy and Growth Strategy.

What are the target strategies: Private equity and private credit.

What is the Technology Readiness Level: TRL9.

How crowded is the investment space: Crowded.

What is the investment maturity: Probably late.

10.3 ELECTRIC GRID INFRASTRUCTURE UPGRADE

What is electric grid infrastructure upgrade: In this case the definition is all technologies, products, and services required to allow the existing electric grid installations worldwide to increase their capacity to meet increased demands (Figure 10.3).

What is the climate driver: Transition risk.

What is the root problem: Transition scenarios require moving away from fossil fuels in all but current policies. All the alternative energy

---

[11] https://www.alliedmarketresearch.com/carbon-capture-and-utilization-market-A12116

Figure 10.3 Representational views of electric grid infrastructure upgrade.

Generated with AI using Perchance

sources rely on electricity as the final form of energy being produced and utilized.

What does this cause: The reliance on the electrical grid, in all transition scenarios, will increase by orders of magnitude (the electric load on the grid, is expected to increase by 60% over the course of the next 20 years).[12]

What needs to happen to fix the issue: The existing infrastructure needs to be upgraded, and new infrastructure needs to be built and commissioned (both as major infrastructure and last mile infrastructure).

How soon does this need to happen: All scenarios for Net Zero 2050 or disorderly transitions include significant amounts of alternative power between 2030 and 2050. The grid inadequacy is already preventing alternative energy development from coming online today.[13]

What is the opportunity: Invest in electric grid companies to benefit from the future improvements in profitability/usage.

What is the benefit: Ownership of a steady and increasing revenue flow linked to the increasing volumes of electricity being used in transition scenarios.

What is the market size: As all energy theses, the market outlook and growth curves are scenario-driven. For the purposes of level-setting, Siemens[14] states that "By 2050, grids will increase in length by about 90%.

---

[12] https://gridstrategiesllc.com/wp-content/uploads/2023/12/National-Load-Growth-Report-2023.pdf
[13] https://techxplore.com/news/2024-04-solar-limbo-waitlists-grid-barrier.html
[14] https://assets.new.siemens.com/siemens/assets/api/uuid:df95fbbe-640e-40cf-82e6-9dc3f608186b/Electrification-Whitepaper-FINAL.pdf

In the scenario of currently stated policies, the IEA anticipates *annual investments of US$ 770 billion* in infrastructure and storage in this period. In the additional pledges scenario, they are close to *US$ 1 trillion per annum.*" According to GrandViewResearch,[15] the global electrical grid market was valued at US$ 268 billion in 2023, with a projected CAGR of 5.6% from 2024 to 2030, which would land it at US$ 333 billion by the end of the period.

What is the long-term vision: Purchase and hold, or purchase, grow, and exit.
What are the target funds: Infrastructure Strategy.
What are the target strategies: Private equity and private credit.
What is the Technology Readiness Level: TRL9.
How crowded is the investment space: Likely crowded.
What is the investment maturity: Probably late.

10.4 ENERGY STORAGE

What is energy storage: Energy storage solutions[16] are technologies that store extra energy from renewable sources for later use, ensuring grid stability (Figure 10.4).

Figure 10.4 Examples of companies in the energy storage space.

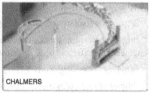

---

[15] https://www.grandviewresearch.com/industry-analysis/electrical-grid-market-report
[16] https://www.nyserda.ny.gov/All-Programs/Energy-Storage-Program/Energy-Storage-for-Your-Business/Types-of-Energy-Storage

What is the climate driver: Transition risk.

What is the root problem: Transition scenarios require significant usage of diffuse and erratic energy sources such as wind, solar, and tidal in all but current policies.

What does this cause: These energy sources have irregular generation patterns and dilute energy concentration, and all require energy storage solutions that are orders of magnitude superior to the current ones in usage (i.e., chemical batteries).

What needs to happen to fix the issue: To meet the energy storage requirements of the transition scenarios, new and improved energy storage solutions need to come online.

How soon does this need to happen: All scenarios for Net Zero 2050 or disorderly transitions include large portions of wind, solar, and tidal from 2030 onward.

What is the opportunity: Identify and invest in new companies and technologies (such as Gravity Storage,[17] EnergyVault,[18] Terrament,[19] sulphur storage,[20] or Molecular Solar Thermal Energy Storage[21]) or emerging players (such as Antora,[22] Kyoto,[23] Heatrix,[24] ODQA,[25] Fluence,[26]

---

[17] https://gravity-storage.com

[18] https://www.energyvault.com

[19] https://www.terramenthq.com/

[20] https://www.solarpaces.org/why-solar-sulphur-cycle-ideal-seasonal-thermal-energy-storage

[21] https://www.sigmaaldrich.com/US/en/technical-documents/technical-article/materials-science-and-engineering/batteries-supercapacitors-and-fuel-cells/molecular-solar-thermal-energy-storage-systems

[22] https://antoraenergy.com

[23] https://www.kyotogroup.no/heatcube

[24] https://heatrix.de

[25] https://www.odqa.com

[26] https://fluenceenergy.com

FormEnergy,[27] Sonnen,[28] and Powin[29]) to gain a foothold in this new market.

What is the benefit: Ownership of a steady and increasing revenue flow linked to the growing need for energy storage solutions.

What is the market size: As with all energy plays, it's the scenario that drives the expected market size and growth. According to Bloomberg,[30] "The global energy storage market almost tripled in 2023, the largest year-on-year gain on record." If we look at the market study on the global size of the market for energy storage systems to 2031, published by Statista[31] in March 2024, we see how they state that "The global energy storage system market is forecast to grow steadily between 2024 and 2031 with a compound annual growth rate of approximately nine percent. Energy storage systems worldwide accounted for a market worth 256 billion U.S. dollars in 2023. The figure was projected to reach over 506.5 billion U.S. dollars by 2031. Energy storage systems include pumped hydropower, electrochemical batteries, electromechanical storage, and thermal storage."

What is the long-term vision: Purchase and hold, or purchase, grow, and exit.

What are the target funds: Infrastructure Strategy and Growth Strategy.

What are the target strategies: Venture capital, private equity, and private credit.

What is the Technology Readiness Level: TRL6.

How crowded is the investment space: Not crowded yet.

What is the investment maturity: In development.

---

[27] https://formenergy.com
[28] https://sonnenusa.com/en
[29] https://powin.com
[30] https://about.bnef.com/blog/global-energy-storage-market-records-biggest-jump-yet
[31] https://www.statista.com/statistics/1395016/energy-storage-market-size-worldwide-forecast

10.5 GEOTHERMAL ENERGY GENERATION COMPANIES

What are geothermal energy generation companies: In this opportunity we cover the End-to-End value chain for extracting energy from the thermal gradient from the earth's crust (Figure 10.5).

What is the climate driver: Transition finance.

What is the root problem: Transition scenarios require moving away from fossil fuels in all but current policies. One of the main mechanisms that the transition scenarios all include is a carbon tax (aka, carbon price).

What does this cause: Energy sources that do not emit CO_2, such as geothermal energy power, will benefit from an overall higher cost of energy, without having to be burdened by the carbon tax, and will have increased profitability.

What needs to happen to fix the issue: Market leaders need to scale up to commercially viable sizes, and new technologies need to progress beyond POC phase.

How soon does this need to happen: All scenarios for Net Zero 2050 or disorderly transitions include significant amounts of alternative power between 2030 and 2050.

Figure 10.5 Representational views of geothermal energy.

Generated with AI using Perchance

What is the opportunity: Identify and invest in new companies (such as Electra Therm[32]) or emerging players (such as Criterion Energy[33] or Bedrock Energy[34]) to gain a foothold in this new market. More details are provided in the deep dive on geothermal in Chapter 12.
What is the benefit: Gain a leading position in a new and growing energy generation field, with increasing energy prices and margins.
What is the market size: See the deep dive on geothermal in Chapter 12.
What is the long-term vision: Purchase and hold, or purchase, grow, and exit.
What are the target funds: Infrastructure Strategy and Growth Strategy.
What are the target strategies: Venture capital, private equity and private credit.
What is the Technology Readiness Level: TRL7.
How crowded is the investment space: Not crowded yet.
What is the investment maturity: In development.

10.6 HYDROELECTRIC POWER GENERATION COMPANIES

What are hydroelectric power generation companies: This opportunity includes all technologies, products, and services tied to harnessing the power of water to generate electricity (Figure 10.6). This includes dams, penstocks, turbines, and generators.
What is the climate driver: Transition risk.

---

[32] https://electratherm.com
[33] https://criterionep.com
[34] https://bedrockenergy.com

Figure 10.6 Representational views of hydroelectric power generation.

Generated with AI using Perchance

What is the root problem: Transition scenarios require moving away from fossil fuels in all but current policies. One of the main mechanisms that the transition scenarios all include is a carbon tax (aka, carbon price).

What does this cause: Energy sources that do not emit CO_2, such as hydroelectric power, will benefit from an overall higher cost of energy, without having to be burdened by the carbon tax, and will have increased profitability.

What needs to happen to fix the issue: Existing hydroelectric plants need to be maintained and potentially expanded, and new ones need to be developed, where feasible.

How soon does this need to happen: All scenarios for Net Zero 2050 or disorderly transitions include significant amounts of alternative power between 2030 and 2050.

What is the opportunity: Invest in hydroelectric power companies to benefit from the future improvement in profitability.

What is the benefit: Ownership of a steady and increasing revenue flow linked to the increasing margins in transition scenarios.

What is the market size: Hydroelectric power generation is often limited mostly by geography and not too much by scenarios, albeit there are some technological developments tied to transition scenarios that could influence the market's trajectory. According to Straits Research,[35] the global

---

[35] https://straitsresearch.com/report/hydropower-generation-market

hydropower generation market was valued at US$ 227 billion in 2023 and is projected to grow to US$ 414 billion by 2032, with a CAGR of 6.91% from 2024 to 2032.

What is the long-term vision: Purchase and hold, or purchase, grow, and exit.

What are the target funds: Infrastructure Strategy.

What are the target strategies: Private equity and private credit.

What is the Technology Readiness Level: TRL9.

How crowded is the investment space: Likely crowded.

What is the investment maturity: Probably late.

10.7 SUSTAINABLE AVIATION FUEL

What is Sustainable Aviation Fuel: By SAF we mean the entire value chain tied to the production of aviation fuel from biologically produced feedstocks of different type, and the technologies, products, and services which are part of it (Figure 10.7).

What is the climate driver: Transition risk.

What is the root problem: Transition scenarios require moving away from fossil fuels in all but current policies. One of the main mechanisms that the transition scenarios all include is a carbon tax (aka, carbon price).

Figure 10.7   Representational views of Sustainable Aviation Fuel.

Generated with AI using Perchance

What does this cause: Sectors, such as aviation, which have high emissions that are hard to abate, will face constantly increasing taxation which will affect their cost structures in dramatic ways.

What needs to happen to fix the issue: Until airliners that rely on alternative energy sources are developed and certified (which can take decades), the current fleets need to operate on fuels that are produced in a sustainable way (or the airlines need to offset their emissions via purchase of VCM credits).

How soon does this need to happen: All scenarios for Net Zero 2050 or disorderly transitions include very significant amounts of emission reduction/offsetting in the airlines sector by 2030.

What is the opportunity: Invest in Sustainable Aviation Fuel companies (at various levels in the chain, such as Helvoil[36] or Lanzajet[37]) to benefit from the projected increase in demand.

What is the benefit: Ownership of a steady and increasing revenue flow linked to the increasing volumes of SAF in transition scenarios.

What is the market size: As with all carbon-linked cases, this is a market that depends on which transition scenario comes to pass. According to GMI Insights,[38] the global sustainable aviation fuel market is valued at US$ 1.7 billion in 2024 and is expected to grow at an impressive CAGR of 46.2% from 2025 to 2034, hitting US$ 74.6 billion by 2034.

What is the long-term vision: Purchase and hold, or purchase, grow, and exit.

What are the target funds: Infrastructure Strategy and Growth Strategy.

What are the target strategies: Venture capital, private equity, private credit.

What is the Technology Readiness Level: TRL9.

---

[36] https://www.helvoil.ch/index-en.html
[37] https://www.lanzajet.com/
[38] https://www.gminsights.com/industry-analysis/sustainable-aviation-fuel-market

Overview of Primarily Infrastructure Strategy Fund Investment Theses

How crowded is the investment space: Crowded.
What is the investment maturity: Probably late.

10.8 BIOFUELS AND WASTE TO ENERGY

What is biofuel and waste to energy: Biofuels are renewable liquid fuels from plants and algae, produced to replace gasoline, diesel, and jet fuel (SAF being covered, however, under a separate opportunity) (Figure 10.8). The same processes that make biofuels can also be used to generate energy from organic waste materials, and the opportunity is therefore addressed collectively.

What is the climate driver: Transition risk

What is the root problem: Transition scenarios require moving away from fossil fuels in all but current policies. One of the main mechanisms that the transition scenarios all include is a carbon tax (aka, carbon price).

What does this cause: Sectors, such as transportation, shipping, and heating, which have high emissions that are hard to abate, will face constantly increasing taxation which will affect their cost structures in dramatic ways.

What needs to happen to fix the issue: Alternative concentrated energy (fuel) that isn't contributing to the increase of GHG levels in the atmosphere

Figure 10.8 Representational views of biofuel and waste to energy.

Generated with AI using Perchance

needs to be developed and manufactured, and replace the current fossil fuels for hard to abate sectors (*biofuels*). Alternative zero emissions solutions for energy generation need to be developed to step in for current heating systems that rely on fossil fuels (*waste to energy*).

How soon does this need to happen: All scenarios for Net Zero 2050 or disorderly transitions include very significant amounts of emission reduction/offsetting in the transportation and energy sectors by 2030.

What is the opportunity: Invest in biofuel companies and waste to energy plants (such as Veolia,[39] Suez,[40] Reworld,[41] Ramboll[42]) to benefit from the projected increase in demand.

What is the benefit: Ownership of a steady and increasing revenue flow linked to the increasing volumes of sustainable fuels and waste to energy in transition scenarios.

What is the market size: In this case we are looking at two separate markets, both scenario-dependent. If we look at the biofuels global market, according to Precedence Research,[43] it is valued at US$ 132 billion in 2024, and expected to reach US$ 141 billion in 2025, and then grow to exceed US$ 257 billion by 2034, at a CAGR of 6.9% over the decade. For the waste-to-energy market, according to the study published by Fortune Business Insights,[44] the global market was valued at US$ 34.5 billion in 2023 and is expected to reach US$ 50.9 billion by 2032, growing at a CAGR of 4.5%.

---

[39] https://www.africa.veolia.com/en/waste-energy
[40] https://www.suez-asia.com/en-cn/our-offering/businesses/what-are-you-looking-for/waste-management/waste-to-energy
[41] https://www.reworldwaste.com/what-we-do/renewable-energy-recovery
[42] https://www.ramboll.com/waste/waste-to-energy
[43] https://www.precedenceresearch.com/biofuels-market
[44] https://www.fortunebusinessinsights.com/industry-reports/waste-to-energy-market-100421

What is the long-term vision: Purchase and hold, or purchase, grow, and exit.
What are the target funds: Infrastructure Strategy and Growth Strategy.
What are the target strategies: Venture capital, private equity.
What is the Technology Readiness Level: TRL7
How crowded is the investment space: Not crowded yet.
What is the investment maturity: In development

10.9 TIDAL POWER GENERATION COMPANIES

What are tidal and wave energy power generation companies: Wave and tidal power technologies share similarities and differences; both extract kinetic energy from the ocean to generate electricity, but they use different locations and methods (Figure 10.9). Wave energy projects capture energy from surface waves or slightly deeper in the ocean. Tidal energy projects generate power by forcing water through turbines or tidal fences, relying on the predictable nature of tidal cycles, which happen at least once a day along coasts. For this opportunity we include all technologies, products, and services tied to the entire value chain for tidal and wave energy generation.

Figure 10.9 Examples of companies in the tidal and wave energy space.

What is the climate driver: Transition risk.

What is the root problem: Transition scenarios require moving away from fossil fuels in all but current policies. One of the main mechanisms that the transition scenarios all include is a carbon tax (aka, carbon price).

What does this cause: Energy sources that do not emit CO_2, such as tidal energy power, will benefit from an overall higher cost of energy, without having to be burdened by the carbon tax, and will have increased profitability.

What needs to happen to fix the issue: Market leaders need to scale up to commercially viable sizes, and new technologies need to progress beyond POC phase.

How soon does this need to happen: All scenarios for Net Zero 2050 or disorderly transitions include significant amounts of alternative power between 2030 and 2050.

What is the opportunity: Identify and invest in new companies (such as Carnegie,[45] EcoWavePower,[46] Panthalassa,[47] Hydrowing,[48] OrbitalMarine,[49] NovaInnovation,[50] or companies using Archimedes screw turbines for hydropower) or emerging players (such as CorPower Ocean,[51] Minesto,[52] Magallanes Renovables,[53] VerdantPower,[54]

---

[45] https://www.carnegiece.com

[46] https://www.ecowavepower.com

[47] https://panthalassa.com

[48] https://hydrowing.tech

[49] https://www.orbitalmarine.com

[50] https://novainnovation.com

[51] https://www.corpowerocean.com

[52] https://minesto.com

[53] https://www.magallanesrenovables.com

[54] https://verdantpower.com

WaveSwell,[55] ORPC,[56] or AW-Energy[57]) to gain a foothold in this new market.

What is the benefit: Secure a leading position in a new and growing energy generation field, with increasing energy prices and margins.

What is the market size: The growth dynamics of both of these renewable energy markets are, as always, scenario dependent. For both wave and tidal energy, Fortune Business Insights[58] estimates that the global wave and tidal energy market was valued at US$ 0.98 billion in 2023 and expected to reach US$ 19.75 billion by 2032, growing at a robust CAGR of 40.75%.

What is the long-term vision: Purchase and hold, or purchase, grow, and exit.

What are the target funds: Infrastructure Strategy and Growth Strategy.

What are the target strategies: Venture capital and private equity.

What is the Technology Readiness Level: TRL7.

How crowded is the investment space: Not crowded yet.

What is the investment maturity: In development.

10.10 WATER

What do we mean by water: Under the generic capstone of "water" we include the entire value chain for both the water and wastewater industries, from technologies and products to infrastructure and services (Figure 10.10). It is, undoubtedly, the amplest of all opportunities that we have identified, as it pertains to the scope of companies that fall under it.

---

[55] https://www.waveswell.com
[56] https://orpc.co
[57] https://aw-energy.com/waveroller
[58] https://www.fortunebusinessinsights.com/industry-reports/wave-and-tidal-energy-market-100584

Figure 10.10 Representational views of water infrastructure.

Generated with AI using Perchance

What is the climate driver: Chronic physical risk.

What is the root problem: Climate change is exacerbating both water scarcity and water-related hazards (such as floods and droughts), as rising temperatures disrupt precipitation patterns and the entire water cycle. Water and climate change are inextricably linked.[59]

What does this cause: Freshwater supplies will decrease over time, making water an increasingly precious commodity.

What needs to happen to fix the issue: More water purification/sanitation facilities and water desalinization solutions need to come online, as well as improvements on existing infrastructure to reduce leakage and improve efficiency of water use across industries, residential usage, and agriculture.

How soon does this need to happen: This is a long-term trend, which will likely accelerate in the coming years and decades, but the need for changes to happen is already ongoing.

What is the opportunity: Identify areas of opportunity in the water sector that will grow due to climate factors and are currently uncovered, under-researched, or misunderstood. Given the vastness of the sector, it would be reductive to choose a few examples from a very richly populated field, and we shall leave it to our readers to focus on areas of interest. As a guideline we can highlight how the global water market is typically segmented into four subsectors, tied to the use of the water, which are then further broken down into technologies, products, services, and infrastructure. The four main segments are:

---

[59] Source: https://www.un.org/en/climatechange/science/climate-issues/water

- Water for residential use (divided in indoor and outdoor use)
- Water for commercial use
- Water for agricultural use
- Water for industrial sectors

What is the benefit: Ownership of critical assets and technologies in a market with structurally growing prices.

What is the market size: The drivers for water are both macro-driven (and not climate scenario–dependent) as well as climate-specific, so the market trajectories and growth will be somewhat less dependent on what scenario is chosen as the most likely. According to Zion Market Research,[60] the global water market was valued at US$ 302.8 billion in 2022 and is expected to reach US$ 430.9 billion by 2030, with a CAGR of 4.51%.

What is the long-term vision: Acquire and hold.

What are the target funds: Infrastructure Strategy, Public Strategy, Growth Strategy, Climate Alternatives, and Physical Assets Plays Strategy.

What are the target strategies: Private equity and private credit.

What is the Technology Readiness Level: TRL9.

How crowded is the investment space: Not crowded yet.

What is the investment maturity: Mature.

10.11　WIND AND SOLAR POWER GENERATION COMPANIES

What are wind and solar power generation companies: Wind and solar power are renewable energy sources generating electricity from wind and sunlight (Figure 10.11). This opportunity includes all technologies, products, infrastructure, and services needed for both industries.

---

[60] https://www.zionmarketresearch.com/report/water-market

Figure 10.11 Representational views of wind and solar power generation.

Generated with AI using Perchance

What is the climate river: Transition risk.

What is the root problem: Transition scenarios require moving away from fossil fuels in all but current policies. One of the main mechanisms that the transition scenarios all include is a carbon tax (aka, carbon price).

What does this cause: Energy sources that do not emit CO_2, such as wind and solar power, will benefit from an overall higher cost of energy, without having to be burdened by the carbon tax, and will have increased profitability.

What needs to happen to fix the issue: Existing wind (on-shore and off-shore) and solar plants need to be maintained and potentially expanded, and new ones need to be developed, where feasible.

How soon does this need to happen: All scenarios for Net Zero 2050 or disorderly transitions include significant amounts of alternative power between 2030 and 2050.

What is the opportunity: Invest in wind and solar power companies to benefit from the future improvement in profitability. As these sectors are both very large and well established, it would be reductive to list a handful of potential targets for investment in this paragraph. As we did for the water opportunity, we can provide a high-level taxonomy to understand the breakdowns.

For wind power, the segmentation is both by application outlook (utility and non-utility) as well as location outlook (on-shore and off-shore).

For solar power, the segmentation is by application outlook (utility, residential, and nonresidential) as well as by technology (solar photovoltaic, divided in mono-Si, thin film, multi-Si and other technologies, and concentrating solar power, divided in parabolic trough, power towers, and linear Fresnel).

What is the benefit: Ownership of a steady and increasing revenue flow linked to the increasing margins in transition scenarios.

What is the market size: As all power market projections, growth rates are tied to how fast alternative energy adoption proceeds, the pace of technological innovation, and the negative externalities placed on usage of fossil fuels (all of which are included in the climate scenarios). The global wind power market, according to Grand View Research,[61] was valued at US$ 97 billion in 2024 and is expected to grow at a CAGR of 4.9% from 2025 to 2030 to reach US$ 156 billion by the end of the period. The global solar power market is approximately 2.5 times larger than wind, as of 2024. Fortune Business Insights[62] estimates the global solar power market to have been US$ 253 billion in 2023, and projects it to reach US$ 436 billion by 2032 at a 6% CAGR.

What is the long-term vision: Purchase and hold, or purchase, grow, and exit.

What are the target funds: Infrastructure Strategy.

What are the target strategies: Private equity and private credit.

What is the Technology Readiness Level: TRL9.

How crowded is the investment space: Crowded.

What is the investment maturity: Probably late.

---

[61] https://www.grandviewresearch.com/industry-analysis/wind-power-industry

[62] https://www.fortunebusinessinsights.com/industry-reports/solar-power-market-100764

PRINCIPLES OF TRANSITION FINANCE INVESTING

10.12 SUSTAINABLE CONCRETE

What is sustainable concrete: Sustainable concrete uses eco-friendly materials and methods to lower its carbon footprint, save natural resources, and enhance durability of structures (Figure 10.12). For the purposes of the opportunity analysis, we use the term to cover the full value chain from raw materials to the finished product on site.

What is the climate driver: Transition risk.

What is the root problem: Climate change due to GHG emissions is steadily warming the planet and increasing temperatures in inhabited zones. Concrete production accounts for 8% of global GHG emissions. Concrete usage and production are projected to increase in scenarios where the economy moves away from fossil fuels.

What does this cause: Demand for sustainable concrete ("green concrete") will grow stronger over time, as traditional concrete will face increasingly high costs to offset carbon emissions.

What needs to happen to fix the issue: Lower-carbon emitting concrete production processes need to come online and scale up.

How soon does this need to happen: All scenarios for Net Zero 2050 or disorderly transitions include very significant amounts of emission reduction/offsetting in the concrete sector from 2030 onwards.

Figure 10.12 Examples of companies in the sustainable concrete space.

Overview of Primarily Infrastructure Strategy Fund Investment Theses

What is the opportunity: Identify and invest in new companies (such as Brimstone,[63] Cambridge Electric Cement,[64] Carbonaide,[65] CemVision,[66] Chement,[67] Leilac,[68] Terra CO2,[69] or Terratico[70]) or emerging players (as Argos,[71] Biomason,[72] CarbonCure,[73] Fortera,[74] Heidelberg Materials,[75] Paebbl,[76] Prometheus Materials,[77] and Sublime Systems[78]) in sustainable concrete to gain a foothold in this new market.

What is the benefit: Ownership of a steady and increasing revenue flow linked to the increasing usage of sustainable concrete.

What is the market size: As per many other cases, market growth is linked to the climate scenario that is chosen. According to research by Market Research Future,[79] the green concrete market was valued at US$ 7.0 billion in 2022 and it is projected to reach US$ 12.0 billion by 2032, growing at a CAGR of 5.5%.

What is the long-term vision: Purchase and hold, or purchase, grow, and sell.

What are the target funds: Infrastructure Strategy and Growth Strategy.

---

[63] https://www.brimstone.com
[64] https://cambridgeelectriccement.com
[65] https://carbonaide.com
[66] https://www.cemvision.tech
[67] https://www.chement.co
[68] https://www.leilac.com
[69] https://terraco2.com
[70] https://terratico.com
[71] https://argos-us.com
[72] https://biomason.com
[73] https://www.carboncure.com
[74] https://forteraglobal.com
[75] https://www.heidelbergmaterials.com/en/sustainability/we-decarbonize-the-construction-industryccus/gezero
[76] https://paebbl.com
[77] https://prometheusmaterials.com
[78] https://sublime-systems.com/technology
[79] https://www.marketresearchfuture.com/reports/green-concrete-market-8699

What are the target strategies: Venture capital, private equity, and private credit.
What is the Technology Readiness Level: TRL8.
How crowded is the investment space: Likely crowded.
What is the investment maturity: In development.

10.13 OCEAN THERMAL ENERGY CONVERSION (OTEC)

What is Ocean Thermal Energy Conversion: Ocean Thermal Energy Conversion (OTEC) is a renewable energy method that generates electricity by using the temperature difference between warm surface water and cold deep water in the ocean (Figure 10.13). For OTEC to work well, the temperature difference must be at least 20 °C (36 °F). OTEC has benefits like providing continuous electricity, offering cooling without using electricity, and producing fresh water that is efficient compared to desalination. However, it has drawbacks such as high costs, limited locations, and the challenge of needing generated power on land while the thermal gradient is at sea. It is a technology that was first experimented with in Cuba in 1930[80] and subsequently by the US Navy in

Figure 10.13 Examples of companies in the OTEC space.

[80] https://en.wikipedia.org/wiki/Ocean_thermal_energy_conversion

the 1970s. There are currently two functioning OTEC power plants in the world, one in Hawaii[81] and one in Japan.[82]

What is the climate river: Transition risk.

What is the root problem: Transition scenarios require moving away from fossil fuels in all but current policies. One of the main mechanisms that the transition scenarios all include is a carbon tax (aka, carbon price).

What does this cause: Energy sources that do not emit CO_2, such as Ocean Thermal Energy Conversion (OTEC), will benefit from an overall higher cost of energy, without having to be burdened by the carbon tax, and will have increased profitability.

What needs to happen to fix the issue: Ocean Thermal Energy Conversion uses the temperature difference between surface and deep-sea water to generate electricity – and though it has an efficiency of just 1–3% – researchers believe an OTEC power plant could deliver up to 250 MW of clean power. The technology needs to be brought to scale and developed into commercial solutions.

How soon does this need to happen: All scenarios for Net Zero 2050 or disorderly transitions include significant amounts of alternative power between 2030 and 2050.

What is the opportunity: Invest in OTEC companies (at various levels in the chain, such as AKUO Energy,[83,84] ENOGIA,[85] Global OTEC,[86] OTEC

---

[81] https://www.makai.com/renewable-energy/otec

[82] http://otecokinawa.com/en/

[83] https://newatlas.com/energy/global-otec-power-dominique

[84] https://www.akuoenergy.com/en

[85] https://enogia.com/en/home

[86] https://globalotec.co

Corporation,[87] UTM Malaysia,[88] and Makai Ocean Engineering[89]) to benefit from the projected increase in demand.

What is the benefit: Ownership of a steady and increasing revenue flow linked to the increasing margins in transition scenarios.

What is the market size: The market for OTEC is very much in the initial stages of development, and the growth it might have is entirely dependent on the need to have alternative energy sources that do not use fossil fuels (and therefore tied to the chosen transition scenario). While it is very difficult to find market data for such a nascent market, with only two functional pilot plants in the world, Fortune Business Insights[90] has aggregated market data and made available a market study that can be used as a baseline reference. According to this study, the shift to renewable energy is likely to boost the global ocean thermal energy conversion plant market. More OTEC plants are also creating opportunities for supporting water desalination. As a result, the Ocean Thermal Energy Conversion plant market is expected to grow from US$ 0.2 billion in 2023 to US$ 1.1 billion by 2033, with a CAGR of 18.9%.

What is the long-term vision: Purchase and hold.

What are the target funds: Infrastructure Strategy and Growth Strategy.

What are the target strategies: Venture capital and private equity.

What is the Technology Readiness Level: TRL6.

How crowded is the investment space: Not crowded yet.

What is the investment maturity: In development.

---

[87] https://otecorporation.com/otec

[88] https://research.utm.my/otec/page/8/

[89] https://www.makai.com

[90] https://www.globenewswire.com/news-release/2023/02/14/2607349/0/en/Ocean-Thermal-Energy-Conversion-Plant-Market-Size-2023-2030-Industry-Growth-Share-And-Trends-Forecast-Analysis-Report.html

10.14 COASTAL TIDAL PROTECTION

What is coastal tidal protection: By coastal tidal protection, we refer to flood barriers created to prevent or lessen flooding by holding back or redirecting floodwater and tidal water (Figure 10.14). These are typically built in flood-prone areas, like riverbanks or coastlines, to protect homes, buildings, and people from flooding damage. Types of flood barriers include flip-up, removable, self-closing, and drop-down barriers. Flip-up barriers are level with the ground when not in use and can be raised during floods. They are made from materials like aluminum, steel, concrete, and polymers, and they serve residential, commercial, industrial, and government needs.

What is the climate driver: Chronic physical risk.

What is the root problem: With the increasing warming of the global climate, the frequency of extreme flooding events in coastlines and rivers has increased over the last several decades and, in at least half of the monitored locations in the United States, floods are now at least five times more common than they were in the 1950s.[91] In addition to this trend, expectations are that the melting of Antarctic ice in the years to come will also contribute to higher sea levels, and more coastal flooding.

Figure 10.14 Examples of use cases in the coastal tidal protection space.

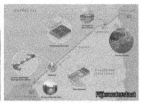

---

[91] https://www.epa.gov/climate-indicators/climate-change-indicators-coastal-flooding

What does this cause: Real estate in areas that were, in decades past, at acceptable levels of flood risk, are now becoming flooded with increased frequency and severity. This is often in densely populated, high-value real-estate areas, where relocation to more inland areas is a very costly solution.

What needs to happen to fix the issue: Technological solutions to adapt to the rising sea levels and frequency of floods, and mitigate the effects of both, need to be developed and implemented to protect the areas at risk.

How soon does this need to happen: This is an urgent matter, as the trend has been in place for over 50 years, and shows signs of speeding up.

What is the opportunity: Invest in companies and technologies (such as those deployed in Venice and in the Netherlands) that cater to the flood barrier market globally, to benefit from the projected increase in demand. There are several up-and-coming players in the field (Barrier Solution,[92] Bloebel,[93] Dam Easy Flood Barriers,[94] Flood Control Asia RS,[95] Flood Control International,[96] Megasecur,[97] MM Engineering,[98] Mobildeich,[99] Muscle Wall,[100] StormMeister,[101] U.S. Flood Corporation[102]), as well as many well-established ones (Aquabarrier,[103] AquaFence,[104] AWMA

---

[92] https://www.floodstopbarrier.com
[93] https://www.blobel.com
[94] https://dameasyfloodbarriers.com
[95] https://rsfloodcontrol.com
[96] https://floodcontrolinternational.com
[97] https://www.megasecur.com
[98] https://www.mmengineering.co.uk
[99] https://www.structure-flex.co.uk/Mobildeich
[100] https://www.musclewall.com
[101] https://www.stormmeister.com
[102] https://usfloodcontrol.com
[103] https://aquabarrier.com
[104] https://www.aquafence.com

Water Control Solutions,[105] Denilco Environmental Technology,[106] FloodBreak,[107] HydroResponse,[108] IBS Technics,[109] NoFloods,[110] PS Flood Barriers,[111] Self Closing Flood Barrier [SCFB][112]), which our readers can review.

What is the benefit: Ownership of a steady and increasing revenue flow linked to the increasing margins in proven climate scenarios.

What is the market size: The flood barrier market is segmented by type, material, and end user. Types include flip-up, removable, self-closing, drop-down, and other types. Materials are aluminum, steel, concrete, and polymer composites. End users consist of residential, commercial, industrial, and government and municipalities. According to The Business Research Company,[113] the flood barrier market has expanded significantly in recent years. It will increase from US$ 1.72 billion in 2024 to US$ 1.85 billion in 2025, with a CAGR of 7.7%. By 2029, it is expected to reach US$ 2.63 billion, with a CAGR of 9.1%.

What is the long-term vision: Purchase and hold, or purchase, grow, and sell.

What are the target funds: Infrastructure Strategy and Growth Strategy.

What are the target strategies: Private equity and private credit.

What is the Technology Readiness Level: TRL8.

How crowded is the investment space: Not crowded yet.

What is the investment maturity: Mature.

---

[105] https://www.awmawatercontrol.com.au
[106] https://en.denilco.com
[107] https://floodbreak.com/about
[108] https://www.hydroresponse.com/water-gate-barrier
[109] https://www.ibs-technics.com/en
[110] https://nofloods.com
[111] https://www.psfloodbarriers.com
[112] https://selfclosingfloodbarrier.com
[113] https://www.thebusinessresearchcompany.com/report/flood-barrier-global-market-report

CHAPTER ELEVEN
OVERVIEW OF PRIMARILY CLIMATE ALTERNATIVES (PHYSICAL ASSETS PLAYS) INVESTMENT THESES

How to invest in real assets that will generate alpha due to climate change

11.1 WHICH OPPORTUNITIES ARE PRIMARILY CLIMATE ALTERNATIVES/ PHYSICAL ASSETS FUND OPPORTUNITIES?

This fund includes compelling climate-driven investment theses in the physical assets space, which include a range of investments from traditional property transactions in the farmland and agriculture space, the timberland space and climate-sanctuary cities, to more transition-focused plays such as paper-recycling facilities and abandoned subterranean mines, for usage for long-term carbon sequestration and carbon credits.

The revenue model is a buy and hold, which can be broken down into buy and operate, and buy and lease (or some combination thereof).

Table 11.1 lists the main opportunities in the Climate Alternatives/ Physical Assets Fund.

The total size of the current market for opportunities in the Growth Fund is US$ 1.265 trillion as of 2024 (multiple sources, details in individual overview paragraphs), and is predicted to grow at a 7.43% CAGR to reach US$ 2.245 trillion by 2032 (in a baseline, non-climate adjusted scenario).

Table 11.2 provides a view of the opportunities for which data is available, and the comparisons to the other funds, as well as to the overall totality of transition finance opportunities.

Figure 11.1 shows the data by year and opportunity, in graph form, and shows that the plantation forest space is, by far, the largest market (albeit the one with lowest growth).

Table 11.1 Primarily Climate Alternatives and Physical Assets Strategy Fund opportunities.

Investment Opportunity	Climate Driver	Investment Horizon	How Crowded Is the Space	Maturity for Investment	TRL
Abandoned subterranean mines	Transition risk	Medium term	Not crowded yet	Ready	7
Forest land – plantation forest	Transition risk	Immediate	Not crowded yet	Ready	7
Forest land – primary	Transition risk	Immediate	Unclear	Ready	9
Northern latitudes farmland	Chronic physical risk	Immediate	Unclear	Ready	9
Paper-recycling facilities	Transition risk	Immediate to medium term	Not crowded yet	Ready	7
Real estate in climate sanctuary cities	Acute and chronic physical risk	Immediate to medium term	Not crowded yet	Ready	9

Table 11.2 Market projections for Climate Alternatives and Physical Assets Plays Fund opportunities, baseline scenario 2024–2032, and comparison to aggregate values for all funds.

Market	2024 Size Estimate (US$ Billions)	CAGR (%)	Target Size (US$ Billions)	Target Year
Plantation forest	$ 1.90	4.97%	$ 2.80	2032
Primary forest for carbon credits	$ 331.00	6.41%	$ 544.00	2032
Paper recycling for biomass feed for carbon credits	$ 8.80	19.75%	$ 37.20	2032
Total Growth Fund	$ 365.60	8.37%	$ 695.67	2032
Total Infrastructure Fund	$ 3,113.05	7.55%	$ 5,572.00	2032
Total Public Strategy Fund	$ 1,013.95	7.93%	$ 1,866.49	2032
Total Climate Alternatives Fund	**$ 1,265.88**	**7.43%**	**$ 2,245.29**	**2032**
TOTAL OVERALL FOR TRANSITION	**$5,758.48**	**7.64%**	**$ 10,379.45**	**2032**

Figure 11.1 Market growth projections for transition finance Climate Alternatives and Physical Assets Plays Fund opportunities, 2024–2032 baseline scenario.

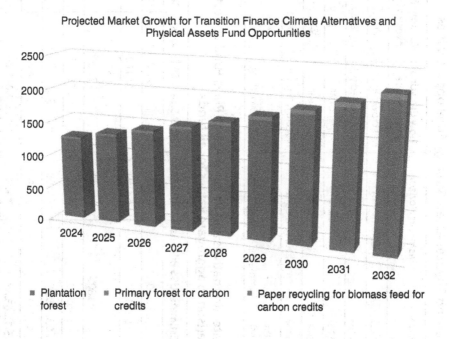

11.2 ABANDONED SUBTERRANEAN MINES

What are abandoned subterranean mines: By abandoned subterranean mines we mean the vast number of underground spaces that were formerly used for mining purposes of one kind or another and have been subsequently abandoned over time (Figure 11.2). These are assets that can be purchased for often nominal fees and repurposed to a variety of uses within transition finance.

Overview of Primarily Climate Alternatives (Physical Assets Plays) Investment Theses

Figure 11.2 Representational views of abandoned subterranean mines.

Generated with AI using Perchance

What is the climate driver: Transition risk.

What is the root problem: Transition scenarios require carbon removal credits in all but current policies. Additionally, energy storage is required in transition finance to allow electrification to occur.

What does this cause: Long-term storage of land-based biomass will be required for some carbon removal technologies, and geological, long-term solutions will be preferred. Gravitational energy storage (either as pumped hydro or mass storage) will increase in demand and value.

What needs to happen to fix the issue: Currently, the VCM market is voluntary-only, and it needs to merge with the mandatory (offsets/cap-and-trade) markets for this market to truly take off (MRV and certification will follow). For energy storage, there are no specific triggers that are waiting for activation.

How soon does this need to happen: All scenarios for Net Zero 2050 or disorderly transitions include significant amounts (Gt) of carbon removal/avoidance credits by 2030. For energy storage, the timeline is tied to the increase of wind and solar, which has already been growing dramatically in the last 20 years, a trend which is expected to continue.

What is the opportunity: Purchase abandoned underground mines, at currently very low evaluations, and hold for when the value of long-term storage of biomass for carbon credits will increase, as predicted by all transition scenarios. Alternatively, convert abandoned subterranean mines of convenient layout into energy storage locations (i.e., gravitational batteries),[1] either by moving water from the deeper regions to the surface and back (pumped hydro) or by moving mass (of different possible kinds) from the entrance to the deeper recesses (generating electrical energy in the process) and back (consuming electrical energy).

What is the benefit: Ownership of an asset that will increase in value over time.

What is the market size: As this is an asset-play, there isn't any specific market information available, or market projections. It is estimated that, worldwide, there are over a million abandoned mines[2] with the top five countries[3] in the world being the following:

- US – 500,000+ mines
- Australia – ~60,000 mines
- Canada – ~10,000 mines
- Africa – ~6,000 mines
- Japan – ~5,000 mines

What is the long-term vision: Purchase and hold.
What are the target funds: Climate Alternatives and Physical Assets Plays Strategy.
What are the target strategies: Venture capital, private equity.
What is the Technology Readiness Level: TRL7.
How crowded is the investment space: Not crowded yet.
What is the investment maturity: Ready.

---

[1] https://en.wikipedia.org/wiki/Gravity_battery
[2] https://globalchallenges.ch/issue/6/abandoned-mines-the-scars-of-the-past/
[3] https://miningdigital.com/top10/top-5-locations-abandoned-mines

Overview of Primarily Climate Alternatives (Physical Assets Plays) Investment Theses

11.3 FOREST LAND – PLANTATION FOREST

What is plantation forest: By tree plantation we refer to a forest planted primarily for wood production, often using one type of tree (Figure 11.3). The products of such plantations are typically lumber for dimensional wood or mass timber, as well as byproducts (tops, branches, sawdust) which are often used for energy production or biomass.

What is the climate driver: Transition risk.

What is the root problem: Transition scenarios require carbon removal credits in all but current policies.

What does this cause: Plantation forest will increase in value, for the potential it holds as a renewable source of biomass, and for the carbon credits this biomass can be used to generate (both in BECCS, biochar, land-based biomass, and ocean-based biomass).

What needs to happen to fix the issue: Currently, the VCM market is voluntary-only, and it needs to merge with the mandatory (offsets/cap-and-trade) markets for this market to truly take off (MRV and certification will follow).

How soon does this need to happen: All scenarios for Net Zero 2050 or disorderly transitions include significant amounts (Gt) of carbon removal/avoidance credits by 2030.

Figure 11.3 Representational views of forest land – plantation forest.

Generated with AI using Perchance

What is the opportunity: Purchase plantation forest land at currently undervalued prices due to the reduced usage of paper in the current economy and hold it for when the value of the carbon credits it will generate will increase, as predicted by all transition scenarios.

What is the benefit: Ownership of a steady and increasing revenue flow of renewable biomass for carbon credits (with an increasing price of carbon).

What is the market size: According to the Food and Agriculture (FAO) organization of the United Nations,[4] "The outlook for primary wood products consumption [...] shows an increase of 0.8 billion m^3 (+37%) [...] from 2.3 billion m^3 Roundwood equivalents in 2020 to 3.1 billion m^3 Roundwood equivalents in 2050." This growth rate corresponds to a 1.15% CAGR over the entire period. This projection is for volume of wood only. If we expand the definition to account for pricing, technology and services tied to the industry, according to The Business Research Company,[5] the forestry and logging market size has increased significantly, rising from US$ 1.16 trillion in 2024 to US$ 1.26 trillion in 2025, with a growth rate of 8.5%. Factors driving this growth include rising residential construction, higher demand for cruise ships, and increased needs for tissue and paper products. The market is projected to reach US$ 1.75 trillion in 2029, maintaining a CAGR of 8.5%. Both of these sets of data cover the whole forestry market, and not just the plantation forest side.

What is the long-term vision: Purchase and hold.

What are the target funds: Climate Alternatives and Physical Assets Plays Strategy.

What are the target strategies: Private Equity.

What is the Technology Readiness Level: TRL9.

How crowded is the investment space: Not crowded yet.

What is the investment maturity: Ready.

---

[4] https://www.fao.org/3/cc2265en/cc2265en.pdf

[5] https://www.thebusinessresearchcompany.com/report/forestry-and-logging-global-market-report

11.4 FOREST LAND – PRIMARY FOREST

What is forest land – primary: According to the FAO,[6] a primary forest is defined as "Naturally regenerated forest of native tree species, where there are no clearly visible indications of human activities and the ecological processes are not significantly disturbed." Besides being very large reservoirs of carbon (over 150 gigatons[7]), primary forests also play a key role in the preservation of both local and global biodiversity (Figure 11.4).

What is the climate driver: Transition finance.

What is the root problem: Transition scenarios require carbon removal and carbon avoidance credits in all but current policies.

What does this cause: Primary forest will increase in value, for the potential it holds as a carbon sink, and for the carbon credits it can generate.

What needs to happen to fix the issue: Currently, the VCM market is voluntary-only, and it needs to merge with the mandatory (offsets/cap-and-trade) markets for this market to truly take off (MRV and certification will follow).

Figure 11.4 Representational views of forest land – primary forest.

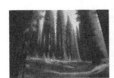

Generated with AI using Perchance

---

[6] https://www.fao.org/fsnforum/consultation/towards-improved-reporting-primary-forests
[7] https://iucn.org/sites/default/files/2023-11/iucn-cop-28-technical-brief-wcpa-primary-forests-ecosystem-integrity-and-climate-change.pdf

How soon does this need to happen: All scenarios for Net Zero 2050 or disorderly transitions include significant amounts (Gt) of carbon removal/avoidance credits by 2030.

What is the opportunity: Purchase primary forest land at currently undervalued prices and hold it for when the value of the carbon credits it will generate will increase, as predicted by all transition scenarios.

What is the benefit: Ownership of a steady and increasing revenue flow of avoidance carbon credits (with an increasing price of carbon).

What is the market size: The projected values of a purely carbon-based play such as primary forest (excluding the possibility of monetization of the biodiversity angle, which is somewhat remote at the moment of writing this book) is entirely dependent on what transition scenario is selected. As a baseline, we can look at Global Market Insights,[8] that estimates that the forestry and land use carbon credit market was US$ 22.4 billion in 2023 and is expected to grow at a CAGR of over 13.9% from 2024 to 2032, reaching US$ 72.4 billion, due to the urgent need to address climate change and the role of carbon credits in promoting sustainable land management practices.

What is the long-term vision: Purchase and hold.

What are the target funds: Climate Alternatives and Physical Assets Plays Strategy.

What are the target strategies: Private equity.

What is the Technology Readiness Level: TRL9.

How crowded is the investment space: Not crowded yet.

What is the investment maturity: Ready.

---

[8] https://www.gminsights.com/industry-analysis/forestry-and-landuse-carbon-credit-market

Overview of Primarily Climate Alternatives (Physical Assets Plays) Investment Theses

11.5 NORTHERN LATITUDES FARMLAND

What is Northern Latitudes Farmland: By Northern Latitudes Farmland (NLF) we mean the areas of farmland in the northern reaches of the world that are experiencing increasing warming and milder conditions, which lead to improved fertility and productivity (Figure 11.5). Greater details are provided in the deep dive on this opportunity in Chapter 13.
What is the climate driver: Chronic physical risk

Figure 11.5 Representational views of Northern Latitudes Farmland and changes in US hardiness zones, 1990–2012.

Generated with AI using Perchance

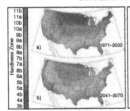
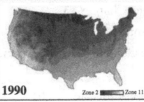
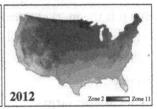

1990   2012

National Oceanic Atmospheric Administration

What is the root problem: Climate change is shifting hardiness zones toward the north, in the northern hemisphere (the southern hemisphere, due to geographical constraints, has much minor impact, as there are limited landmasses in southern latitudes).

What does this cause: Arable land is shifting northward, expanding the wheat belt into higher and higher latitudes. Scientists project it could go from about 55°N today to as much as 65°N – the latitude of Fairbanks, Alaska – by 2050.

What needs to happen to fix the issue: The shift in hardiness zones is good news for perennial cash crops in certain US states and Canadian provinces, and northern latitudes in general and presents a long-term investment opportunity.

How soon does this need to happen: This is a long-term trend, which will likely accelerate in the coming years and decades.

What is the opportunity: Acquire land in northern latitudes that is currently underpriced as it is not fully useable yet and hold it long-term as it becomes more productive and valuable over time, with the increasing temperature and northward shift of the hardiness zones.

What is the benefit: Ownership of productive land will come at a premium in climate transition scenarios, given the expected desertification and loss of productivity of currently high-yield areas.

What is the market size: See Chapter 13.

What is the long-term vision: Acquire and hold.

What are the target funds: Climate Alternatives and Physical Assets Plays Strategy.

What are the target strategies: Private equity.

What is the Technology Readiness Level: TRL9.

How crowded is the investment space: Unclear.

What is the investment maturity: Ready.

11.6 PAPER RECYCLING FACILITIES

What are paper-recycling facilities: By paper-recycling facilities we mean the gathering locations involved in amassing and storing recycled paper, either for reuse or final disposal in landfill (Figure 11.6). These are an opportunity to acquire biomass at one of the lowest price points possible and use it to generate carbon credits in one form or another.[9]

What is the climate driver: Transition risk.

What is the root problem: Transition scenarios require carbon removal credits in all but current policies.

What does this cause: Recycled paper will increase in value, for the potential it holds as a renewable source of cheap wood-based biomass, and for the carbon credits this biomass can be used to generate (both in BECCS, biochar, land-based biomass storage, and ocean-based biomass storage).

What needs to happen to fix the issue: Currently, the VCM market is voluntary-only, and it needs to merge with the mandatory (offsets/cap-and-trade) markets for this market to truly take off (MRV and certification will follow).

Figure 11.6 Representational views of paper recycling facilities.

Generated with AI using Perchance

---

[9] https://www.thehappyturtlestraw.com/the-carbon-footprint-of-paper-decomposition

How soon does this need to happen: All scenarios for Net Zero 2050 or disorderly transitions include significant amounts (Gt) of carbon removal/avoidance credits by 2030.

What is the opportunity: Purchase paper-recycling facilities (gathering and processing) at currently undervalued prices due to the reduced usage of paper in the current economy, and hold them for when the value of the carbon credits they can generate will increase, as predicted by all transition scenarios.

What is the benefit: Ownership of a steady and increasing revenue flow of renewable biomass for carbon credits (with an increasing price of carbon).

What is the market size: The projected value of a purely carbon-based play such as paper recycling facilities, is entirely dependent on what transition scenario is selected. According to Grand View Research,[10] the global carbon credit market was valued at US$ 479 million in 2023 and is projected to grow at a very strong CAGR of 39.4% from 2024 to 2030, reaching US$ 4.89 billion in this baseline, short-term scenario. For specific transition finance scenario price trajectories and longer projections, the NGFS scenario explorer provides all the relevant values.[11]

What is the long-term vision: Purchase and hold.

What are the target funds: Climate Alternatives and Physical Assets Plays Strategy.

What are the target strategies: Private equity.

What is the Technology Readiness Level: TRL7.

How crowded is the investment space: Not crowded yet.

What is the investment maturity: Ready.

---

[10] https://www.grandviewresearch.com/industry-analysis/carbon-credit-market-report
[11] https://data.ene.iiasa.ac.at/ngfs

Overview of Primarily Climate Alternatives (Physical Assets Plays) Investment Theses

11.7 REAL ESTATE IN CLIMATE SANCTUARY CITIES

What is real estate in climate sanctuary cities: Climate sanctuary cities are areas expected to be comfortable and safe to live in as the climate changes, as visualized in Figure 11.7. For the United States these are often located in the Midwest and northern regions of the country.[12] The criteria for a city to be considered a climate sanctuary include resilience (capacity to survive, adapt, and thrive despite climate change), currently having a continental climate (i.e., moderate heat in summer), and be naturally disaster-free (not in areas at risk for flooding, wildfire, hurricanes, etc.). A good reference to understand climate sanctuary cities is the excellent book by Jake Bittle, *The Great Displacement: Climate Change and the Next American Migration*.[13]

What is the climate driver: Acute and chronic physical risk.

What is the root problem: Climate change is increasing the risk of living in areas that are under the threat of extreme weather events.

What does this cause: Inhabitants of areas that are increasingly being hit by climate-linked disasters will eventually seek to relocate to areas that are at lower risk, both due to losses sustained as well as because of increasingly unaffordable costs for insurance in high-risk areas.

What needs to happen to fix the issue: Real estate needs to be developed in climate sanctuary cities to provide housing to the additional residents that are expected to relocate due to extreme climate events.

How soon does this need to happen: Disasters have been on the rise for the last quarter century, and insurance for many high-risk areas is becoming

---

[12] https://yaleclimateconnections.org/2023/11/why-climate-havens-might-be-closer-to-home-than-youd-think

[13] Bittle, J. (2023). *The Great Displacement: Climate Change and the Next American Migration*. Simon & Schuster.

Figure 11.7 Representational views of climate sanctuary cities.

Generated with AI using Perchance

increasingly expensive or outright unavailable, driving people to move to cities and regions that are perceived to be less prone to climate risk.

What is the opportunity: Invest in real estate in climate sanctuary cities (both existing and new developments).

What is the benefit: Benefit from the increase of residents that are expected to relocate to climate sanctuary cities in great numbers, driving values of real estate up.

What is the market size: There isn't much in terms of market research to size the opportunity; however, a study from ProPublica from 2020 estimated that at least 13 million Americans would be forced to relocate due to climate change by 2030.[14] A certain number of locations have been identified[15] in the United States, and can be used as a global blueprint for desirable characteristics, such as:

Ann Arbor, Michigan, has a temperate climate and access to Great Lakes water. It is known for education and innovation, particularly through the University of Michigan.

Asheville, North Carolina, located in the Blue Ridge Mountains, is less at risk for sea-level rise and extreme weather, with a mild climate and vibrant culture.

Boise, Idaho's, dry climate with four seasons that reduces natural disaster risks, with growth in sustainable practices.

---

[14] https://www.propublica.org/article/climate-change-will-force-a-new-american-migration
[15] https://www.causeartist.com/top-climate-haven-cities-usa/

Overview of Primarily Climate Alternatives (Physical Assets Plays) Investment Theses

Boulder, Colorado's, high altitude results in a cooler climate, with less vulnerability to extreme weather and a focus on sustainability and environmental preservation.

Buffalo, New York, benefits from the Great Lakes for a steady water source and cooler temperatures, along with strong community ties and revitalization efforts.

Burlington, Vermont, near Lake Champlain has a stable water supply and moderate climate, emphasizing environmental sustainability.

Columbus, Ohio, is located inland, with a moderate climate and various sustainability programs enhancing resilience.

Duluth, Minnesota, is a safe choice due to its distance from coastlines and wildfire zones, along with an abundance of fresh water from Lake Superior. Its cool climate is likely to stay stable, making it appealing for those avoiding extreme heat.

Eugene, Oregon, has a temperate climate and focuses on environmental sustainability, with community engagement in green initiatives.

Fayetteville, Arkansas, has a moderate climate and emphasizes natural beauty and sustainability initiatives.

Ithaca, New York, is in the Finger Lakes region, providing a stable water supply and temperate climate, with strong sustainability efforts driven by educational institutions like Cornell University.

Kansas City, Missouri, has a moderate climate and reliable water from nearby rivers, making strides in sustainability and green infrastructure.

Madison, Wisconsin, is also shielded from hurricanes and sea-level rise, focusing on sustainability and community resilience, appealing to climate-aware individuals.

Minneapolis, Minnesota's, northern location provides cooler temperatures and abundant freshwater from the Mississippi River and nearby lakes. Its strong sustainability initiatives make it a resilient choice.

Pittsburgh, Pennsylvania's, inland position protects against hurricanes and flooding. The city focuses on green technology and sustainable urban development, supported by a resilient community.

Portland, Maine, offers a coastal location with reduced hurricane risk and a cooler climate, supported by strong infrastructure and sustainability initiatives.

Rochester, New York, near Lake Ontario has a stable water supply and cooler temperatures, as well as a strong economy and sustainability commitment.

Seattle, Washington's, marine climate avoids inland heatwaves, with investments in green infrastructure and renewable energy.

Spokane, Washington, enjoys a dry, temperate climate, being less vulnerable to wildfires with solid infrastructure and economic growth, making it suitable as a climate haven.

What is the long-term vision: Purchase and hold.
What are the target funds: Climate Alternatives and Physical Assets Plays Strategy.
What are the target strategies: Private equity.
What is the Technology Readiness Level: TRL9.
How crowded is the investment space: Not crowded yet.
What is the investment maturity: Ready.

CHAPTER TWELVE

SAMPLE DEEP DIVE: GEOTHERMAL ENERGY

How can we tap into the endless power of the earth's core as a profitable investment

12.1 WHICH IS THE CLIMATE DRIVER FOR GEOTHERMAL ENERGY?

The transition finance driver for geothermal energy (Figure 12.1) is transition risk.

Figure 12.1 Descriptive views of geothermal energy applications.

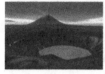

Generated with AI using Perchance

12.2 WHICH FUNDS DO GEOTHERMAL ENERGY FALL UNDER?

Geothermal energy is a transition finance opportunity that falls both in the Growth Strategy Fund and in the Infrastructure Strategy Fund, depending on which companies are being considered.

12.3 WHAT IS THE TRL FOR GEOTHERMAL?

The Technology Readiness Level for geothermal varies, depending on which technology, company, and geography is being assessed. As a sector, the average can be estimated as being a TRL 7, system prototype demonstration in operational environment, despite a few operational systems being already deployed in select locations.

12.4 DETERMINE THE INVESTMENT HORIZON FOR GEOTHERMAL

Geothermal requires long-term investment, and has long-term return profiles, as most infrastructure investments do. As a result, the estimated investment horizon for geothermal is the entire 30-year transition climate span.

12.5 WHAT IS THE INVESTMENT MATURITY FOR GEOTHERMAL?

Geothermal, as an average sector, is estimated to be an "in development" opportunity in terms of investment maturity, meaning that some subsectors and opportunities are ripe for investment in the short term, while others are still in earlier phases and will be ripe in 24/36 months or longer.

12.6 HOW CROWDED IS GEOTHERMAL?

In general terms, geothermal is not considered to be a crowded investment space, as of April 2024.

12.7 WHAT IS THE ROOT PROBLEM FOR GEOTHERMAL?

Transition scenarios require moving away from fossil fuels in all but current policies. One of the main mechanisms that the transition scenarios all include is a carbon tax (aka, carbon price). The levying of a carbon tax, while likely to not be a coordinated effort across all geographies, is expected to be a monotonically growing function, and will impact the affordability of all fossil-fuel-based energy sources. As of 2019, 77 countries and over 100 cities have committed to achieving net-zero emissions by 2050[1] and carbon taxes have been implemented or scheduled to be implemented in 25 countries.[2]

12.8 WHAT DOES THE ROOT PROBLEM FOR GEOTHERMAL CAUSE?

Energy sources that do not emit CO_2, such as geothermal energy power, will benefit from the overall higher cost of energy caused by the carbon tax, without having to be burdened by it, and will benefit from increased profitability and growing demand. As a result, geothermal business models that are not viable today, due to competition from cheap oil, will reach equal footing, and then become highly competitive against fossil fuels, the higher the price of carbon goes.

---

[1] https://sdg.iisd.org/news/77-countries-100-cities-commit-to-net-zero-carbon-emissions-by-2050-at-climate-summit/

[2] https://openknowledge.worldbank.org/entities/publication/0a107aa7-dcc8-5619-bdcf-71f97a8909d6

IRENA[3,4] presents the competitive advantages of geothermal energy as follows:

> The technical potential of hydrothermal geothermal resources is estimated at around 200 gigawatts electric (GWe) and over 5,000 gigawatts thermal (GWth). The Intergovernmental Panel on Climate Change projects that geothermal energy **can supply about 18% of the world's electricity demand** and **meet the electricity needs of 17% of the world's population**. Geothermal is a sustainable energy resource that is widespread in different geological and geographical settings. It occurs over a wide range of temperatures that enables it to be utilized as a renewable and clean energy for electricity generation and heat and cooling applications. In addition, critical minerals such as lithium can be extracted from geothermal brines.
>
> Geothermal energy is considered environmentally benign. The life cycle emissions of geothermal binary electricity plants with 100% reinjection are estimated to be as low as 11.3 grams of CO_2 per kWh, and the water consumption of a similar plant is estimated to be 0.66 liters/kWh. The land requirement of a geothermal power plant is around 7.5 square kilometers/terawatt hour.
>
> With proper reservoir management, geothermal power plants can provide stable and reliable electricity and heat with a capacity factor of more than 80%. At the same time, binary technology can allow geothermal power plants to be operated in flexible mode, which is ideal for grids with a diverse energy mix that includes variable renewable sources.

---

[3] IRENA. (2021). Geothermal: The Solution Underneath. International Renewable Energy Agency. Abu Dhabi. www.globalgeothermalalliance.org/-/media/Files/IRENA/GGA/Publications/Geothermal---The-Solution-Underneath.pdf

[4] IRENA. (2022). Renewable Power Generation Costs in 2021, International Renewable Energy Agency, Abu Dhabi. www.irena.org/Publications/2022/Jul/Renewable-Power-Generation-Costs-in-2021

Geothermal energy competitively generated electricity at a LCOE of US$ 0.068/kWh for new plants commissioned in 2021.[5] Given its high availability, it is estimated that integrating geothermal electricity into grids in the United States will save the system around US$ 41/kWh, mainly through avoidance of installing ancillary services to stabilize the grid.

12.9 WHAT NEEDS TO HAPPEN TO FIX THE ROOT PROBLEM FOR GEOTHERMAL?

Market leaders need to scale up from the current to commercially viable sizes, and new technologies need to progress beyond POC phase.

As of 2022, worldwide geothermal power capacity amounted to 14.8 gigawatts (GW), of which 17% or 2.6 GW were in the United States.[6]

The projection of how large geothermal will become, and in which countries the growth will be focused, depends on the scenario that is selected.

For the purposes of this deep dive exercise, we shall choose two scenarios, the Net Zero 2050 (which has a low probability of occurring) and the delayed transition (which is significantly more probable).

These two scenarios are both NGFS scenarios, which we are using here for ease of presentation, but could be also replaced by custom scenarios run through IAMs such as GCAM (if the likely scenario we want to use is not one that aligns to any "pre-canned" scenario from NGFS).

The NGFS (Network for Greening the Financial System) is an important authoritative source of scenarios for all the financial industry (and

---

[5] https://www.irena.org/News/articles/2023/May/Boosting-the-Global-Geothermal-Market-Requires-Increased-Awareness-and-Greater-Collaboration

[6] https://ourworldindata.org/grapher/installed-geothermal-capacity

beyond) and has developed a common set of scenarios designed to act as a foundation for analysis across many institutions, creating much-needed consistency and comparability of results.

Financial regulators, as well as banks, use these NGFS scenarios to better understand the risks to the financial system, economies, and the banks' own business and balance sheets.

The NGFS scenarios demonstrate a range of potential lower-risk and higher-risk outcomes. It is useful to classify the seven standard

Figure 12.2 NGFS Phase IV scenarios.
Source: NGFS/Source https://www.ngfs.net/ last Accessed on February 17, 2025.

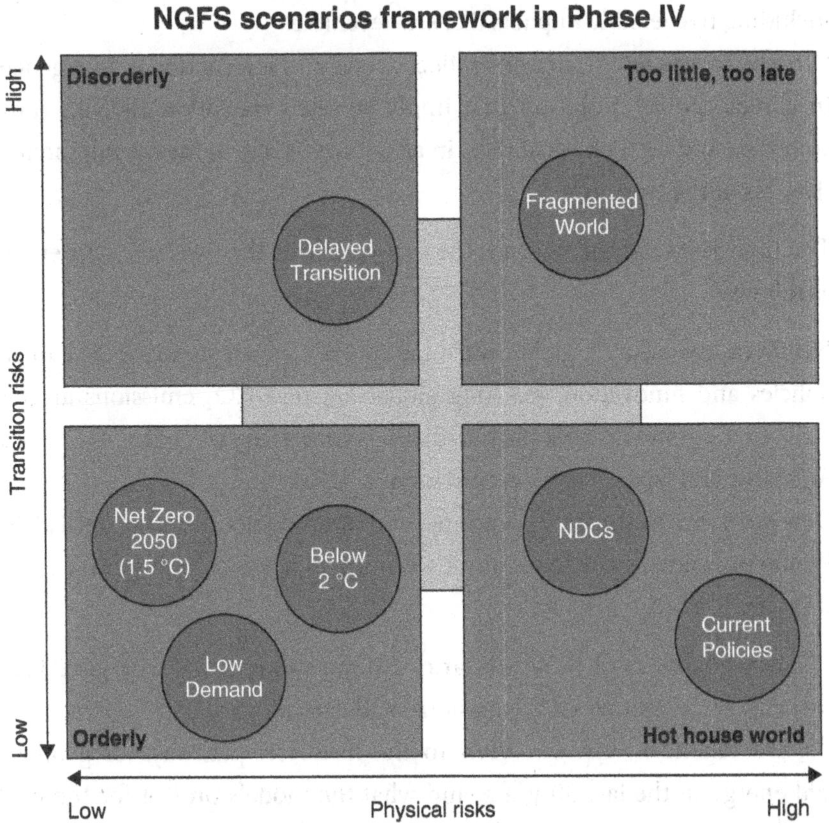

NGFS scenarios framework in Phase IV

Quadrants (Transition risks on y-axis Low→High, Physical risks on x-axis Low→High):
- Top-left (Disorderly): Delayed Transition
- Top-right (Too little, too late): Fragmented World
- Bottom-left (Orderly): Net Zero 2050 (1.5 °C), Below 2 °C, Low Demand
- Bottom-right (Hot house world): NDCs, Current Policies

NGFS scenarios along two dimensions, as illustrated in Figure 12.2. Furthermore:

"Orderly" scenarios assume climate policies are introduced early and become gradually more stringent. Both physical and transition risks are relatively subdued.

"Disorderly" scenarios explore higher transition risk due to policies being delayed or divergent across countries and sectors. For example, carbon prices increase abruptly after a period of delay.

"Hothouse world" scenarios assume that some climate policies are implemented in some jurisdictions, but globally efforts are insufficient to halt significant global warming. The scenarios result in severe physical risk including irreversible impacts like sea-level rise.

"Too little, too late" scenarios reflect delays and international divergences in climate policy ambition that imply elevated transition risks in some countries and high physical risks in all countries due to the overall ineffectiveness of the transition.

The high-level narratives from the two scenarios that we have chosen are as follows:

Net Zero 2050: limits global warming to 1.5 °C through stringent climate policies and innovation, reaching global net-zero CO_2 emissions around 2050. In these scenarios, some jurisdictions such as the US, EU, UK, Canada, Australia, and Japan reach net zero for all GHGs.

Delayed Transition: assumes annual emissions do not decrease until 2030. Strong policies are needed to limit warming to below 2 °C. Negative emissions are limited.

The overall effects of these scenarios can be summarized in Figure 12.3, covering temperature, CO_2 emissions, and carbon price.

We can now shift our view to the historical pathways of geothermal energy in the last 30 years, and what the models project for the next 30 years.

Sample Deep Dive: Geothermal Energy

Figure 12.3 Temperature evolution, global CO₂ emissions and shadow carbon price for NGFS Phase V scenarios.

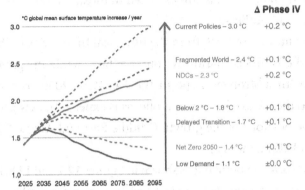

Temperature Evolution by Scenario
AR6 Surface Temperature (GSAT) increase (50th), MAGICC with REMIND-MAgPIE emission inputs

Scenario	Δ Phase IV
Current Policies – 3.0 °C	+0.2 °C
Fragmented World – 2.4 °C	+0.1 °C
NDCs – 2.3 °C	+0.2 °C
Below 2 °C – 1.8 °C	+0.1 °C
Delayed Transition – 1.7 °C	+0.1 °C
Net Zero 2050 – 1.4 °C	+0.1 °C
Low Demand – 1.1 °C	±0.0 °C

Sources: IIASA NGFS Climate Scenarios Database, MAGICC model (with REMIND-MAgPIE emissions inputs). MAGICC provides a range of temperature increase compared to the pre-industrial levels. The temperature paths displayed here follow the 50th percentile.

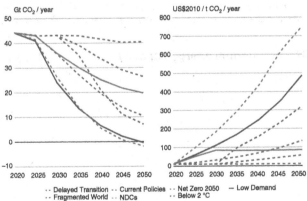

Global Yearly CO₂ Emissions
REMIND-MAgPIE

Shadow Carbon Price
REMIND-MAgPIE

-- Delayed Transition -- Current Policies -- Net Zero 2050 — Low Demand
-- Fragmented World -- NDCs -- Below 2 °C

Source: IIASA NGFS Climate Scenarios Database, REMIND-MAgPIE model. World aggregates mask strong differences across sectors and jurisdictions. Regionally and sectorally granular information is available in the IIASA Portal. End of century warming outcomes shown. 5-year time interval data.

Source: IIASA NGFS Climate Scenarios Database, REMIND-MAgPIE model. Shadow carbon prices are weighted global. Regionally and sectorally granular information is available in the IIASA Portal. End of century warming outcomes shown. 5-year time interval data.

NGFS SCENARIOS

Figures 12.4 and 12.5, show the growth of geothermal energy usage globally and by selected countries between 2000–2022 and the global utilization, and installed capacity for geothermal heating and cooling between 1995 and 2020, and paint a picture of steady and accelerating growth which, as is shown in Figure 12.6, is still localized in mostly developed countries, with a handful of outliers.

Once we move, however, from the historical time series to the projections from the NGFS scenarios, we observe how, while the growth trend continues (with a stronger slope in the Net Zero 2050 scenario, when compared to the Delayed Transition one, as is expected), new geographies pick up large portions of the growth (Middle East and Africa, OECD and Europe, and Latin America).

It is noteworthy to point out as shown in Figures 12.7 and 12.8, that while the end state for Net Zero 2050 and Delayed Transition for geothermal differs

Figure 12.4 Growth of geothermal globally and by selected countries, 2000–2022.
Source: Installed geothermal energy capacity, 2022 / https://ourworldindata.org/grapher/installed-geothermal-capacity?time=2022, last accessed on 9 May 2025 / Our World in Data / CC BY 4.0.

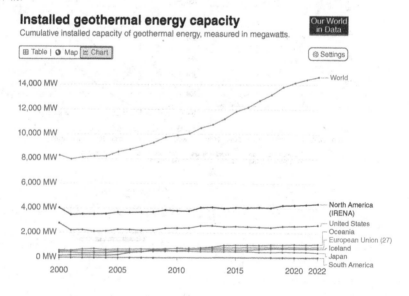

Figure 12.5 Global utilization and installed capacity for geothermal heating and cooling, 1995–2020.
Source: IRENA.org, 2023/.

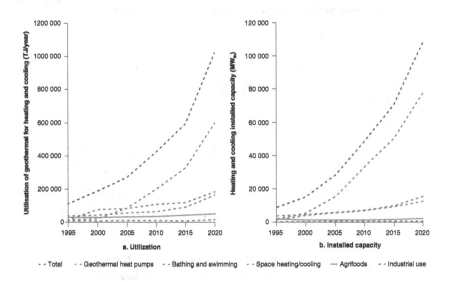

by approximately a factor of two (global geothermal average of 6 IAMs is 62.5 EJ/year in Net Zero and 32.7 EJ/year in Delayed Transition), *both scenarios start their most significant growth in 2030*, albeit with different slopes.

12.10 HOW SOON DOES THE FIX NEED TO HAPPEN FOR GEOTHERMAL?

All scenarios for Net Zero 2050 or disorderly transitions include significant amounts of alternative power between 2030 and 2050, as we have observed. The nature of geothermal investments, which require setting up

PRINCIPLES OF TRANSITION FINANCE INVESTING

Figure 12.6   Installed capacity for geothermal energy, by region.

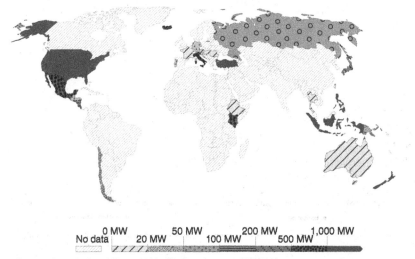

Figure 12.7   NGFS Phase 4 geothermal energy projections, 2025–2055 averages of 6 IAM models for Net Zero 2050 scenario.
Source: Banque de France / https://www.ngfs.net / last accessed February 19, 2025.

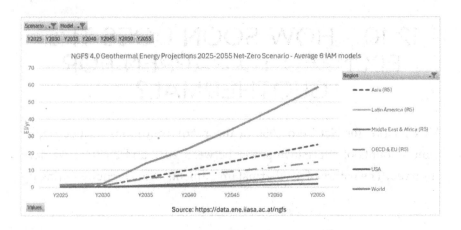

Sample Deep Dive: Geothermal Energy

Figure 12.8   NGFS Phase 4 geothermal energy projections, 2025–2055 averages of 6 IAM models for transition scenario.
Source: Banque de France / https://www.ngfs.net / last accessed February 19, 2025.

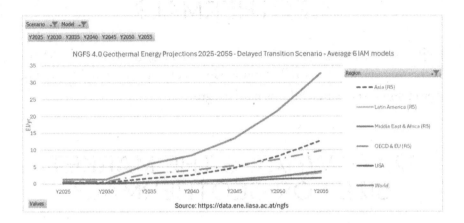

of infrastructure, pilot plants, and scaling up to production levels, translates into a fairly shorter timeframe than what would appear from the relatively faraway date for the pickup of volumes, as five years to develop and achieve scale is not a very long time for new energy infrastructure projects, especially for those which might require implementation of novel technologies and solutions.

12.11   WHAT IS THE INVESTMENT OPPORTUNITY FOR GEOTHERMAL?

Identify and invest in new companies (such as presented in section 12.16) or emerging players (as identified in section 12.17) to gain a foothold in this new market.

12.12 WHAT IS THE BENEFIT FROM INVESTING IN GEOTHERMAL?

Gain a leading position in a new and growing energy generation field, with increasing energy prices and margins. Generate alpha from higher pricing power and revenue potential as markets grow.

12.13 WHAT IS THE MARKET SIZE FOR GEOTHERMAL?

The market size for the future of geothermal, as a transition finance opportunity, is linked to which transition scenario is chosen, and how wide a definition we decide to use for the opportunity. Market information is relatively easy to find for geothermal power itself, and will be presented in this section, and less so for the technology and infrastructure that is needed to support it.

According to StraitsResearch[7] the size of the geothermal power global market was valued at US$ 8.4 billion in 2023, and estimated to reach US$ 12.1 billion, growing at a CAGR of 4.2% during the forecast period (2024–2032), as shown in Figure 12.9. This forecast is for the power market alone, and does not include technology and installations.

The *StraitsResearch Geothermal Power Market Size Report* provides the following Regional Analysis for the 2023–2032 projections (*which are not aligned to a specific NGFS scenario*, and should therefore only be used as a general indication of ongoing projects):

---

[7] https://straitsresearch.com/report/geothermal-power-market

Sample Deep Dive: Geothermal Energy

Figure 12.9 Projected geothermal power market size, 2023-2032.
Source: FirstView Media Ventures Private Limited / (source: https://straitsresearch.com/) / last Accessed on February 17, 2025.

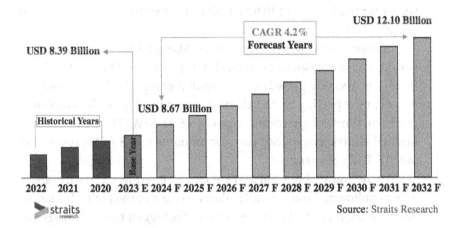

Based on region, the global market is segmented into North America, Europe, Asia-Pacific, Latin America, and the Middle East and Africa.

North America is the most significant global geothermal power market shareholder and is estimated to grow at a **CAGR of 4.2%** over the forecast period. The growth of the North American geothermal energy market is driven by increased efforts taken by scientists and developers to meet the growing demand for energy in the Western United States and Mexico. Several geothermal projects are ongoing in the United States and Mexico, further fueling the demand for geothermal energy. At the end of 2013, the capacity of geothermal power was 3,440 MW in the Western United States, with new or renovated power plants in Utah, Nevada, California, and New Mexico.

Furthermore, the Mexican Department of Energy will likely have 35% of Mexico's energy production from renewable energy sources by 2024. Mexico is making reforms such as Energy Reform 2013-2018 and Estrategia Nacional de Energía 2013-2027 to open the power market for private and outside organizations. Such initiatives are forecasted to drive the demand for geothermal power and thus contribute toward the market's growth.

Moreover, Canada is making a material contribution to boosting the market growth. For instance, GEA's April 2014 International Projects List has displayed nine current geothermal power generation projects at early or prospective stages. These projects include six geothermal plants in British Columbia, two in Saskatchewan, and one in Alberta.

Europe is anticipated to exhibit a **CAGR of 3.6%** over the forecast period. The European Geothermal Energy Council (EGEC) stated that there was a steady growth of geothermal energy in Europe, with 16 new plants expecting to start their operation in 2017, with a combined geothermal power generation capacity of 33 MW. The installed geothermal electricity capacity per year amounts to 2.8 GWe, producing over 15 TWh of energy.

Furthermore, about 330 MWe of new geothermal electricity capacity was online in Turkey in 2019. Europe is one of the global leaders in investments in renewable energy. One of the biggest research programs in the EU in the last decade is "Horizon 2020"/"Horizon Europe" the former of which had a budget of 80 billion Euro, and covered renewable energy for 2014–2020. Europe has aimed to cut its greenhouse gas emissions by 80%. To achieve this, the share of renewables is expected to grow significantly, not only in power but also in the transportation, heating, and cooling industries. This factor is expected to contribute to the geothermal power market's growth significantly.

The **Asia-Pacific** market is analyzed across China, Japan, India, South Korea, Australia, and the rest of Asia-Pacific. The geothermal power market is strong in Indonesia. In addition, when the 330 MW Sarulla geothermal power plant went online in May 2018, it denoted another achievement in Indonesia's geothermal power sector. The US$ 1.7 billion venture of over 2.1 million Indonesian family units is considered the nation's world's biggest single-contract geothermal power plant. This project is driving growth across the whole Asia-Pacific geothermal power market.

The **Latin America, Middle East and Africa** geothermal power market is also growing. In 2015, around 13% of Costa Rica's energy was generated from geothermal power plants using the country's abundant volcanic resources. With five million inhabitants, Costa Rica is the seventh largest geothermal producer out of 25 countries with available data. As per the Inter-American Development Bank (IADB) and the World Bank, Latin America uses around 5% of its geothermal potential of 300 terawatt-hours per year. There is less scope for geothermal power generation in the Latin America, Middle East, and Africa region; however, the market is expected to grow with growth initiatives and investment toward energy development.

IRENA[8] presents their view of Geothermal energy in the context of the renewable energy ecosystem as follows:

Many countries have set targets for geothermal energy development. In the United States, for instance, the GeoVision analysis conducted by the United States Department of Energy's Geothermal Technologies Office (US DoE 2019) evaluated future geothermal deployment opportunities. It concluded that the use of geothermal energy could be significantly increased through wider access to geothermal resources, improvements in project economics, and enhanced education and outreach. With technological improvements, geothermal electricity generation in the United States could rise to 60 gigawatts electric (GWe) of installed capacity by 2050, and the potential for geothermal heating and cooling is significant. The GeoVision report considers deep EGSs [Enhanced Geothermal Systems] to have the greatest potential to drive growth.

In 2017, China adopted its "13th Five-Year Plan for Geothermal Energy Development and Utilization," which promoted the development of geothermal to reduce air pollution and supply continuous base-load electricity and heat (Jianchao, Mengchao and Liu, 2018).[9] The 14th five-year plan for renewable energy calls for the development and use of geothermal energy

---

[8] IRENA and IGA. (2023). Global geothermal market and technology assessment. International Renewable Energy Agency. Abu Dhabi; International Geothermal Association, The Hague. https://www.irena.org/Publications/2023/Feb/Global-geothermal-market-and-technology-assessment

[9] https://ideas.repec.org/a/eee/renene/v125y2018icp401-412.html

(Nextrends Asia, 2021),[10] focusing on optimizing geothermal heating and cooling deployment.

In **Europe**, the IEA (International Energy Agency) and ADEME (French Environment and Energy Management Agency) have found geothermal to be the cheapest option for heating (EU Reporter, 2022). The European Geothermal Energy Council (EGEC) seeks to use Europe's geothermal energy for renewable heating, cooling, and electricity, and to extract lithium and other minerals. It also urged the European Commission to create a strategy to this purpose by 2023 (Renewables Now, 2022).[11]

In **Africa**, Kenya plans to double geothermal electricity capacity by 2030, reaching 1.6 GWe.[12]

Many countries, such as Indonesia, Kenya, New Zealand, and Turkey, have greatly increased their geothermal electricity capacity in the past 10 years. Some, like China and Turkey, have advanced geothermal heating and cooling. Geothermal development is uneven, but there are good prospects for growth due to climate change goals, oil price fluctuations, and new technologies.

In countries with deregulated electricity markets, various electricity sources compete to access the grid. Renewable sources have become competitive due to falling technology costs, if viewed by measuring the LCOE (Levelized Cost of Electricity). In 2021, the average LCOE for geothermal energy was US$ 0.068 per kWh, making it cheaper than fossil fuels. However, geothermal's actual LCOE varies based on specific conditions for power plants, including well depth, number of wells, electricity output, technology used, and whether the field is green or brown. In the decade between 2014 and 2024, the LCOE for geothermal stayed between US$ 0.05-0.07/kWh.

---

[10] https://nextrendsasia.org/energy-in-chinas-14th-five-year-plan

[11] https://www.ren21.net/wp-content/uploads/2019/05/GSR2022_Full_Report.pdf

[12] Burkardt, P. and Herbling, D. (2021). "The world's no. 1 in geothermal electricity, Kenya aims to export its know-how." Bloomberg. https://furtherafrica.com/2021/07/21/kenya-looking-to-export-its-know-how-as-worlds-no-1-in-geothermal-electricity/

In the same period, on the other hand, the LCOEs for utility-scale solar PV, onshore wind, concentrated solar power, and offshore wind dropped by 88%, 68%, 67%, and 60%, respectively. As a result, in 2021, about 225 Gwe of wind and solar was deployed, making up 88% of new renewable capacity, while only around 370 Mwe of geothermal was deployed (IRENA).[13] The low deployment level is likely due to the historically high initial costs and lengthy development times for geothermal resources.

The potential exists to lower the LCOE of geothermal projects and maintain the competitiveness of energy prices from geothermal, particularly on drilling costs, which accounts for a significant share of project costs. Project developers in Indonesia and elsewhere are implementing measures to reduce the costs associated with developing new and makeup geothermal wells through the application of best practices, including:

1. Foreseeing and avoiding potential drilling issues to shorten drilling time;
2. Using advanced subsurface modeling techniques to focus on permeable structures for drilling efficient wells;
3. Properly managing the geothermal reservoir to slow down well production decline and lessen the need for additional wells (Star Energy Geothermal, 2022).[14]

Geothermal energy has many benefits beside the LCOE that make it competitive. It can produce both electricity and heat and allows for mineral extraction. It provides reliable electricity generation with high efficiency, low greenhouse gas emissions, and a small ecological impact. Unlike variable sources, it offers a continuous supply, requiring less complex integration with the grid and is also a sustainable heat source with low operating costs and

---

[13] https://www.irena.org/-/media/Files/IRENA/Agency/Publication/2023/Feb/IRENA_Global_geothermal_market_technology_assessment_2023.pdf

[14] https://www.starenergygeothermal.co.id/

improved efficiency. As a result of these advantages, geothermal can enhance energy access, air quality, food systems, and help decarbonize cities.[15]

Geothermal projects have high initial costs and risks, as mentioned earlier, often requiring a long-term power purchase agreement (PPA) of 15–25 years with an electric utility or off-taker to secure financing for the initial stages. Though this precondition may not be excessively difficult to secure in countries with strong supportive policies for geothermal development, the PPA process can still slow project start times. In countries with weaker policies, long-term PPA signing may be restricted by electricity market conditions, like deregulation.

When PPAs are exclusively assigned through price-based, technology-neutral auctions, geothermal cannot compete with cheaper solar PV and wind projects. This puts geothermal projects at higher financial risks due to completion deadlines and power delivery obligations, as not meeting requirements can lead to fines for developers. Some countries, like Chile, have partly solved this issue by setting special conditions that consider the characteristics and risks of geothermal resource projects during their development stages, including uncertainties about resource capacity and development timeframe tied to drilling results.

12.14 WHAT IS THE LONG-TERM VISION FOR GEOTHERMAL INVESTMENTS?

The long term-vision for investing in geothermal, depending on the individual investment, is purchase and hold, or purchase, grow, and exit.

---

[15] Vargas, C.A., Caracciolo, L. and Ball, P.J. (2022). Geothermal energy as a means to decarbonize the energy mix of megacities. *Commun Earth Environ* 3, 66. https://doi.org/10.1038/s43247-022-00386-w

12.15 WHAT IS THE TRIGGER FOR GEOTHERMAL INVESTMENTS, AND HAS IT ALREADY OCCURRED?

The trigger is a joint rise in demand for renewable energy and an increase in price/cost for fossil-fuel based energy. The first part of the trigger (rise in demand) has already been activated, while the second part is in process of activation in different areas of the world and is expected to hit full activation by 2030 both in the Net Zero 2050 and delayed transition scenarios.

12.16 WHICH NEW COMPANIES HAVE BEEN IDENTIFIED IN EARLY STAGES FOR GEOTHERMAL (VC TARGETS)?

As early-stage VC targets in geothermal, we have identified the following:

Sage Geosystems uses an enhanced geothermal approach, Geopressured Geothermal Systems, to harvest both heat and pressure for increased energy output. https://www.sagegeosystems.com

GreenFire Energy is a closed-loop geothermal company that develops Advanced Geothermal Systems (AGS) called GreenFire's GreenLoop®. They have spent over a decade refining their thermodynamic modeling to reduce project risk and enhance production output. https://www.greenfireenergy.com

XGS is a closed-loop geothermal company that drills a directional well to reach hot rock at 250 °C or higher. They create a network of special material around the well to collect heat, which is used to heat water in a closed-loop system. The hot water can be used directly or converted to electricity. In January 2024, they secured $9.7 million in financing to speed up their North American prototype showing Thermal Reach Enhancement™ technology at full commercial scale. https://www.xgsenergy.com

AltaRock Energy focuses on Superhot Rock Geothermal (SHR) to access hotter, deeper rock. SHR can produce up to 10 times more energy than traditional wells. SHR resources serve half the global population within 10 km and 95% within 20 km. AltaRock has developed engineered geothermal systems and collaborates on drilling and power conversion. SHR can provide low-cost, carbon-free power, reduce need for infrastructure, and repurpose traditional power plants for renewable energy. https://altarockenergy.com

Teverra is a geo-informatics tech company focused on the geothermal energy market. They work on subsurface solutions for carbon storage, geothermal, energy storage, and greener oil and gas projects. Their clean energy initiative includes carbon sequestration solutions and converting late-stage oil and gas wells to renewable geothermal resources. They explore and produce geothermal energy from low-temperature sedimentary formations and hot dry rocks. https://www.teverra.com

ElectraTherm, based in Flowery Branch, Georgia, offers top heat recovery solutions using the Organic Rankine Cycle (ORC) and unique technologies to turn low temperature heat, like waste heat and micro geothermal, into clean electricity. They have delivered over 100 ORC systems to more than 13 countries, with many more on order, and have logged over 2,000,000 hours of operation, making them a leader in low temperature waste heat recovery. https://electratherm.com

Bedrock Energy creates geothermal systems with ground-source heat pumps to offer renewable, emission-free heating and cooling for urban buildings. https://bedrockenergy.com

12.17 WHICH NEW COMPANIES HAVE BEEN IDENTIFIED AS EMERGING PLAYERS FOR GEOTHERMAL (PE TARGETS)?

As emerging players PE targets in geothermal, we have identified the following:

Baseload Capital is a geothermal developer focused on financing. They raise funds and develop geothermal projects. They also own Baseload Power, which operates the plants funded by Baseload Capital. They have power companies in Japan, Taiwan, the United States, and Iceland. In October 2022, they raised $24 million in funding. https://www.baseloadcap.com

Eavor uses closed-loop geothermal systems. An EavorLoop™ connects two vertical wells with horizontal multilateral wellbores to form a closed buried-pipe system. Their proprietary working fluid is added at the surface and circulated to gather heat from deep earth for electricity or heating/cooling. The Eavor-Lite™ Demonstration Project, located near Rocky Mountain House, Alberta, began drilling in August 2019 and includes two vertical wells with multilateral legs at 2.4 km depth, linked by a surface pipeline. https://www.eavor.com

Quaise Energy is a geothermal drilling tech company using millimeter wave technology to access super hot rock geology. They raised $21 million in a Series A1 financing round led by Prelude Ventures and Safar Partners, with participation from Mitsubishi Corporation and Standard Investments. The A1 funding will boost field operations and strengthen the supply chain, while product development will keep moving forward with existing capital. https://www.quaise.energy

Fervo Energy focuses on enhanced geothermal technology, using over 10 years of advancements in drilling and production from oil and gas.

Their precision directional drilling technology allows for horizontal drilling in geothermal reservoirs, which means they can drill multiple wells from one spot, reducing surface impact and risks. This method increases access to difficult geologies, boosting geothermal energy resources. They install fiber optic cables in the wells to collect real-time data on flow, temperature, and performance, providing deep insights. Fervo uses advanced data analytics to locate the best resources and improve heat mining efficiency, gaining access to larger resource areas. https://fervoenergy.com

GA Drilling is a drilling tech company, founded in 2008, that is similar to Quaise, but further ahead in their development. It focuses on conventional drilling and is also developing technology similar to Quaise. The company announced a $15 million capital round with investors including Nabors, Christian Oldendorff's Family Office, alfa8, Thomas von Koch, Underground Ventures, and Neulogy Ventures. https://www.gadrilling.com

Criterion is a mixed solar and geothermal company. Criterion announced a partnership with Chesapeake Energy Corporation (NASDAQ:CHK) to support geothermal energy development. The partnership involves an investment by Chesapeake to help plan an initial test well, advancing Criterion Energy Partner's mission of making geothermal energy commercially viable everywhere. https://criterionep.com

12.18 WHICH ESTABLISHED PLAYERS EXIST IN GEOTHERMAL (PRIVATE CREDIT TARGETS)?

The key established players in the global geothermal market include:

Ormat leads the global geothermal sector by exploring, designing, developing, building, owning, and operating geothermal power plants worldwide. The company focuses on advancing geothermal technology and offers customized solutions. With experience in over 30 countries, Ormat helps clients maximize their geothermal resources. https://www.ormat.com/en/home/a/main

ABB   https://new.abb.com/power-generation/segments/geothermal-power

EDF   https://www.edf.fr/en/the-edf-group/producing-a-climate-friendly-energy/doubling-the-share-of-renewable-energies-by-2030/geothermal-energy-an-inexhaustible-renewable-energy-source

Enel SPA (Enel)   https://www.enelgreenpower.com/learning-hub/renewable-energies/geothermal-energy/geothermal-plants

General Electric (GE)   https://www.gevernova.com/steam-power/products/steam-turbines/stf-g220

Mitsubishi Hitachi Power Systems Inc.   https://power.mhi.com/products/geothermal

Toshiba Corporation   https://www.global.toshiba/ww/products-solutions/renewable-energy/products-technical-services/geothermal-power.html

Siemens AG   https://www.siemens-energy.com/global/en/home/stories/swm-geothermal-plants-in-munich.html

Yokogawa Electric Corporation   https://www.yokogawa.com/us/industries/renewable-energy/geothermal-power

CHAPTER THIRTEEN

SAMPLE DEEP DIVE: NORTHERN LATITUDES FARMLAND

Harnessing the northward shirt of the corn belt

13.1 WHAT IS NORTHERN LATITUDES FARMLAND?

By northern latitudes farmland we mean the areas of farmland in the northern reaches of the world that are experiencing increasing warming and milder conditions as a result of climate change, which lead to improved fertility and productivity (Figure 13.1).

Figure 13.1   Descriptive views of Northern Latitudes Farmland.

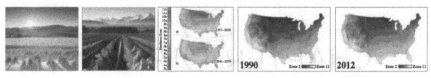

Generated with AI using Perchance

13.2   WHICH IS THE CLIMATE DRIVER FOR NORTHERN LATITUDES FARMLAND?

The transition finance driver for Northern Latitudes Farmland is chronic physical risk.

13.3   WHICH FUNDS DO NORTHERN LATITUDES FARMLAND FALL UNDER?

Given the nature of investment in farmland, the Northern Latitudes Farmland investment thesis falls under the Climate Alternatives/Physical Assets Plays Fund.

13.4 WHAT IS THE TRL FOR NORTHERN LATITUDES FARMLAND?

While it is somewhat counterintuitive to use a Technology Readiness Level for investment in farmland as a thesis, we can still follow the methodology and assign a value of TRL9 ("actual system proven in operational environment") to this thesis, as it is, effectively, one of the most ancient and well-known activities that mankind has engaged in since around 12,000 years ago.[1]

13.5 DETERMINE THE INVESTMENT HORIZON FOR NORTHERN LATITUDES FARMLAND

The investment horizon for Northern Latitudes Farmland (NLF) is the entire transition finance investment horizon (30 years or more), as it is based on a slow and irreversible shift that will continue for decades into the future (effectively for the entire century and further). It is well suited to an evergreen investment opportunity, where investors can enter and exit the fund at different points in time, via secondary market transactions, while the fund holds on to the assets that keep increasing in value over time, at a higher rate than the risk-adjusted benchmark.

---

[1] Zeder, Melinda A. (2011). The origins of agriculture in the Near East. *Current Anthropology* 52, no. S4: S221–35. https://doi.org/10.1086/659307

13.6 WHAT IS THE INVESTMENT MATURITY FOR NORTHERN LATITUDES FARMLAND?

The shift northward of hardiness zones (in the Northern Hemisphere, and southward in the southern) due to climate change is a well-established and observed phenomenon,[2] with relevant backward and forward looking analytics published since the early 2000s, as shown in Figure 13.2.

This shift is stronger in the global north, and has been documented[3] as far back as 2013 by NASA, showing how vegetation growth in the northern latitudes increasingly resembles what it was in much lusher southern latitudes, with conditions measured in 2013 matching those found 4–6° further south in 1984, as can be seen in Figure 13.2.

To put this data into perspective, NASA's study stated that:

> As a result of enhanced warming and a longer growing season, large patches of vigorously productive vegetation now span a third of the northern landscape, or more than 3.5 million square miles (9 million square kilometers). That is an area about equal to the contiguous United States. This landscape resembles what was found 250 to 430 miles (400 to 700 kilometers) to the south in 1982.

This trend has been further corroborated by recent studies that show how, since 1979, the Arctic, and by extension northern latitudes, has warmed nearly four times faster than the rest of the globe,[4] in a phenomenon known as "Arctic Amplification," which is a subset of the more generic

---

[2] Parker, Lauren E., and Abatzoglou, John T. (2016). Projected changes in cold hardiness zones and suitable overwinter ranges of perennial crops over the United States. *Environ. Res. Lett.* 11 034001 (2016). DOI 10.1088/1748-9326/11/3/034001 https://iopscience.iop.org/article/10.1088/1748-9326/11/3/034001

[3] https://climate.nasa.gov/news/880/amplified-greenhouse-effect-shifts-norths-growing-seasons/

[4] Rantanen, M., Karpechko, A.Y., Lipponen, A. et al. (2022). The Arctic has warmed nearly four times faster than the globe since 1979. *Commun Earth Environ* 3, 168. https://doi.org/10.1038/s43247-022-00498-3

Figure 13.2   Polar amplification at northern latitudes.

Note: **Left:** Annual mean temperature trends for the period 1979–2021, derived from the average of the observational datasets. Areas without a statistically significant change are masked out.
Right: Local amplification ratio calculated for the period 1979–2021, derived from the average of the observational datasets. The dashed line in both images depicts the Arctic Circle (66.5°N latitude).
Source: Rantanen et al., Commun Earth Environ 3, 168 (2022) / Springer Nature / CC BY 4.0

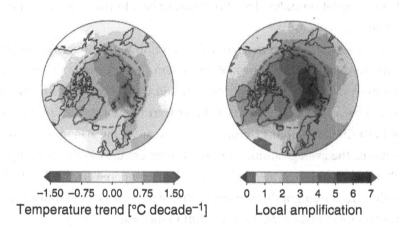

"Polar Amplification" phenomenon, that occurs in GHG driven planetary warming (this same phenomenon has been observed, at an extreme level on planet Venus).

On earth, this effect is much stronger in the northern latitudes, with the effects spilling into Canada, North America, and the Eurasian Continent, while of much smaller amplitude in the Southern Hemisphere, where, even within Antarctica itself, it is primarily confined to the area of West Antarctica (Figure 13.2).

While this is somewhat positive under the lens of reducing the speed of rising sea levels, since as the rise is driven, primarily, by the amount of South Pole ice that melts and which experiences much less polar amplification than the north pole (ice sheets in Greenland are the other driver, and are fully affected by northern polar acceleration), it further reduces the viability of Southern Latitudes Farmland as an investment opportunity.

Of the 10 million square miles (26 million square kilometers) of northern vegetated lands, 34–41% showed increases in plant growth (light shading), 3–5% showed decreases in plant growth (darker shading), and 51–62% showed no changes (white) over 1983–2013. Satellite data in Figure 13.3 are from the AVHRR and MODIS instruments, which contribute to a vegetation index that allows researchers to track changes in plant growth over large areas.

If we look at the average annual minimum temperatures as reported by the Applied Climate Information System,[5] which gathers temperature data from over 242 climate stations around the United States from 1950 onward, we can see how the data shows warming for 95% of locations in the 1950–2022 timeframe (looking at a 30-year rolling average). Across all locations, the average annual minimum temperatures in the last 30 years (1993–2022) were warmer by 1.7°C when compared to the 1950–1980 baseline. As a result of this warming, 50% of all measuring stations experienced an increased hardiness zone shift in the observation period.

The historical measured data in Figure 13.4 shows how *arable land is quickly moving northward, shifting the wheat belt into higher and higher latitudes*. Long-running projections, based on current pace of around 160 miles per decade, predict it could go from about 55°N (the current limit) to around 65°N by 2050.

This shift, which we are delving into for the United States, is also observed (and is left to our readers to research if of interest) in the Northern Hemisphere in Europe, Russia, and China, and, in the Southern Hemisphere, in South America (Chile and Argentina, primarily), and Australia. For the Southern Hemisphere, however, the geography is such (only 32% of the overall global landmass is in the Southern Hemisphere, and almost 10% of the hemisphere is in Antarctica, which is uninhabited

---

[5] https://scacis.rcc-acis.org/

and not farmable) that this shift is effectively negligible in terms of shifting the areas of growth, and mostly will result in a diminishing amount of farmland overall, as areas that are currently fertile will become too hot/dry

Figure 13.3 Changes in plant growth over 1983–2013 in northern latitudes.

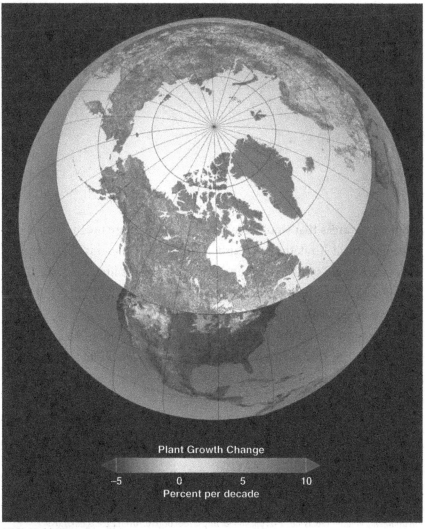

NASA / Public Domain

Figure 13.4 Shifting of hardiness zones in North America -
a) Hardiness zones for the US 1971–2000 and projection 2041–2070.
b) Global warming and potential northward expansion of wheat mega-environment 6 in North America by 2050.[6]

Source: Parker & Abatzoglou – "Projected changes in cold hardiness zones and suitable overwinter ranges of perennial crops over the United States", 2016 / IOP Publishing / CC BY 4.0

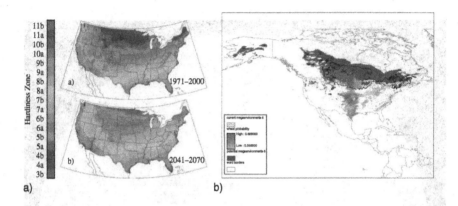

and the new areas that would benefit from the shift are much smaller due to geographical limitations. (South America becomes rapidly narrower with increasingly southern latitudes, and Australia is limited by the Great Australian desert which changes dynamics of potentially fertile land drastically, independently of the latitude.)

The results of this analysis tell us that the investment maturity of NLF is "ready" given that *the shift in hardiness is well established and ongoing since many decades*, and all the pre-requisites for investing in farmland in the areas of interest are in place.

The specific choices of which countries and types of farmland are dependent on the risk appetite and nature of the fund that is investing and will not be covered in this deep dive.

---

[6] Ortiz, Rodomiro et al. (2008). Climate change: Can wheat beat the heat? *Agriculture, Ecosystems & Environment*, Volume 126, Issues 1-2, pp. 46–58. https://doi.org/10.1016/j.agee.2008.01.019

13.7 HOW CROWDED IS NORTHERN LATITUDES FARMLAND?

At the time of writing this book, the assessment of the crowding for NLF as an investment thesis, the call is "unclear." The decision to not call this opportunity with one of the standard levels of crowdedness is due to the fact that there are a wide range of investors that are aggressively investing in farmland in many of the target countries that this thesis targets, but it isn't clear if their investments fall under this thesis or not. Bill Gates, with 275,000 acres owned in July 2024, is the largest farmland investor in the United States,[7] and has often been in the limelight for his choice of large-scale investment in this asset class. Other large investors in this space include several REIT vehicles such as Farmland Partners (FPI), which is the largest in the United States (175,000 acres and ~300 farms) and Gladstone Land Corp. (LAND), which owns ~170 farms and 112,000 acres.

At a global level, there are multiple asset managers focusing on farmland, led by Nuveen which, as per the 2023 Pensions & Investments,[8] is the #1 manager of farmland assets worldwide, with $11.6 billion under management[9] and over 2 million gross acres managed globally.[10]

While these three investors are clearly big players in the general farmland space, they do not appear to be purely focused on the northern latitudes play as such and are rather generalist investors in farmland as a relatively low-risk, low-correlation, stable return investment, without a specific climate angle.

---

[7] https://finance.yahoo.com/news/bill-gates-owns-275-000-150012766.html
[8] https://www.pionline.com/largest-money-managers/2023
[9] AUM is represented by Fair Market Value as of 31 Dec 2023.
[10] As of 31 Dec 2023.

13.8 WHAT IS THE ROOT PROBLEM FOR NORTHERN LATITUDES FARMLAND?

The root problem for NLF is the fact that climate change has been steadily shifting hardiness zones northward in the Northern Hemisphere, and southward in the Southern Hemisphere, and is expected to continue to do so for the remainder of the century.

13.9 WHAT DOES THE ROOT PROBLEM FOR NORTHERN LATITUDES FARMLAND CAUSE?

The shift in latitude for hardiness zones expands arable land to higher and higher latitudes over time (at a pace of ~160 miles per decade), and, concurrently, makes land in lower latitudes drier, hotter, and less productive than what it currently is.

As a result of this, the expectation is that regions of the earth that exhibit relatively low productivity (and, by consequence, value), will become increasingly more similar to current prime agricultural land, while land that is at the warmer/lower latitude extreme of the hardiness belt today will lose value and, over time, fall into desertification.

An example of where northern US states can evolve into can be provided by looking at the vegetation in the Latah formation in Washington State during the Miocene epoch[11] from ~15 million years ago, where the

---

[11] Berry, Edward Wilber. (1928). A REVISION OF THE FLORA OF THE LATAH FORMATION. Chapter H of "Shorter contributions to general geology." 10.3133/pp154H. https://pubs.usgs.gov/publication/pp154H

landscape was dominated by temperate forests and species that are similar to what is currently found in California and the Mediterranean basin.

It is worthy to note that the Miocene (specifically the Middle Miocene Climate Optimum, or MMCO), which we are using in this example, is very close in CO_2 concentration, and projected temperatures, to where the end of the 21st century is expected to settle at (i.e., a global annual mean surface temperature of 18.4°C, ~3°C higher than the beginning of the 21st century and as expected for the end of the century, with a CO_2 concentration between 460 and 580 compared to the current ~420 as of early November 2024).[12]

13.10 WHAT NEEDS TO HAPPEN TO FIX THE ROOT PROBLEM FOR NORTHERN LATITUDES FARMLAND?

This is an unusual case of issue fix question, within the transition finance investing methodology, as the shift in hardiness zones is simply good news for arable land, perennial cash crops, and pastureland in certain US states and northern latitudes in general, and presents a long-term investment opportunity for investors to benefit from.

---

[12] You, Y. and Ribbe et al. (2009), Simulation of the Middle Miocene Climate Optimum. *Geophys. Res. Lett.*, 36, L04702, doi:10.1029/2008GL036571.

13.11 HOW SOON DOES THE FIX NEED TO HAPPEN FOR NORTHERN LATITUDES FARMLAND?

This is a long-term ongoing trend, which will likely accelerate in the coming years and decades, and no specific "fix" is required for this opportunity.

13.12 WHAT IS THE INVESTMENT OPPORTUNITY FOR NORTHERN LATITUDES FARMLAND?

Acquire land in northern latitudes that is currently underpriced when considering the trajectory of improving productivity it is set on, and hold it long term as it becomes more productive and valuable over time, with the increasing temperature and northward shift of the hardiness zones and the increased needs for agricultural produce that will be driven by the global population growth in the 2024–2040 time horizon.

13.13 WHAT IS THE BENEFIT FROM INVESTING IN NORTHERN LATITUDES FARMLAND?

The benefit of investing in NLF is the ownership of productive land that will increasingly come at a premium in climate transition scenarios, given the expected desertification and loss of productivity of currently high-yield areas, and the increased demand for agricultural produce, only partially offset by the projected growth in vertical farming output.

To provide a quantitative assessment of the possible returns for this strategy, we can focus on the United States, for which data is easily available via the US Department of Agriculture National Agricultural Statistics Service,[13] and with a very long track of historical data (some data going back to 1850).

Similar data can be found for Canadian land, at Statistics Canada, the Canadian National Statistical Office, which publishes the Census of Agriculture[14] as well as for many other countries that are in scope for NLF, which we shall leave to our readers to review, in the spirit of not overburdening this book with too much data.

We shall analyze the historical performance of the different types of farmland in the United States under three lenses, respectively, *land value appreciation, return from rental as percentage of land value*, and *Risk-Adjusted Return for the overall investment*, and one forward-looking metric, which is tied to the *projected improvement of the hardiness zone*, and the incremental increase in value that shifting to a more productive hardiness zone would bring.

Farmland Returns for the United States: Land Value

If we take the data from the USDA NASS, we see that there are four separate categories of farmland for which value data is reported, which are, nominally:

AG Land, Cropland: Asset value, measured in $ /acre. As per the USDA: "This category includes cropland harvested, other pasture and

---
[13] https://quickstats.nass.usda.gov
[14] https://www.statcan.gc.ca/en/census-agriculture?MM=as

grazing land that could have been used for crops without additional improvements, cropland on which all crops failed or were abandoned, cropland in summer fallow, and cropland idle or used for cover crops or soil improvement but not harvested and not pastured or grazed."

AG Land, Cropland, Irrigated: Asset value, measured in $ / acre. As per the USDA: "This category includes all land watered by any artificial or controlled means, such as sprinklers, flooding, furrows or ditches, subirrigation, and spreader dikes. Included are supplemental, partial, and preplant irrigation. Each acre was counted only once regardless of the number of times it was irrigated or harvested. If an operation reported less than one acre irrigated, the irrigated land for the operation *was rounded to* one acre. Livestock lagoon wastewater distributed by sprinkler or flood systems was also included."

AG Land, Cropland, Non-irrigated: Asset value, measured in $ / acre. Cropland that is not irrigated.

AG Land, Pastureland: Asset value, measured in $ / acre. Grazable land, inclusive of woodland pasture and cropland pasture. It may be irrigated or dry land.

The values for each of these types of land are not inclusive of buildings, which are available as separate time series if required, but bring in additional complexities tied to the size of the farm being assessed and the age of the building and are therefore germane to the pure farmland analysis that is being reviewed here.

As would be expected, cropland is typically more valuable than pastureland, and irrigated is more valuable than non-irrigated, for obvious reasons.

To keep the analysis to manageable and relevant data, we shall identify a subset of northern US states that stand to benefit from the shift in hardiness zones driven by climate change, and focus on historical and forward-looking data for these.

Sample Deep Dive: Northern Latitudes Farmland

The states that we have selected are:

- Iowa
- Michigan
- Minnesota
- Montana
- Nebraska
- North Dakota
- South Dakota
- Wisconsin
- Wyoming

It is worthy to note that data is available for all states for the generic "cropland" category, but many states do not have data for irrigated/non-irrigated breakdowns, and the starting years for data availability vary between 1998 and 2008, depending on the state we are looking at.

Let's begin by looking at the land value for the selected states between 1996 and 2024 as shown in Figure 13.5 for all cropland. The data shows that between 1996 and 2024, the value of all cropland in these selected states increased by a MOIC of 4.46 over 28 years (not inflation adjusted), with a period (2014–2020) where the growth was slower, and for certain states such as Iowa, South Dakota, and North Dakota, at times negative. The average yearly appreciation for these select states over the period was 6.58%.

Once we observe the Year-Over-Year (YOY) change in value, as shown in Figure 13.6, we see a somewhat cyclical nature of bouts of significant appreciation (at times hitting 40% yearly) centered around 2006, 2013, and 2022.

Once we shift to irrigated farmland we notice how the sample of data from the USDA shrinks dramatically, and we only have data for Montana, Nebraska, and Wyoming (only from 2008), which, however, shows a similar profile, albeit at higher land values as shown in Figure 13.7.

The YOY change analysis, albeit limited to only three states, as shown in Figure 13.8, shows again a peak of appreciation in the 2006–2008 frame,

Figure 13.5 Cropland select US states, value per acre (US$) 1996–2024.

Source: U.S. Department of Agriculture (USDA) / https://www.nass.usda.gov / last accessed February 19, 2025.

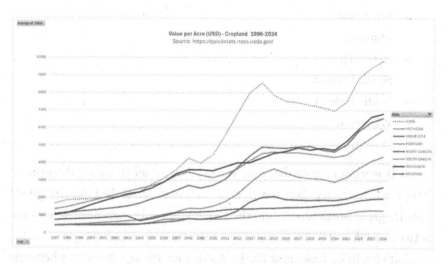

Figure 13.6 Cropland select US states, value YOY Change % 1996–2024.

Source: U.S. Department of Agriculture (USDA) / https://www.nass.usda.gov / last accessed February 19, 2025.

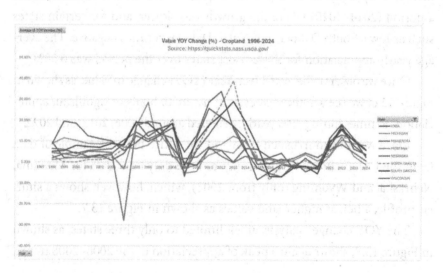

Sample Deep Dive: Northern Latitudes Farmland

Figure 13.7   Irrigated cropland select US states, value per acre (US$) 1996–2024.
Source: U.S. Department of Agriculture (USDA) / https://www.nass.usda.gov / last accessed February 19, 2025.

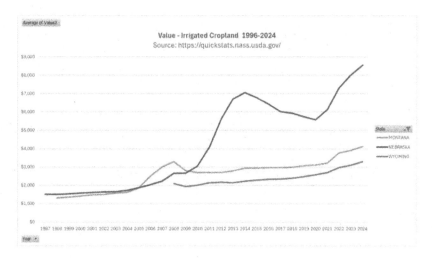

around 2012 and then again around 2022, in line with what was observed for generic cropland. The average yearly appreciation, for this reduced sample, was 5.37%.

Shifting to non-irrigated cropland, the dataset expands slightly, with the addition of South Dakota to the list of states that have reported data to the USDA at this level of granularity. The data for these four states, as per Figure 13.9, breaks down into two distinct patterns, one where there is a steady, but slow appreciation, which we see in Wyoming and Montana, and one of speedy appreciation until 2014, followed by a course correction and decreasing values for ~5 years, and increasing values until 2024, as seen for Nebraska and South Dakota.

The analysis of the YOY change graph in Figure 13.10 allows us to remove the scale effect of the large differences in land value between South Dakota and Nebraska (2024 average value $4,840/acre) and Wyoming and Montana (2024 average value $1,060/acre) and see how all the states

Figure 13.8 Cropland irrigated, select US states, value YOY change % 1996–2024.
Source: U.S. Department of Agriculture (USDA) / https://www.nass.usda.gov / last accessed February 19, 2025.

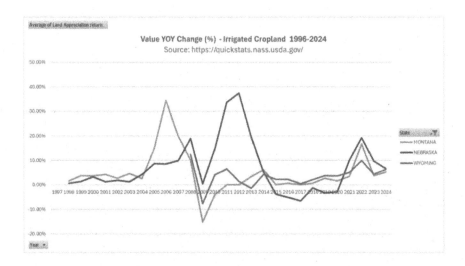

Figure 13.9 Non-irrigated cropland select US states, value per acre (US$) 1998–2024.
Source: U.S. Department of Agriculture (USDA) / https://www.nass.usda.gov / last accessed February 19, 2025.

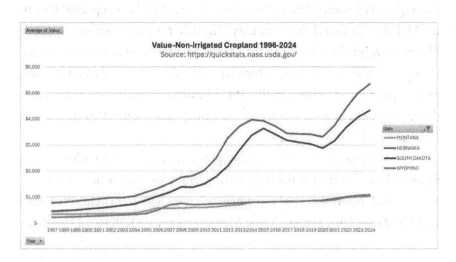

Sample Deep Dive: Northern Latitudes Farmland

Figure 13.10 Non-irrigated cropland, select US states, value YOY change % 1998–2024.
Source: U.S. Department of Agriculture (USDA) / https://www.nass.usda.gov / last accessed February 19, 2025.

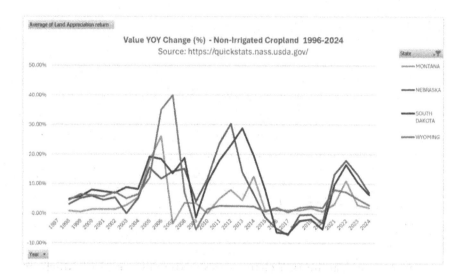

performed as investments over the time period. As per prior asset classes, we observe three peaks in appreciation, centered around 2006, 2012, and 2022. The average yearly appreciation for these four states over the 1998–2024 timeframe has been 6.92%.

Moving to the last asset class, pastureland, we have a full complement of data once again, albeit many states only start reporting from 2008 onward. The picture that the data paints is somewhat different from cropland, as the appreciation slope is not as steep, but the depreciation in the 2014–2020 period is hardly present at all in most states, as can be seen in Figure 13.11, with Iowa being the only state that shows a significant reduction in value during that period. Given the lack of data prior to 2008 for many states, it is not worthwhile to calculate the MOIC for the entire period, but the 2008–2024 window gives an average total appreciation of 33% over 17 years.

Figure 13.11   Pastureland select US states, value per acre (US$) 1998–2024.
Source: U.S. Department of Agriculture (USDA) / https://www.nass.usda.gov/ last accessed February 19, 2025.

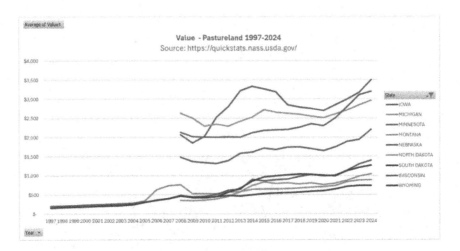

Once we look at the YOY changes, as shown in Figure 13.12, which are mostly limited to post-2008, we notice how this asset class, with the exception of an outlying dataset for Montana in 2006–2010 that seems at odds with the overall performance, is very stable in the level of appreciation, and doesn't show the periodic peaks and troughs that cropland has exhibited over the same period.

Farmland Returns for the United States: Rental

The second major source of investment return on farmland, besides the land appreciation, is whatever income can be obtained either by farming the land or renting it out. For practical investors, who do not have an interest in directly becoming farmers or owning farms as enterprises, this stream of income is achieved via rental of the farm to third parties, which provides potentially less income than direct farming but reduces volatility

Sample Deep Dive: Northern Latitudes Farmland

Figure 13.12   Pastureland, select US states, value YOY Change % 1998–2024.
Source: U.S. Department of Agriculture (USDA) / https://www.nass.usda.gov / last accessed February 19, 2025.

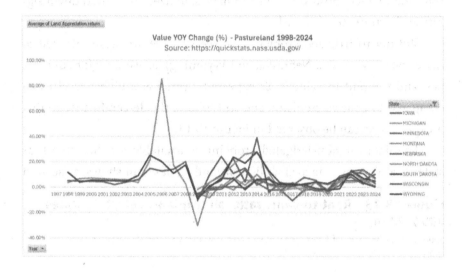

and risk. (There is an additional cost for farmland management companies that needs to be deducted from the rental income, which is not included in the USDA figures, but is not of such entity to change the overall picture.)

As was the case for the land value series, we have data for all four types of land, with the same data limitations that we have seen in the previous sections, and, overall, we can observe a 30-year decline in rent-to-value ratio (as a matter of fact, this trend has been observed for almost half a century), and is due to multiple factors, including the general faster increase in land value compared to the potential return from farming it, due to non-agricultural reasons (potential to develop land as opposed to farm it), interest rates, propensity to invest in short-term assets with lower yields, and low-cost competition from imported crops reducing the appeal and cash value of farming per acre (after all, independently of what an acre of land might be worth, a farmer will only pay the landlord a fraction of what they can make by farming it, as it has to be an economically viable proposition).

If we start by observing the overall rent-to-value series for all Cropland, as shown in Figure 13.13, where we have a full set of data, we see how the average went from ~6.2% in 1997 to ~2.9% today, on a steadily decreasing trajectory, which, however, seems to have stabilized, or slowed down significantly, from 2014 onward.

Shifting to irrigated cropland, we see how we are, again, limited to three states (Montana, Nebraska, and Wyoming), as we were for land values, and the rent-to-value is, as expected, overall at a higher level when compared to generic cropland, and still follows the descending trend that is expected, as can be observed in Figure 13.14.

The data for non-irrigated cropland is available for the same four states that we saw data availability for land values, and shows, as seen in

Figure 13.13   Rent-to-value ratio, all cropland, select US states 1996–2024.
Source: U.S. Department of Agriculture (USDA) / https://www.nass.usda.gov/ last accessed February 19, 2025.

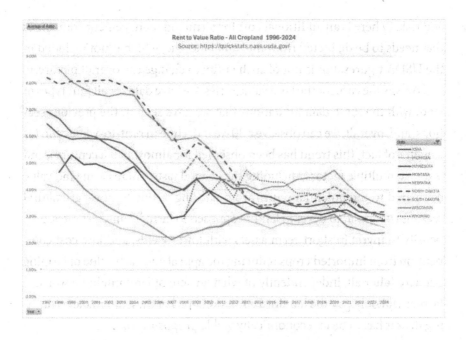

Figure 13.15, similar paths as irrigated cropland, with surprising differences for certain states (Wyoming shows lower rent-to-value for non-irrigated, but Nebraska doesn't, and South Dakota actually has higher rent-to-value for non-irrigated when compared to irrigated).

When we shift to pastureland, we observe, as per Figure 13.16, similar values as cropland, with higher variability between states, and an overall lower starting high mark (~6% compared to ~8%). The downward curve for RTV in the case of pastureland seems to have ended in 2008, in stark contrast with other types of farmland, and a few states show upward trending ratios in the recent decade. This is a very interesting set of data, as

Figure 13.14 Rent-to-value ratio, irrigated cropland, select US states 1996–2024.
Source: U.S. Department of Agriculture (USDA) / https://www.nass.usda.gov/ last accessed February 19, 2025.

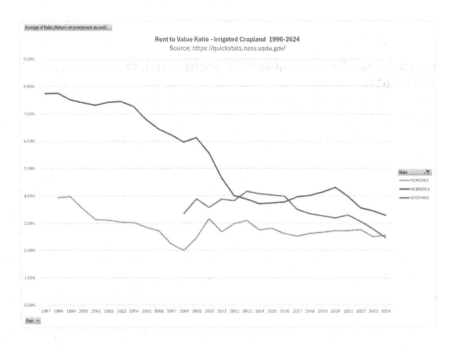

Figure 13.15 Rent-to-value ratio, non-irrigated cropland, select US states 1996–2024.
Source: U.S. Department of Agriculture (USDA) / https://www.nass.usda.gov/ last accessed February 19, 2025.

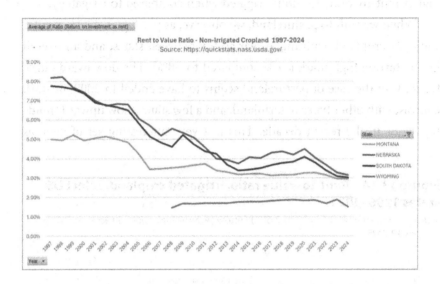

Figure 13.16 Rent-to-value ratio, pastureland, select US states 1996–2024.
Source: U.S. Department of Agriculture (USDA) / https://www.nass.usda.gov / last accessed February 19, 2025.

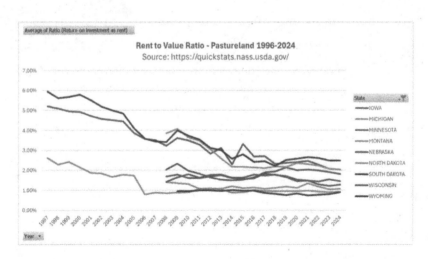

pastureland is the *asset that has the lowest carry costs* of all the four categories that we have observed, *and the least value volatility*.

Farmland Returns for the United States: RAR

The third series of historical data that we will analyze is the Risk-Adjusted Returns (RAR) for the four classes of farmland, where we will aggregate the returns on value appreciation, rental income, and deduct a standardized risk-free rate (we have chosen 90-day US Treasury bills). For the purposes of this analysis, we shall also compare the returns to the S&P yearly returns (also risk adjusted) and will calculate the Sharpe ratio[15] for each.

The data used for S&P, Risk-Free Returns, and Risk-Adjusted S&P are shown in Table 13.1.

Table 13.1 Reference return rates, 1996–2024.

Year	S&P YEARLY Return	S&P Risk Adjusted	Risk-Free Return (90 Day T-Bills)
1996	20.26%	15.04%	5.22%
1997	31.01%	25.78%	5.23%
1998	26.67%	21.48%	5.19%
1999	19.53%	14.92%	4.61%
2000	−10.14%	−16.06%	5.92%
2001	−13.04%	−17.64%	4.60%
2002	−23.37%	−25.14%	1.77%
2003	26.38%	25.28%	1.10%
2004	8.99%	7.91%	1.08%
2005	3.00%	0.25%	2.75%
2006	13.62%	8.98%	4.64%

(Continued)

---
[15] https://en.wikipedia.org/wiki/Sharpe_ratio

Table 13.1 (*Continued*)

Year	S&P YEARLY Return	S&P Risk Adjusted	Risk-Free Return (90 Day T-Bills)
2007	3.53%	−1.45%	4.98%
2008	−38.49%	−40.72%	2.23%
2009	23.45%	23.29%	0.16%
2010	12.78%	12.66%	0.12%
2011	0.00%	−0.08%	0.08%
2012	13.41%	13.33%	0.08%
2013	29.60%	29.55%	0.05%
2014	11.39%	11.35%	0.04%
2015	−0.73%	−0.75%	0.02%
2016	9.54%	9.31%	0.23%
2017	19.42%	18.70%	0.72%
2018	−6.24%	−7.96%	1.72%
2019	28.88%	26.54%	2.34%
2020	16.26%	15.52%	0.74%
2021	26.89%	26.84%	0.05%
2022	−19.44%	−20.40%	0.96%
2023	24.23%	19.16%	5.07%
2024	20.00%	16.00%	4.00%

We can start our analysis, as per prior format, with all cropland data, and review the Risk-Adjusted Returns for selected states, as shown in Figure 13.17.

As we did in previous paragraphs, we notice how there is cyclicality in the returns profile, with 2006, 2012, and 2022 showing marked peaks of returns in most states, and, overall, a better Sharpe ratio and average RAR in almost all states when compared to the S&P 500, as can be observed in Table 13.2, where the average RAR for all the states is 8.7% (versus 6.3 for the S&P 500) and the Sharpe ratio is 1.51 against 0.36.

Figure 13.17   Risk-Adjusted Returns, all cropland, selected states 1998–2024.

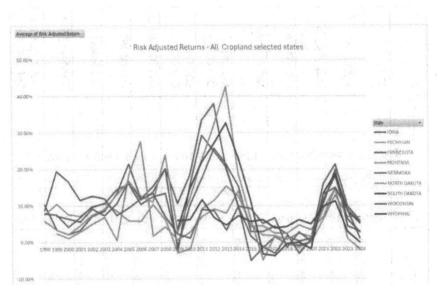

Once we move to irrigated cropland, as show in Figure 13.18, with the smaller sample of states reporting data, we see a peak and trough event for Montana (2006–2009) which is much larger than what is observed for Nebraska, a 2012 peak for Nebraska, that is hardly present in Montana, and the common 2022 lesser peak that has been observed across the board.

Overall, even with the reduced sample of states, we can still determine that irrigated cropland overperforms the S&P 500 in average RAR for all states (7.5% versus 6.3%), albeit this average is entirely driven by Nebraska's outsized contribution (10.4% RAR) while Montana and Wyoming are both slightly lower than the S&P 500, as Table 13.3 shows. The Sharpe Ratios, however, are superior to the S&P (0.36) in all states, and can be considered Adequate/Good for Wyoming (1.53) and the average of all three states (1.25).

Table 13.2 Risk-Adjusted Returns: All cropland and selected benchmarks, 1998–2024.

		IOWA	MICHIGAN	MINNESOTA	MONTANA	NEBRASKA	NORTH DAKOTA	SOUTH DAKOTA	WISCONSIN	WYOMING	ALL States	Risk Free Rate	Risk Adjusted S&P 500
Average RAR 1998-2024		9.12%	6.4%	9.3%	5.9%	11.2%	10.6%	10.7%	8.3%	6.1%	8.7%	2.0%	6.3%
	SD	9.1%	4.8%	6.9%	6.3%	9.8%	10.2%	11.2%	5.2%	2.9%	5.7%	2.0%	17.6%
Sharpe Ratio		1.00	1.35	1.35	0.94	1.15	1.04	0.96	1.61	2.10	1.51	0.00	0.36
Sharpe Ratio Grading		Adequate/Good	Adequate/Good	Adequate/Good	Bad	Adequate/Good	Adequate/Good	Bad	Adequate/Good	Very Good	Adequate/Good	Bad	Bad

Table 13.3 Risk-Adjusted Returns: Irrigated cropland and selected benchmarks, 1998–2024.

	MONTANA	NEBRASKA	WYOMING	ALL States	Risk Free Rate	Risk Adjusted S&P 500
Average RAR 1998-2024	5.7%	10.4%	5.5%	7.5%	2.0%	6.3%
SD	8.0%	11.0%	3.6%	6.0%	2.0%	17.6%
Sharpe Ratio	0.72	0.95	1.53	1.25	0.00	0.36
Sharpe Ratio Grading	Bad	Bad	Adequate/Good	Adequate/Good	Bad	Bad

Figure 13.18   Risk-Adjusted Returns, irrigated cropland, selected states 1998–2024.

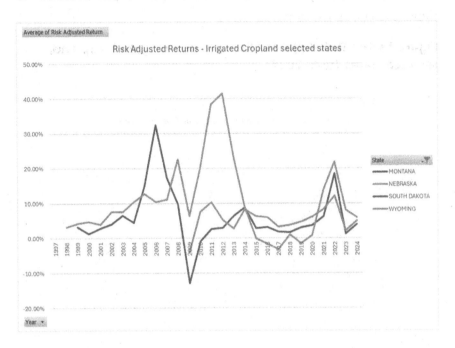

Shifting our attention to non-irrigated cropland, we have, as seen before, a slightly larger sample, as South Dakota reports data for this asset class (Wyoming data, however, is fragmentary), as can be seen in Figure 13.19. In general terms, we can observe the usual three peak (2006, 2012, and 2022) pattern, with some slight changes in magnitude and timing between individual states.

Looking at the detailed analysis of RAR and Sharpe ratios for non-irrigated cropland, as reported in Table 13.4, it is evident how all states that report data have much better Sharpe ratios than the S&P 500 benchmark, and the returns are superior (8.8% average against 6.3% average). The only cases with lower average RAR are Montana (6.1% average against the 6.3% average for the S&P, but with a Sharpe of 0.98) and Wyoming,

PRINCIPLES OF TRANSITION FINANCE INVESTING

where the average of reported data is 3.3%, but data for 2010–2015 is missing (and likely to coincide with a well-recognized spike in returns, as shown in many other states).

Figure 13.19 Risk-Adjusted Returns, non-irrigated cropland, selected states 1998–2024.

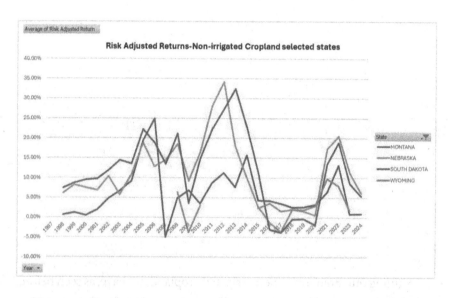

Table 13.4 Risk-Adjusted Returns: Non-irrigated cropland and selected benchmarks, 1998–2024.

	MONTANA	NEBRASKA	SOUTH DAKOTA	WYOMING	Grand Total	Risk Free Rate	Risk Adjusted S&P 500
Average RAR 1998–2024	6.1%	10.9%	11.9%	3.3%	8.8%	2.0%	6.3%
SD	6.2%	8.6%	9.3%	3.3%	6.8%	2.0%	17.6%
Sharpe Ratio	0.98	1.26	1.29	0.99	1.30	0.00	0.36
Sharpe Ratio Grading	Bad	Adequate/ Good	Adequate/ Good	Bad	Adequate/ Good	Bad	Bad

Sample Deep Dive: Northern Latitudes Farmland

As we finally look at the RAR for pastureland, we see the returns in line with the other asset classes, but with a large variability across states. Individual yearly RAR values have surpassed 80% in specific cases (Montana in 2006), as is evident in Figure 13.20. While this is certainly not the norm, we can, however, clearly notice how the returns do not show the marked cyclicality that cropland returns have highlighted. (The 2006, 2012, and 2022 peaks are still present but muted when compared to cropland.)

Figure 13.20   Risk-Adjusted Returns, pastureland, selected states 1998–2024.

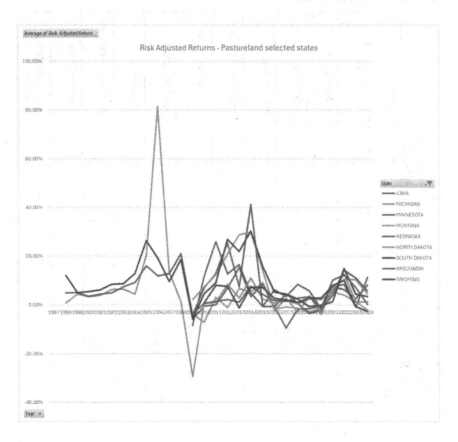

The analysis of the RAR and Sharpe ratios for pastureland between 1998 and 2024, as highlighted in Table 13.5, shows that the average of the nine states that we are reviewing has a RAR of slightly below the S&P 500 benchmark (6.1% against 6.3%), but this average is hampered by the extremely low performance of Michigan (0.9%).

At an individual state level, the differences can be dramatic, with North Dakota recording a 43% better return on a yearly basis (9.06% RAR against 6.3% RAR for the S&P), Nebraska with 44% better returns (9.15% RAR vs.

Table 13.5 Risk-Adjusted Returns: Pastureland and selected benchmarks, 1998–2024.

	IOWA	MICHIGAN	MINNESOTA	MONTANA	NEBRASKA	NORTH DAKOTA	SOUTH DAKOTA	WISCONSIN	WYOMING	All States average	Risk Free Rate	Risk Adjusted S&P 500
Average RAR 1998–2024	4.5%	0.9%	3.3%	6.2%	9.1%	9.1%	10.0%	3.2%	3.7%	6.1%	2.0%	6.3%
SD	8.9%	4.2%	5.7%	16.8%	8.9%	9.9%	8.9%	4.0%	3.8%	8.1%	2.0%	17.6%
Sharpe Ratio	0.51	0.24	0.58	0.37	1.03	0.91	1.12	0.80	0.97	0.76	0.00	0.36
Sharpe Ratio Grading	Bad	Bad	Bad	Bad	Adequate/Good	Bad	Adequate/Good	Bad	Bad	Bad	Bad	Bad

6.3% RAR), and South Dakota posting the highest differential with a 58% improvement on the baseline (10.02% RAR against 6.3% RAR).

Looking at the Sharpe ratios, we see how, for pastureland, every state, except Michigan (0.24), beats the S&P, and certain states, such as Nebraska (1.03) and South Dakota (1.12) posting Adequate/Good Sharpe ratios exceeding the value of 1.0.

It is relevant to note how the pastureland asset class is the one that has the lowest carrying cost, in terms of Farmland Management Companies (FMC), as there is a much less amount of work needed per acre when compared to cropland of different types (the cost of FMC has not been included in this analysis).

Forward-Looking Appreciation Due to Hardiness Zone Improvements

The fourth analysis that is relevant to the NLF opportunity is the one that focuses on the forward-looking appreciation due to the projected hardiness zone improvement in the medium to long term. While the scope and speed of the improvement are dependent on how much additional GHG emissions are produced in the upcoming years,[16] the direction of the trend is unmistakable, and the linkage between hardiness, productivity, and land value is well established.

---

[16] Matthews, Stephen N. et al. (2018). Assessing potential climate change pressures across the conterminous United States: mapping plant hardiness zones, heat zones, growing degree days, and cumulative drought severity throughout this century. RMAP-NRS-9, p. 31. Newtown Square, PA: U.S. Department of Agriculture, Forest Service, Northern Research Station. https://doi.org/10.2737/NRS-RMAP-9

PRINCIPLES OF TRANSITION FINANCE INVESTING

Figure 13.21 Baseline and projections of hardiness zones for the United States in low and high climate-change scenarios.[17]

Source: Matthews et al. (2018). "Assessing potential climate change pressures across the conterminous United States: mapping plant hardiness zones, heat zones, growing degree days, and cumulative drought severity throughout this century."

Note: If we take the values per acre of cropland for the states in NLF that we are studying, and similar states that have higher hardiness zones (i.e., states that currently look like what these states will look like in mid-century or later), and observe the average value per acre by average hardiness zone, we can highlight the patterns that we see in Table 13.6.

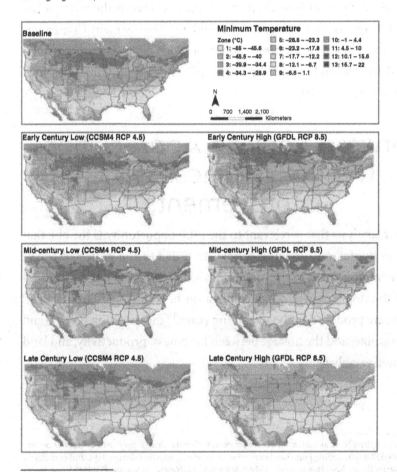

[17] Note: To define the coldest day per year, daily minimum temperatures were identified within the period July 1 to June 30, with the year assigned to the first 6 months of the 12-month period. Zone categories follow the USDA definitions (Cathey 1990). Time periods: baseline (1980–2009); early century (2010–2039); mid-century (2040–2069); late century (2070–2099).

Table 13.6 Value per acre and increase in value by average hardiness zone at state level.

State Hardiness Zone Average	All Cropland Value per Acre Average	Delta % Increase from Lower to Higher Bucket	Pastureland Value per Acre Average	Delta % Increase from Lower to Higher Bucket
Average 6+	$ 6,624.00	11%	$ 2,922.00	39%
Average 5–6	$ 5,962.50	26%	$ 2,100.00	20%
Average 4–5	$ 4,742.50	154%	$ 1,749.25	87%
Average 3–4	$ 1,870.00		$ 934.50	

If we observe Figure 13.21, taken from Matthews et al., we can see the baseline hardiness zones (2018) and the different projections both for RCP (Representative Concentration Pathway) 4.5, a scenario that stabilizes radiative forcing at 4.5 watts per square meter in the year 2100 without ever exceeding that value, as well as for RCP 8.5 (where the forcing is 8.5 watts per square meter). For perspective, RCP 4.5 is the equivalent of a 2–3 °C warming by 2100, which is a very likely scenario (given 1.5 ° have already been achieved at the moment of writing this book), while RCP 8.5 is in the region of ~4.5 °C, representing the current consensus for a "worst-case scenario" for global warming. The time projections are for early-century (current to 2040), mid-century (2040–2070), and late-century (2070 to 2100), with the early-century being the most relevant to short-term investments.

It is interesting to notice how the largest changes occur in the middle of the country, in the northern latitudes, where the mitigating effects of the coastal climate are less evident.

The table shows us, once we calculate the average hardiness zone for a specific state (which is done by averaging the hardiness zones across the entire state), what the average land value for the bucket (3–4 hardiness average, has an average value of $1,870 per acre of cropland and $934 per acre of pastureland) and what the change in average value is when moving to the following bucket (for example, if moving to the 4–5 hardiness average, i.e., an average between 4.0 and less than 5.0, the increase of value for cropland is 154% and for pastureland is 87%).

This table allows us to forecast, once we have an estimate of where the average hardiness of a state will be by a certain date, the approximate increase in land value that needs to be added to the baseline, as a result of the shift to a more valuable hardiness zone.

As is intuitive, the biggest jump in value happens from the hardiness zones of 3 to 4, which are low-value, low-productivity farmland, into the 4 to 5 hardiness zones, which become much more valuable and productive farmland, with further increases being less impactful at a percentage level.

Once we apply these percentages to the NLF states that we have selected, for cropland and farmland, we obtain the additional projections to 2040 that are shown in Table 13.7.

Table 13.7 Projected increases in land value due to hardiness zone improvements, 2023–2040.

State	Average Hardiness Zone 2023	Projected Average Hardiness Zone 2040	Jump Zone	Delta Increase Value Expected Cropland 2023–2040	Delta Increase Value Expected Pastureland 2023–2040
IOWA	5	6.65	5 to 6	11%	39%
MICHIGAN	5.25	8	5 to 8	33%	117%
MINNESOTA	4	5	4 to 5	26%	20%
MONTANA	3.9	5.6	3 to 5	179%	107%
NEBRASKA	5.1	6.6	5 to 6	11%	39%
NORTH DAKOTA	3.8	4.5	3 to 4	154%	87%
SOUTH DAKOTA	4.5	5.7	4 to 5	26%	20%
WISCONSIN	4.05	6	4 to 6	37%	59%
WYOMING	4.7	5.75	4 to 5	26%	20%

Once we convert these 2023–2040 projected value increases to annual CAGR, we obtain the data presented in Table 13.8, which varies from an additional 0.65% annual projected appreciation for Iowa cropland, up to 6.00% for North Dakota cropland, showing effects of improving hardiness zones as a result of climate shifting trends.

Once we join the historical returns (Risk-Adjusted Returns from land appreciation and rental) together with the projected appreciation due to hardiness zone improvements (assuming the 1998–2024 average will stay

Table 13.8 Estimated CAGR due to projected shifts in hardiness zones, 2024–2040 for selected states within the NLF investment opportunity, based on RCP 4.5.

State and Asset	Projected Additional CAGR 2024–2040 Due to Hardiness Zone Improvements
Iowa Crop	0.65%
Iowa Pasture	2.08%
Michigan Crop	1.80%
Michigan Pasture	4.96%
Minnesota Crop	1.45%
Minnesota Pasture	1.15%
Montana Crop	6.62%
Montana Pasture	4.65%
Nebraska Crop	0.65%
Nebraska Pasture	2.08%
North Dakota Crop	6.00%
North Dakota Pasture	3.99%
South Dakota Crop	1.45%
South Dakota Pasture	1.15%
Wisconsin Crop	1.99%
Wisconsin Pasture	2.94%
Wyoming Crop	1.45%
Wyoming Pasture	1.15%

stable in the 2024–2040 timeframe, which is a conservative assumption), we see an estimate of the possible CAGR for the different types of farmland assets by state, and the relative contribution that the Hardiness shift provides to the total return, as shown in Table 13.9.

The aggregate data show how the picture of returns and relative impact of hardiness shifts, at the aggregate state level at which this analysis has been performed (for the obvious needs to keep it to a short enough size to fit within the allocated space in this chapter), is quite varied, with states such as the Dakotas, Nebraska, and Montana showing projected returns in the mid- and low-teens, both for cropland and pastureland, while certain assets (pastureland in Wyoming and Minnesota, for example) are extremely unappealing even when considering an increase in value due to climate change.

It's worth noting how the relative impact of the increase in hardiness has a significant amount of variability between states, and amongst the high-return states varies from 10% for South Dakota Pastureland all the way up to 52% for Montana Cropland.

Table 13.9 Aggregate effect of 1998–2024 average RAR for farmland coupled with projected impact of shift in hardiness zones for selected NLF states in the United States.

State and Asset	Projected Additional CAGR 2024–2040 Due to Hardiness Zone Improvements	1998–2024 Historical Yearly Return (RAR)	% of Ttal Projected Return Due to Hardiness Improvement	Historical + Expected CAGR by Hardiness Increase	RANK
Iowa Crop	0.65%	9.12%	6.65%	**9.77%**	11
Iowa Pasture	2.08%	4.54%	31.41%	**6.62%**	14
Michigan Crop	1.80%	6.43%	21.87%	**8.23%**	12
Michigan Pasture	4.96%	0.98%	83.45%	**5.94%**	16

Sample Deep Dive: Northern Latitudes Farmland

State and Asset	Projected Additional CAGR 2024–2040 Due to Hardiness Zone Improvements	1998–2024 Historical Yearly Return (RAR)	% of Ttal Projected Return Due to Hardiness Improvement	Historical + Expected CAGR by Hardiness Increase	RANK
Minnesota Crop	1.45%	9.33%	13.45%	**10.78%**	9
Minnesota Pasture	1.15%	3.31%	25.78%	**4.46%**	18
Montana Crop	6.62%	5.94%	52.70%	**12.56%**	3
Montana Pasture	4.65%	6.24%	42.69%	**10.89%**	8
Nebraska Crop	0.65%	11.24%	5.47%	**11.89%**	5
Nebraska Pasture	2.08%	9.15%	18.52%	**11.23%**	6
North Dakota Crop	6.00%	10.63%	36.08%	**16.63%**	1
North Dakota Pasture	3.99%	9.06%	30.58%	**13.05%**	2
South Dakota Crop	1.45%	10.72%	11.92%	**12.17%**	4
South Dakota Pasture	1.15%	10.02%	10.30%	**11.17%**	7
Wisconsin Crop	1.99%	8.33%	19.29%	**10.32%**	10
Wisconsin Pasture	2.94%	3.23%	47.64%	**6.17%**	15
Wyoming Crop	1.45%	6.08%	19.26%	**7.53%**	13
Wyoming Pasture	1.15%	3.71%	23.67%	**4.86%**	17

13.14 WHAT IS THE MARKET SIZE FOR NORTHERN LATITUDES FARMLAND?

In order to keep the length of this deep dive to a manageable size, we shall only look at the market size for farmland in the United States, with the understanding that similar analysis can and should be performed, if of interest, for any other applicable geography.

Farmland in the United States: Current State

According to the 2022 Census of Agriculture,[18] published by the US Department of Agriculture:

> In 2022, the United States had just over **1.9 million farms**, down 6.9% from 2017. These farms accounted for 880.1 million acres of land in farms, or 39% of all US land. This was a decline of 20.1 million acres (2.2%) from the 2017 level Table 13.10.
>
> During the same time, the **average farm size** increased 5.0%, from 441 acres in 2017 to **463 acres** in 2022.
>
> Between 2017 and 2022, almost all of the size classes decreased in number of farms. **Only the largest class (5,000 acres or larger) increased in number of farms.**

The definition of farm, as used for this data, is "any place from which $1,000 or more of agricultural products were produced and sold, or normally would have been sold, during the census year."

The decline in active farms in the United States is a long-term trend, which has been observed since the turn of the century, with a fairly constant declining slope as shown in Figure 13.22.

---

[18] https://www.nass.usda.gov/AgCensus/

Sample Deep Dive: Northern Latitudes Farmland

Table 13.10 Farms and farmland key metrics and changes, 2017–2022.

Farms and Farmland, 2017 and 2022			
Metric	2017	2022	% change
Number of farms	2,042,220	1,900,487	−6.9
Land in farms (acres)	900,217,576	880,100,848	−2.2
Average farm size (acres)	441	463	+5.0

Source: United States Department of Agriculture / www.nass.usda.gov/AgCensus / Public Domain

Figure 13.22 Twenty-year trends for farmland in the United States.
Source: United States Department of Agriculture / www.nass.usda.gov/AgCensus / Public Domain

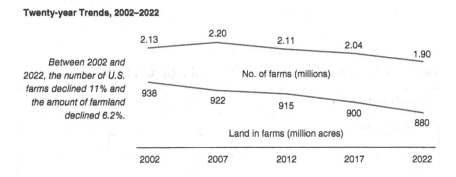

Farmland is mostly concentrated in the center of the country, as seen in Figure 13.23, with almost 40% of land being considered farmland, but a great variability between states, with counties in the central area from North Dakota to Texas with over 70% of the land used for agriculture.

If we look at the breakdown of land use within the farmland across the nation, as we can see in Table 13.11, we observe how cropland and permanent pasture represent almost 90% of the total, with Woodland covering 8% and the remaining 4% allocated in land in farmsteads, buildings, livestock facilities, etc. Cropland is primarily concentrated in midwestern states, while permanent pasture is more common in western states.

Figure 13.23 Farmland as percent of land area by county, 2022.
Source: United States Department of Agriculture / www.nass.usda.gov/AgCensus / Public Domain

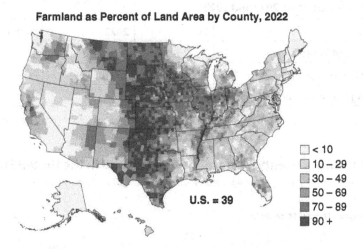

Table 13.11 Land use for farmland in the United States, 2022.

Type of Land Use	acres (million)	% of total
Permanent pasture	393	45
Cropland	382	43
Harvested	*301*	*34*
Woodland	72	8
Other	33	4
Total	880	100

Source: United States Department of Agriculture / www.nass.usda.gov/AgCensus / Public Domain

In terms of *Farm Specialization*, using the North American Industry Classification System (NAICS), we can observe how *Oilseed and grain production* and *Cattle and dairy production* represent almost 75% of the totality of land usage, with 32% and 41% respectively, with other usages shown in Table 13.12. To put this data into perspective, the number of farms specializing in cattle and dairy production in the 2022 census was 568,972.

Sample Deep Dive: Northern Latitudes Farmland

The distribution of land by size of farms is skewed toward the tails, with very large farms (over 5,000 acres) owning 42% of the land, and very small farms (1–49 acres) representing the plurality of farms (42%), as shown in Figure 13.24.

Table 13.12 Farm Specialization in the United States in 2022, by land usage.

NAICS category	% of farmland	% of farms
Cattle and dairy	41	30
Oilseeds and grains	32	18
Other crops	14	23
Other animals	7	10
Specialty crops (fruits, vegetables, nursery)	3	10
Hogs and pigs	1	1
Poultry and eggs	1	4
Sheep and goats	1	4

Source: United States Department of Agriculture / www.nass.usda.gov/AgCensus / Public Domain

Figure 13.24 Distribution of US farms by size and % of farmland owned.
Source: United States Department of Agriculture / www.nass.usda.gov/AgCensus / Public Domain

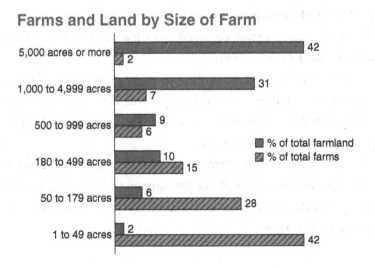

Table 13.13 Land ownership by percentage of farms and land.

Land Ownership	% of farms	% of farmland	Average size acres	Average size dollars
Full owners	72	35	230	$ 144,502
Part owners	22	56	1,155	$ 688,285
Tenants	6	9	655	$ 461,354

Source: United States Department of Agriculture / www.nass.usda.gov/AgCensus / Public Domain

The 2022 snapshot of ownership of land for US farms shows a mixed picture of full owners, part owners and tenants, with 39% of the farmland being actively farmed being rented from others. The part owner model, while only representing 22% of the number of farms, covers over half the land in the country (56%) showing that this setup leads to typically larger farms in both acreage and sales. Detailed data can be seen in Table 13.13.

Farmland in the United States: Projections

The forward-looking projections for agribusiness in general are dominated by the drivers of *global population* growth, *expected to reach 9.7 billion by 2050*, and *agricultural production needs*, which are also *expected to grow, by as much as 60% by mid-century*.

Expectations are that the evolution of large portions of the global population into middle-class conditions will drive a requirement for higher-quality diets, more proteins, and increased grain and high-value agricultural production in general.

Within this framework, further exacerbated by water scarcity, partially driven by global warming itself, the pressure on the agricultural sector will be strong, and the demand for land and agricultural products is expected to be solid and growing.

Figure 13.25   1961–2050 Population and arable land per capita data (and projections).
Sources: https://population.un.org/ & https://www.fao.org/faostat

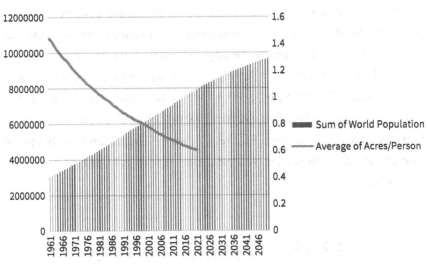

As shown in Figure 13.25, if we turn to the Food and Agriculture Organization of the United Nations (FAOSTAT)[19] and to the UN World Population[20] we can see how, since 1961, while the population has grown in a stable fashion and is projected to hit almost 10 billion people by 2050, the number of acres of arable land has not followed the same trend, resulting in the ratio of arable land per capita steadily declining (which has required constant improvement in agriculture to keep

---

[19] https://www.fao.org/faostat/en/
[20] https://population.un.org/

up with the food production requirements). Given the finite nature of arable land (and farmland in general), there is no reasonable case to be made to expect this trend to change direction in any meaningful way, setting the stage for increasing values and desirability for farmland in the years to come.

Part of the additional demand for agricultural produce will be generated by the increased productivity that higher levels of CO_2 will entail, which is estimated to be approximately 13% by 2050 for most crops,[21] but this effect is not sufficient to offset the projected increase in demand and will need to be coupled with additional factors such as the growth of indoors farming (vertical farming) and technology-driven improvements to improve efficiency, water usage, and recovery of drought-stricken areas (to increase the overall amount of farmland available).

13.15 WHAT IS THE LONG-TERM VISION FOR NORTHERN LATITUDES FARMLAND INVESTMENTS?

Given the type of investment, trends, and horizons that are typical of farmland investments, and the investor lens, as opposed to an operator type approach, the natural long-term vision for NLF is *buy and rent*, with the rental portion managed via the services of a Farm Management Company.

---

[21] Jaggard, KW, Qi, A, and Ober, ES. (2010). Possible changes to arable crop yields by 2050. *Philos Trans R Soc Lond B Biol Sci.* Sep 27; 365(1554): 2835-51. doi: 10.1098/rstb.2010.0153. PMID: 20713388; PMCID: PMC2935124.

The concentration of investment in select states also allows for using a limited number of FMC relationships, thus reducing the expenditure of time and money via economy of scale.

13.16 WHAT IS THE TRIGGER FOR NORTHERN LATITUDES FARMLAND INVESTMENTS, AND HAS IT ALREADY OCCURRED?

The trigger for NLF if the ongoing warming of the planet, which has started with the Industrial Revolution, and accelerated dramatically in the last 60 years. The trigger therefore has been fully activated, and the investment opportunity doesn't require any further tipping point for it to be viable. The overall growth of the global population and economy, both of which are generally expected to continue for at least a few decades, are additional force multipliers, as they will increase the demand for agricultural products, in a world where the overall amount of productive farmland is stable or decreasing (due to the nature of the Southern Hemisphere that we have discussed earlier). Vertical farming (i.e., indoor farming in multilayered setups) has the potential to somewhat ease and reduce the pressure that will be generated by the population growth and supply crunch on traditional agricultural land, but it cannot counterbalance the need for pastureland, and for specialty crops which are not suitable to short-term automated production in indoor settings.

13.17 WHICH GEOGRAPHIES HAVE BEEN IDENTIFIED FOR NORTHERN LATITUDES FARMLAND?

As an overall strategy, the geographies that are targets for NLF across the world are (independently of geopolitical considerations):

- Northern Hemisphere:
  - Canada
  - Northern United States
  - United Kingdom
  - Ireland

Figure 13.26 NASA GISS temperature trend, 2000–2009.
Source: Robert Simmon / NASA / Public Domain
Note: There's a strong Arctic amplification compared to the weak Antarctic amplification.

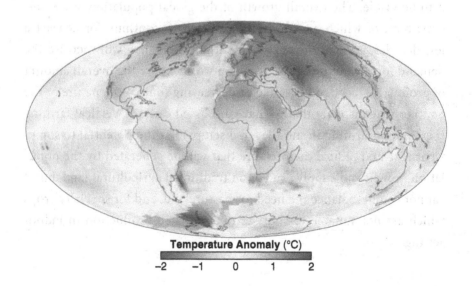

- Northern European countries
- Baltic countries
- Russia
- Mongolia
- Kazakhstan
- Southern Hemisphere
  - Chile
  - Argentina
  - Australia
  - New Zealand

For the Southern Hemisphere, besides the already mentioned geography-driven constraints, the warming trends are less accelerated by the much weaker polar amplification that is observed in the Antarctic, when compared to the Arctic, as can be seen in Figure 13.26.

CHAPTER FOURTEEN

SAMPLE DEEP DIVE: ENERGY EFFICIENCY FOR BUILDINGS

Ensuring your property doesn't become a stranded asset

14.1 WHICH IS THE CLIMATE DRIVER FOR ENERGY EFFICIENCY FOR BUILDINGS?

The transition finance driver for Energy Efficiency for Buildings (Figure 14.1) is primarily transition risk, as the mechanism via which the driver is transmitted is increasing regulation, albeit there is a smaller driver which is chronic physical risk, as the global warming of the environment in general drives Energy Efficiency for Buildings, as the need to cool

Figure 14.1   Descriptive views of Energy Efficiency for Buildings.

Generated with AI using Perchance

buildings down will become more widespread, and inefficient buildings cost more to cool than efficient ones, independently of the presence or absence of a carbon tax.

14.2   WHICH FUNDS DO ENERGY EFFICIENCY FOR BUILDINGS ENERGY FALL UNDER?

Energy Efficiency for Buildings is an opportunity that is primarily a Growth Strategy Fund opportunity, and, secondarily, a Public Strategy Fund opportunity.

14.3   WHAT IS THE TRL FOR ENERGY EFFICIENCY FOR BUILDINGS?

On average, the Technology Readiness Level of Energy Efficiency for Buildings is considered TRL 9 (*actual system proven in operational environment*) as most of the technologies (insulation, solar panels, energy storage solutions) are currently developed and in growth stages.

Sample Deep Dive: Energy Efficiency for Buildings

14.4   DETERMINE THE INVESTMENT HORIZON FOR ENERGY EFFICIENCY FOR BUILDINGS

The investment horizon for Energy Efficiency for Buildings is determined to be 5–10 years, as most of the opportunities are standard technology development opportunities, which do not require the typical Transition Finance long-term investment horizons of 15–20 years.

14.5   WHAT IS THE INVESTMENT MATURITY FOR ENERGY EFFICIENCY FOR BUILDINGS?

The investment maturity of Energy Efficiency for Buildings is estimated, as of 2024, to be "ready," as investment opportunities are currently ready for investment in this space.

14.6   HOW CROWDED IS ENERGY EFFICIENCY FOR BUILDINGS?

As of year-end 2024, the crowdedness of Energy Efficiency for Buildings is evaluated as "not crowded yet," meaning that the opportunity has not yet become known to many investors, the number of VC deals is small, and there aren't any significant PE deals to be found. No companies have gone public doing exclusively what this opportunity focuses on. As a quantitative measure, a Google News search for "energy efficiency buildings capital raise announced" returns ~40 hits as of March 2025.

14.7 WHAT IS THE ROOT PROBLEM FOR ENERGY EFFICIENCY FOR BUILDINGS?

Transition scenarios require emissions reduction targets for GHG over time. Additionally, the overall warming of the global climate will increase the requirements for building cooling, which will increase operating energy consumption costs.

14.8 WHAT DOES THE ROOT PROBLEM FOR ENERGY EFFICIENCY FOR BUILDINGS CAUSE?

Existing buildings will face increasingly steep costs tied to their CO_{2e} emissions used for heating/cooling. High-emissions buildings will lose value and might end up as stranded assets altogether.[1] Energy usage for building cooling will increase (building heating requirements, on the other hand, will decrease, and will somewhat offset this effect).

---

[1] Zimmerman, Greg. Buildings Go Net-Zero Energy, Tackle Climate Change.- *No longer just for boutique buildings, net-zero energy is a goal increasingly within reach. Even existing buildings that plan for "zero over time" can get to net-zero energy.* https://www.facilitiesnet.com/green/article/Buildings-Go-Net-Zero-Energy-Tackle-Climate-Change--18034

Sample Deep Dive: Energy Efficiency for Buildings

14.9 WHAT NEEDS TO HAPPEN TO FIX THE ROOT PROBLEM FOR ENERGY EFFICIENCY FOR BUILDINGS?

Building owners will either have to offset their increased and baseline emissions (via VCM), reduce their emissions (via conversion of buildings to improve efficiency) or face steep penalties.

As an example of this mechanism and how it works, we can observe the French case where any property is required to have a third-party issued Energy Performance Diagnostic (in French, DPE, recorded at the French Agency for Ecological Transition),[2] as a mandatory requirement since 2006 for properties to be sold, and since 2007 for rental properties. The rating is based both on energy consumption (A-G, the DPE certificate, on the left in Figure 14.2) and on direct GHG emissions (A-G, the GES certificate, on the right).

As of 2024, any property that uses over 450 kWh/m^2/year (F and G classes) is under prohibition to rent to third parties, which affects 81% of small homes in France (small homes, due to hot water and gas usage,

Figure 14.2 French DPE and GES certification example.
Source: DPE GES: définition, différences, objectifs et évolutions 2025 / https://www.dimo-diagnostic.net/actualite-diagnostic-immobilier/dpe-ges, Last accessed on April 11, 2025 / Dimo Diagnostic.

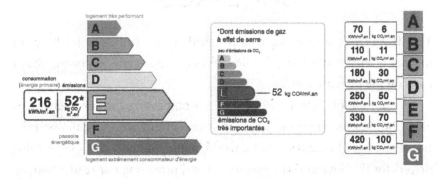

---

[2] https://www.ademe.fr/en/frontpage/

are more energy inefficient than large ones, as the energy usage for these specific applications is diluted over a smaller number of square meters).

Any sale of a property that is classed as G or F will require, starting April 2025, a mandatory energy audit, and the 2025 limit for energy efficiency will be lowered to 421 kWh/m^2/year, making 7% of all apartments and houses in the French territories unfit for rental.

By 2028, the limit will be lowered to properties in the F class of energy consumption (331 to 420 kWh/m^2/year) and in 2034 the Category E (251 to 330 kWh/m^2/year) properties will also be considered unsuitable.

As a data point, for the Paris region, residential properties classified G, F, or E cover approximately 45% of the total market, giving a clear estimate of how large the market for energy-efficiency retrofitting in France will be in the next decade, especially considering that the French government is actively encouraging subsidies and tax reduction credits to property owners who embark in investments to improve energy consumption on residential buildings.

14.10 HOW SOON DOES THE FIX NEED TO HAPPEN FOR ENERGY EFFICIENCY FOR BUILDINGS?

This is already an ongoing concern, with many countries pushing for increased energy efficiency in the real estate space and imposing higher costs on the higher emitters.

As an example, not meant to be all-encompassing and comprehensive, Table 14.1 shows a current snapshot of energy efficiency regulation for a select number of countries in the world, highlighting the kind of ongoing drivers for this investment opportunity, and providing our reader with an idea of the state of play in the field.

Sample Deep Dive: Energy Efficiency for Buildings

Table 14.1 Select list of Energy Efficiency for Buildings laws by countries/regions.

Country/Region	Standard/Law	Impact
Belgium	Renovation Requirement Law	In 2020, Belgium created an economic recovery plan that focuses on energy renovation of buildings, offering help and incentives for property owners. In January 2023, the Flemish government made a rule that all homes bought from that year with class E or F must be upgraded to class D or better within five years. They also froze rental prices for class E and F properties for one year. Authorities can deny permits for projects not meeting energy efficiency standards, with rent limits for class D and E, and a ban for class F. Since October 2022, Brussels has also banned rent indexation for class F and G housing.
Canada - Quebec	Montreal's Building Emissions Bylaw[3]	The bylaw created by the City of Montreal about disclosing greenhouse gas emissions and rating large buildings was enacted in 2021 to help the city reach carbon neutrality by 2050. This regulation requires owners of large buildings to: • Show the types and amounts of energy used in their buildings • Get a greenhouse gas emission performance rating from the city • Display their rating and make it accessible on the city's official website.
Cyprus	National Action Plan	The National Action Plan for Nearly Zero Energy Buildings (NZEBs) includes measures for after 2020. These rules apply to both new and existing buildings but differ by their use. Buildings with major renovations over 1,000 m^2 must meet energy performance standards, insulation levels of new constructions, and achieve at least a B rating on the Energy Performance Certificate (EPC).[4]

(Continued)

---

[3] https://montreal.ca/en/articles/law-concerning-ghg-emission-disclosures-and-ratings-large-buildings-20548

[4] Olasolo-Alonso, López-Ochoa, L.M., and Las-Heras-Casas, Jesús et al. *Energy & Buildings* 281 (2023) 112751.

Table 14.1 (Continued)

Country/Region	Standard/Law	Impact
England/Wales	Minimum Energy Efficiency Standard [MEES]	MEES was introduced in April 2018, setting a scale from A (most efficient) to F (least efficient) for energy ratings. It is illegal for landlords to renew or issue leases for properties rated F or G, with severe penalties for non-compliance. From April 2023, landlords need a minimum rating of E, risking 10% of London offices becoming unviable without upgrades. By April 2030, all commercial buildings must have a rating of B or higher, requiring significant improvements for many properties.
European Union	Energy Performance of Buildings Directive	The European Green Deal is the main growth strategy to make the EU economy sustainable, aiming for net zero emissions by 2050. This is crucial for real estate firms as it will change their business models, market demand, and financing. The revised Energy Performance of Buildings Directive set new Minimum Energy Performance Standards: from 2027, commercial properties need an EPC rating of C; from 2030, a rating of B; and by 2035, as many residential properties as possible should have a rating of C when cost-effective and practical.
Germany	Buildings Energy Act (Gebäudeenergiegesetz, or GEG)	The Buildings Energy Act, effective November 1, 2020, updates regulations on building efficiency and meets European energy performance standards. It sets criteria for energy use in new and old buildings and promotes advanced technology and renewable energy to tackle inefficiency. Germany struggles to reach a 65% to 73% energy reduction goal due to many older buildings and inefficient heating systems.

Sample Deep Dive: Energy Efficiency for Buildings

Country/Region	Standard/ Law	Impact
Greece	Law 4122/2013 and Law 3661/2008	In Greece, Law 4122/2013 follows Directive 2010/31/EU. Law 3661/2008 requires new buildings to use solar thermal systems for part of their hot water needs, with a minimum solar contribution of 60% annually. Existing buildings being renovated must improve energy efficiency if feasible. The Ministry of Environment and Energy provides support and has set an energy efficiency target for 2020.[5]
Italy	EPBD Adoption law	Italy must reduce energy use in existing residential buildings by at least 16% by 2030, with even higher targets later. The focus should be on cutting energy consumption by at least 55% in the worst-performing 43% of these buildings. Similar goals apply to nonresidential buildings. Starting January 1, 2030, all new private buildings must be zero-emission, and public buildings must meet this standard by January 1, 2028, achieving nearly zero-energy status. For major renovations, where costs exceed 25% of the building's value or surface area, measures must be taken to improve energy performance in line with the Energy Performance of Buildings Directive.
Malta	Legal Notice 238 of 2006, Legal Notice 261 of 2008, Legal Notice 376 of 2012, Legal Notice 47 of 2018	The Maltese legal framework assigns the Building Regulation Board the responsibility of revising the existing minimum energy performance standards based on findings from cost-optimal studies. A working group, comprising representatives from the Building Regulation Board, the Building Regulation Office, and the Ministry of Energy and Health, has prepared the Technical Document F. The stipulations outlined in this document pertain to fixed building services that are either being designed or installed in both new and existing structures.[6]

(Continued)

---

[5] Olasolo-Alonso, P. et al. *Energy & Buildings* 281 (2023) 112751.

[6] Olasolo-Alonso, P. et al. *Energy & Buildings* 281 (2023) 112751.

Table 14.1 (*Continued*)

Country/Region	Standard/Law	Impact
Portugal	National System of Energy Certification and Indoor Air Quality in Buildings	The Portuguese State improves energy efficiency and indoor air quality in buildings through the National System of Energy Certification and Indoor Air Quality. This includes rules from Directive 2002/91/CE and Directive 2010/31/EU. The regulations cover design specs for HVAC systems, energy consumption limits, maintenance requirements, performance monitoring, and training standards for technicians.
Spain	EPBD adoption law (Urban Rehabilitation and Regeneration Plan)	The main goals of this initiative are to improve Spain's current buildings and increase the availability of social rental housing in energy-efficient structures, with a total planned investment of 15.3 billion Euros. The Regeneration Plan includes various reforms and investments, including the "Energy Rehabilitation of Buildings Program," which focuses on energy efficiency and renewable energy. The Spanish government has also started a "Program for the Construction of Social Rental Housing in Energy-Efficient Buildings" with a budget of 1 billion Euros to develop about 25,000 affordable rental homes through public-private partnerships, contributing 50,000 Euros per unit.
UAE - Dubai	Dubai's Green Building Regulations and Specifications	In 2011, Dubai introduced the Dubai Green Building Regulations and Specifications to reduce energy demand by 30%. Initially focused on government buildings, the regulations expanded in 2014 to cover all new commercial, public, and industrial buildings, along with many existing properties. The aim is for new buildings to achieve net-zero carbon by 2030 and for all buildings to reach this status by 2050. The regulations include requirements for HVAC systems and energy-efficient zoning in buildings. By 2022, these regulations influenced over 289 million square feet of properties.

Sample Deep Dive: Energy Efficiency for Buildings

Country/Region	Standard/ Law	Impact
US - New York	New York's Local Law 97	In 2019, the city passed Local Law 97 (LL97) to cut emissions by 40% by 2030 and 80% by 2050. This law is part of Mayor de Blasio's New York City Green New Deal, which aims for carbon neutrality by 2050. LL97 sets carbon emission limits for larger buildings, which include those over 25,000 square feet and groups of buildings on the same lot that exceed 50,000 square feet. Landlords not complying will face fines starting in 2024, with higher penalties by 2030. By May 2025, affected buildings must submit an annual Greenhouse Gas Emission report. The goal is to encourage sustainable practices and energy efficiency.

14.11 WHAT IS THE INVESTMENT OPPORTUNITY FOR ENERGY EFFICIENCY FOR BUILDINGS?

Identify and invest in companies or emerging players in the "Zero over Time" building conversion field (focusing both on the new building technologies as well as the renovation of existing buildings to upgrade energy efficiency) to gain a foothold in this new market.

The fields that this opportunity includes are, among others, listed in Table 14.2.

Table 14.2 Examples of Energy Efficiency for Buildings (EEB) opportunities.

Type	Description
Building Energy Management Systems	Building Energy Management Systems (BEMS) encompass the installation of sensors, meters, and control mechanisms to gather real-time information regarding electricity usage within a building. This information is subsequently analyzed to identify trends, inefficiencies, and potential areas for enhancement. Additionally, the system facilitates the automated management of various building elements, including heating, ventilation, air conditioning (HVAC), lighting, and other systems that contribute to overall energy consumption.
Building Insulation Improvements	Roof, window, and wall insulation plays a primary role in decreasing the energy needed for cooling, heating, or humidity control. By optimizing insulation, it is possible to significantly enhance energy efficiency. Key areas within buildings, including walls, windows, roofs, and floors, should be prioritized to minimize heat transfer, prevent energy loss, and maintain a comfortable indoor climate, all while reducing energy consumption for heating or cooling. Common insulation materials, such as fiberglass, cellulose, and spray foam, are frequently utilized to improve the energy efficiency of buildings, while triple glazing for windows is the preferred solution.
Analytics, Audit, and Energy Certification	Part of the energy efficiency ecosystem requires assessment, measure, monitoring, and certification of energy efficiency, which is a third-party run activity that is necessary both for regulatory bodies and for real estate owners, and provides actionable insights on potential areas of improvement, as well as certified assessments that determine the taxation levels for the property.
Building Lighting Improvements	Adopt energy-efficient lighting solutions. Lighting constitutes a substantial portion of energy usage in office buildings, accounting for approximately 11% of the overall energy consumption. By replacing outdated and power-hungry lighting systems with more energy-efficient alternatives, such as LED or CFL technology, energy efficient outdoor lighting and smart-lighting systems that only stay on when presence of people is detected, considerable improvements in energy savings can be achieved.

Sample Deep Dive: Energy Efficiency for Buildings

Type	Description
Building Ventilation Improvements	The incorporation of efficient ventilation using fans and vents significantly enhances the energy efficiency of buildings. These solutions are low-energy alternatives that substantially reduce heating and cooling expenses. By expelling hot or stale air, they also eliminate excess moisture and allergens, thereby enhancing indoor air quality and fostering a healthier living environment. Optimizing a fan system, which involves aligning fan capacity more closely with the specific demands of the load, further contributes to energy savings in air distribution systems. Additionally, heat recovery ventilators, which utilize the outgoing air from buildings to warm incoming air, play a crucial role in boosting energy efficiency. During the summer months, these systems can also utilize cooler air from the building to pre-cool incoming outside air before it is processed by the HVAC units for additional cooling.
Improved Efficiency Equipment and Appliances	Upgrading outdated and inefficient equipment to high-efficiency alternatives is a highly effective strategy for minimizing energy consumption in buildings. Conducting an energy audit is essential to pinpoint the least efficient equipment, which should then be replaced with modern, more efficient models. This transition can lead to significant energy and cost reductions for owners and operators of commercial buildings. In addition to lowering the energy required for building operations, it also mitigates heating losses caused by air leaks. By addressing these heat losses, the demand for heating is decreased, further contributing to energy savings. Consequently, the facility will experience a reduction in exhaust emissions due to the lower fuel consumption for heating purposes.
Improved HVAC Systems	HVAC systems represent typically 25% of a building's energy consumption and are therefore a prime target for energy efficiency improvement. New technologies that reduce the energy usage of the HVAC units themselves or allow for improved tailoring of temperature regulation by smaller and more target zones are typical examples of ways to reduce this large portion of energy usage in buildings, while improving livability and comfort.

(Continued)

Table 14.2 (Continued)

Type	Description
Installation of Local Renewable Energy	Any addition of local generation of energy for the building, be this in the form of roof-mounted solar panels, roof-mounted wind turbines, or ground-based geothermal heating systems, will improve the energy efficiency of the building, as the certification is based upon the amount of energy that is taken from the grid or from delivered fossil fuel/external energy.
Leak and Draft Prevention and Fixing	Energy loss and inefficiency in buildings are often due to leaks or drafts. Common sources of heat loss include the regions surrounding doors and windows. Implementing various types of weatherstripping, along with enhancing doors and windows and properly sealing the entry points for utilities, can effectively mitigate this issue.
Passive Cooling Technologies	Passive cooling strategies for buildings can significantly decrease energy consumption and reliance on air conditioning. These techniques utilize natural elements such as wind, shading, insulation, and thermal mass to lower indoor temperatures. To optimize the effectiveness of passive cooling methods, designers should consider the temperature variations between day and night and implement appropriate solutions. This approach guarantees that the cooling systems employed will operate more efficiently, leading to a reduction in overall energy usage.
Usage of Carbon Neutral Materials for Construction Purposes	When engaging in new construction, or working on significant structural rebuilding, it is necessary to also look at the overall carbon footprint of the materials being used, in addition to the energy efficiency of the finished product, as production of materials such as concrete and steel are responsible for a combined total of 16% of the global GHG emissions, while usage of alternative materials, such as green concrete, sustainable steel, and mass timber, the latter of which, besides providing comparable structural benefits and improved insulation, is carbon neutral, or even, if sustainably sourced, carbon-negative.

14.12 WHAT IS THE BENEFIT FROM INVESTING IN ENERGY EFFICIENCY FOR BUILDINGS?

The benefit of investing in Energy Efficiency for Buildings, as a captive, regulation-driven market, is ownership of a market position in a field that is set to grow sizably in all transition scenarios.

14.13 WHAT IS THE MARKET SIZE FOR ENERGY EFFICIENCY FOR BUILDINGS?

The market size for Energy Efficiency for Buildings is dependent on how large a net we want to cast to define the opportunity, as this can be very wide, as we have seen in Table 14.2. In order to keep this deep dive to a manageable size, we shall choose some select few of the EEB opportunities that we have identified, and evaluate the market sizes and trends for them, with the understanding that our readers can perform similar analytics for the others as they choose.

Building Energy Management Systems (BEMS) Market 2023–2032

According to Allied Market Research,[7] the BEMS market was valued at $6.5 billion globally in 2022 and is projected to grow at a CAGR of 11.2% to reach $18.5 billion by 2032, driven primarily by the ongoing trend toward

---

[7] https://www.alliedmarketresearch.com/bems-building-energy-management-systems-market

Figure 14.3 BEMS market projection, 2022–2032, by end user.
Source: Allied Market Research / https://www.alliedmarketresearch.com/bems-building-energy-management-systems-market / last Accessed on February 17, 2025.

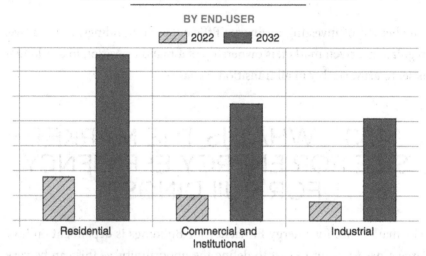

By end-user, residential segment dominated the building energy management system market

smart buildings, rising IoT, cloud computing and incentives toward energy efficiency for buildings.

The main categories that the market is segmented into are Services, Software, and Hardware, and usage in Residential, Commercial and Institutional, and Industrial, as can be seen in Figure 14.3, where we can see that Residential usage is, and will be, the main market component.

According to Allied Market Research, the BEMS marketplace is still highly fragmented, with no individual player dominating the market, and multiple companies with significant market shares such as:

- ABB Group
- Accruent Inc.
- Azbil Corporation

- Daikin Applied
- Acuity Brands Lighting Inc.
- DEXMA
- Albireo Energy LLC
- Airedale International Air Conditioning Ltd.
- IBM Corporation
- Emerson Electric Co
- Distech Controls
- Automated Logic Corporation
- Ecova
- GridPoint
- Echelon Corporation
- Lucid
- Elster Group
- Daintree Networks
- Danfoss
- Legrand
- Carrier
- Osram
- GE Digital
- Iconics
- Tridium
- KMC Controls
- Ameresco

If we observe the regional makeup of the market in 2022, we see how APAC, as seen in Figure 14.4, plays the largest role, due to the rapid economic growth driving new construction, urbanization, and higher-energy requirements.

Figure 14.4 BEMS market by geography, 2022.
Source: Allied Market Research / https://www.alliedmarketresearch.com/bems-building-energy-management-systems-market / last Accessed on February 17,2025.

Region wise, Asia-Pacific was the highest revenue contributor to the market in 2022

Building Thermal Insulation Market 2023–2030

According to Grand View Research,[8] the estimated size of the global building thermal insulation market was US$ 31.40 billion in 2022, as seen in Figure 14.5, with projections indicating a compound annual growth rate (CAGR) of 4.5% from 2023 to 2030, with a target market size of US$ 44.69 billion by 2030. The anticipated growth is primarily attributed to the increasing use of thermal insulation in both residential and commercial sectors to lower overall energy expenses, along with a growing awareness of the importance of energy conservation.

---

[8] https://www.grandviewresearch.com/industry-analysis/building-thermal-insulation-market

Figure 14.5 Global building thermal insulation market, 2022, share by end user.
Source: Grand View Research / https://www.grandviewresearch.com/industry-analysis/building-thermal-insulation-market / last Accessed on February 17,2025.

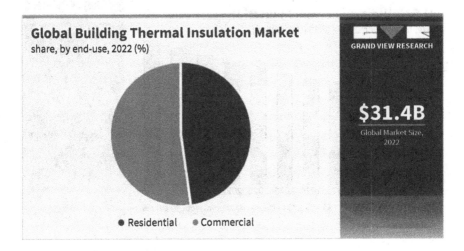

The US market was ~9.0 billion in 2021 and is the largest in North America, expected to grow with a lower CAGR than the global market, at 3.4%, as shown in Figure 14.6, hitting ~12 billion by 2030.

The main categories of product are Glass Wool, Expanded Polystyrene (EPS, which is projected to have the highest CAGR at 5%), Extruded Polystyrene (XPS), Cellulose, Mineral Wool (which has fire safety advantages), and a slew of Other products, including high-tech options such as Aerogels.

From a regional perspective, Europe is one of the leading markets, with 33% of the global share in 2022, and forecast to remain so into 2030, due to strong regulatory initiatives by the European Commission which are expected to fuel growth over time. The fastest growing market, on the other hand, for the same reasons seen for the BEMS market, is Asia-Pacific, as can be seen in Figure 14.7.

Figure 14.6 US BTI market projections, 2020–2030.

Source: Grand View Research / https://www.grandviewresearch.com/industry-analysis/building-thermal-insulation-market / last Accessed on February 17, 2025.

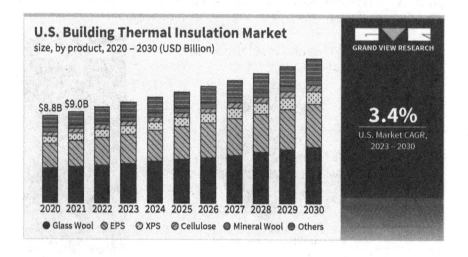

Figure 14.7 Global BTI market projections, 2020–2030, largest and fastest growing markets.

Source: Grand View Research / https://www.grandviewresearch.com/industry-analysis/building-thermal-insulation-market / last Accessed on February 17, 2025.

Sample Deep Dive: Energy Efficiency for Buildings

In terms of players in the market, there is significant fragmentation and price-sensitivity, with many regional suppliers, due to the high volumes and costs of shipping that are intrinsically linked to the type of product. Grandview Research identifies the main global players as:

- Rockwool International A/S
- GAF Materials Corporation
- Guardian Building Products, Inc.
- Huntsman International LLC
- Johns Manville Corporation
- Cellofoam North America, Inc.
- Atlas Roofing Corporation
- CertainTeed Corporation
- Roxul, Inc.
- Dow Building Solutions
- Owens Corning Corporation
- Saint-Gobain S.A.
- Byucksan Corporation
- Kingspan Group PLC
- BASF Polyurethanes GmbH
- Knauf Insulation
- Armacell
- L'Isolante K-Flex
- Kaimann GmbH
- Fletcher Insulation
- Paroc Group
- ThermaXX Jackets
- Bauder Ltd.

HVAC Market 2023–2030

According to Global Markets Insights,[9] the estimated size of the global HVAC market, inclusive of Heating Equipment, Ventilation Equipment, Air Conditioning Equipment, Chillers, and Cooling Towers, in 2023 was valued at approximately US$ 294 billion and expected to grow at a CAGR of 5.6% between 2024 and 2032 on the coattails of building energy efficiency requirements around the world. This growth ratio puts the projected value of the market at US$ 481 billion by 2032, as can be seen in Figure 14.8.

Within the broader HVAC segment, the Air Conditioning Equipment product type segment covers the larger portion and represented revenues of approximately US$ 124 billion in 2024, projected to grow to US$ 210 billion by 2023, because of strong and growing demand for better and more efficient cooling systems for energy-efficient buildings around the world.

Figure 14.8   Projections for global HVAC market, 2024–2032.
Source: Global Market Insights / https://www.gminsights.com/industry-analysis/hvac-market / last Accessed on February 17,2025.

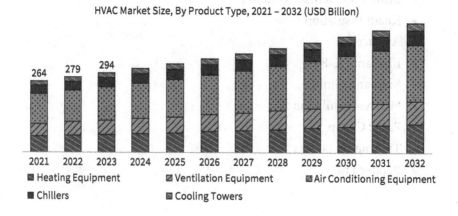

---

[9] https://www.gminsights.com/industry-analysis/hvac-market

Figure 14.9 Projections for North America HVAC market, 2024–2032.
Source: Global Market Insights / https://www.gminsights.com/industry-analysis/hvac-market / last Accessed on February 17,2025.

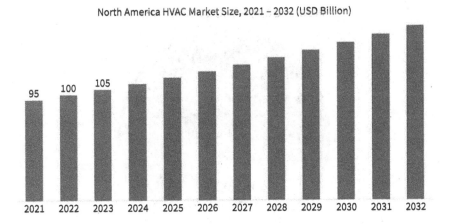

The North America market represents US$ 105 billion in 2023 and is expected to grow to US$ 165 billion by 2032, as shown in Figure 14.9, with a CAGR of 5.15%.

The global breakdown of market shares shows a slight preponderance of the North American market, which at US$ 105 billion represents 39% of the totality, followed by almost equal shares by Europe (US$ 80 billion and 30% of the market share) and Asia Pacific (US$ 81.4 billion and 31% of the global market), as shown in Figure 14.10.

In terms of growth potential, Europe is the lowest, with a projected CAGR of 4.8%, followed by the United States with 5.15% and then by Asia Pacific, which leads the regions with a CAGR of 6.9% due to the well-known rise in urbanization, sustainable infrastructure, and new construction.

The global players that Global Markets Insights has identified are the following:

- Bosch
- Carrier Group

Figure 14.10   2023 Global segmentation of HVAC market by region.
Source: Global Market Insights / https://www.gminsights.com/industry-analysis/hvac-market / last Accessed on February 17,2025.

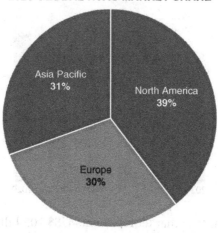

- Daikin Industries Inc.
- Danfoss
- GREE Electric Appliances, inc.
- Haier Group
- Hisense HVAC equipment Co., Ltd.
- Johnson Controls Plc
- Lennox International
- LG Electronics
- Midea Group
- Mitsubishi Electric Group
- Panasonic Corporation
- Rheem Manufacturing Company
- Trane Technologies
- York

14.14 WHAT IS THE LONG-TERM VISION FOR ENERGY EFFICIENCY FOR BUILDINGS INVESTMENTS?

Given the type of rapidly evolving market, and presence of multiple companies in growth stages within this opportunity, the long-term vision for EEB investments is *buy-grow-exit* (with *buy and hold* as a secondary).

14.15 WHAT IS THE TRIGGER FOR ENERGY EFFICIENCY FOR BUILDINGS INVESTMENTS, AND HAS IT ALREADY OCCURRED?

The primary trigger for EEB is the passing of legislation that penalizes energy inefficient buildings around the world. This has already occurred in multiple jurisdictions, as we have seen in other sections of this chapter, and is ongoing in many more, making this trigger partially activated. The secondary trigger, which is the warming of the planet that creates a need for increased cooling in buildings that would have hitherto not required it to the same extent, has already been activated, and is increasing in strength as time goes by.

The third trigger, which is the levying of a carbon tax, has only yet been applied in selected countries, and to limited levels, and will represent an additional accelerant when and where applied, as it will further incentivize energy efficiency by making energy waste even more unaffordable.

PRINCIPLES OF TRANSITION FINANCE INVESTING

14.16 WHICH NEW COMPANIES HAVE BEEN IDENTIFIED IN EARLY STAGES FOR ENERGY EFFICIENCY FOR BUILDINGS (VC TARGETS)?

Table 14.3 lists a (noncomprehensive) list of early stage players in the EEB space that would be valid targets for venture capital investments, ordered by decreasing amount of funding received.

Table 14.3 Early stage players in the Energy Efficiency for Buildings space.

Company	Sector	Fund Target	Estimated Funding Received to Date[10]	Country	Summary
Measurable.energy	BEMS	VC Post Seed	$10,000,000	UK	measurable.energy is a platform using machine learning and hardware to reduce wasted energy and greenhouse gas emissions in commercial and residential buildings.
SkyCool Systems	HVAC	VC Post Seed	$9,300,000	USA	Skycool Systems enhances cooling efficiency by using untapped renewable resources, such as solar energy, reducing electricity use.
Bedrock Energy	Heating	VC Post Seed	$8,500,000	USA	Bedrock Energy produces geothermal systems that use ground-source heat pumps to access the ground's ambient temperatures, offering renewable and emission-free heating and cooling for buildings in urban areas throughout the year.

[10] As per publicly available data, might be inaccurate/incomplete

Sample Deep Dive: Energy Efficiency for Buildings

Company	Sector	Fund Target	Estimated Funding Received to Date	Country	Summary
Conry Tech	HVAC	VC Seed	~$8,000,000	Australia	Conry Tech is changing air conditioning to enhance comfort and sustainability by creating new hardware that addresses key HVAC challenges, offering better energy management and temperature control. It was established by recognized HVAC professionals with many years of experience.
Thalo Labs	BEMS	VC Seed	~$8,000,000	USA	Thalo focuses on improving HVAC performance through constant monitoring. Its advanced mass spectrometry sensors easily attach to current systems, enabling proactive maintenance to save time, money, and reduce emissions. Copilot analyzes data continuously, alerting teams when action is necessary to maintain system efficiency and health.
dPoint Technologies	HVAC	VC Post Seed	$6,100,000	Canada	dPoint manufactures and sells membranes and energy recovery technology that greatly enhance energy efficiency and air quality in buildings. It has modified its patented fuel-cell heat and humidity exchanger technology for use in energy recovery ventilator systems, which shift heat and humidity between incoming and outgoing air in a building's ventilation system.

(Continued)

Table 14.3 (*Continued*)

Company	Sector	Fund Target	Estimated Funding Received to Date	Country	Summary
INOVUES	Windows	VC Post Seed	$5,500,000	USA	INOVUES is a window technology company offering a unique solution that allows existing building facades to be upgraded with the latest energy-saving and smart glass technologies without needing to remove or replace them.
NanoTech Materials	Insulation	VC Seed	$5,000,000	USA	NanoTech is a material science company that uses nano technology to make buildings fireproof and lower global energy use.
Dabbel	BEMS	VC Seed	$4,630,000	Germany	DABBEL uses cloud-based AI technology to manage building energy systems, cutting energy use and CO_2 emissions by up to 40%.
Ento	BEMS	VC Seed	$3,600,000	Denmark	Ento is an AI-based platform designed to find the best methods to construct and enhance buildings to lower carbon emissions. It generates reports showing energy optimization, provides alerts for issues, and includes a tracking area to oversee energy-saving initiatives.
Elyos	BEMS	VC Seed	$3,500,000	United Kingdom	Elyos's platform utilizes machine learning to improve energy use and automate engagement in demand response markets for businesses. It aims to reduce costs and carbon emissions by adjusting energy consumption during peak hours.

Sample Deep Dive: Energy Efficiency for Buildings

Company	Sector	Fund Target	Estimated Funding Received to Date	Country	Summary
Monodraught	Passive lighting	VC Seed	$3,410,000	United Kingdom	Monodraught produces natural lighting, air conditioning, and ventilation technology used by companies like IKEA, Ford, and Waitrose. They design, manufacture, install, and maintain sustainable solutions for commercial buildings. Monodraught aims to reduce the carbon footprint of buildings with various standard and custom products, providing optimized temperature control and indoor air quality while reducing electricity and refrigerant use.
QEA Tech	Services	VC Seed	$3,300,000	Canada	QEA Tech is a software company that uses AI, drone technology, and thermal imaging to give insights on energy efficiency in buildings.
Hydronic Shell	HVAC	VC Seed	$3,250,000	USA	Hydronic Shell Technologies offers HVAC and facade systems for energy retrofits in construction.
Miru	Windows	VC Seed	$3,150,000	Canada	Miru emphasizes the importance of windows in reducing carbon emissions in buildings. They use advanced electrochromic technology to create windows that adjust automatically to varying needs, providing comfortable, attractive, and energy-efficient environments.

(Continued)

Table 14.3 (*Continued*)

Company	Sector	Fund Target	Estimated Funding Received to Date	Country	Summary
Inficold	HVAC	VC Seed	$2,840,000	India	Inficold, located in Uttar Pradesh, India, creates cold storage rooms, milk coolers, and air conditioners that use solar energy, either from the grid or off-grid. Traditional refrigeration systems that depend on diesel generators can be expensive. The company solves this by using thermal energy storage and off-grid solar integration. This technology relies on ice to store cooling energy, needing just 6 to 8 hours of solar or grid power to provide 24/7 cooling without diesel engines or batteries. Their solar systems allow for direct use of solar energy without needing approvals or the frequent replacement of batteries, enabling fast installation and quick returns on investment.
R8tech	BEMS	VC Seed	$2,520,000	Estonia	R8 Digital Operator creates AI software to enhance current Building Automation Systems (BAS, BMS).
Wind my Roof	Wind and solar	VC Seed	$2,310,000	France	WIND my ROOF creates modular wind turbines for flat-roofed buildings to harness wind energy. It aims to provide electricity through a mix of rooftop wind turbines and solar panels.

Sample Deep Dive: Energy Efficiency for Buildings

Company	Sector	Fund Target	Estimated Funding Received to Date	Country	Summary
viboo	BEMS	VC Seed	$2,260,000	Switzerland	viboo provides self-learning predictive control for BEMS using physics-informed machine learning as a cloud service.
TablePointer	BEMS	VC Seed	$2,230,000	Singapore	TablePointer is an AI solution designed for small and medium commercial facilities, assisting them in optimizing energy use and boosting profitability.
Onyx Solar	Solar	VC Seed	$2,100,000	Spain	Founded in 2009, Onyx Solar is a leading company in photovoltaic glass solutions for building-integrated photovoltaics (BIPV). With more than 500 projects in 60 countries, they convert sunlight into clean energy while improving thermal insulation, controlling sound, and filtering ultraviolet (UV) and infrared (IR) radiation. They provide customizable designs to suit various architectural requirements.

(Continued)

Table 14.3 (Continued)

Company	Sector	Fund Target	Estimated Funding Received to Date	Country	Summary
Ampotech	BEMS	VC Seed	$2,080,000	Singapore	Ampotech offers AI-powered Internet of Things solutions for energy management in commercial real estate, utility companies, renewable energy providers, manufacturing and logistics businesses, and public sector agencies. These solutions aim to provide energy and operational cost savings along with remote asset management. Their award-winning devices, data platform, and applications deliver notable cost, performance, and cybersecurity benefits over standard commercial products.
Accelerate Wind	Wind	VC Seed	$1,700,000	USA	Accelerate Wind produces rooftop turbines featuring innovative airfoils that naturally boost wind speed, enhancing power output compared to traditional turbines. These airfoils are developed in collaboration with scientists from Argonne National Lab to ensure they are both efficient and cost-effective.
Wattblock	Services	VC Seed	$1,200,000	Australia	Wattblock offers independent advice to over 85,000 residents in apartment buildings, covering solar, battery studies, and energy efficiency measures. Their fee-for-advice model ensures unbiased recommendations.

Sample Deep Dive: Energy Efficiency for Buildings

Company	Sector	Fund Target	Estimated Funding Received to Date	Country	Summary
Stash Energy	Energy Storage	VC Seed	$1,060,000	Canada	Stash Energy is a Canadian company that creates energy storage and demand response systems for homes and businesses. Its main product is the Stash Energy Mini-Split Heat Pump, which extracts heat from outside air in the winter and releases it outside in the summer. This device lets homeowners save energy during off-peak times for use during peak hours when electricity costs more.
hello energy	SaaS	VC Seed	$1,000,000	Netherlands	hello energy is a software solution for sustainability and portfolio managers in real estate, aimed at creating a positive environmental impact. The company gathers, verifies, and enhances sustainability data from various global sources, linking real estate owners and tenants with insights, stories, and challenges.
Soltell Systems	BEMS	VC Seed	$1,000,000	Israel	Soltell Systems focuses on automating and managing distributed rooftop solar photovoltaic (PV) systems with Industrial Internet of Things (IoT) technology. They cater to commercial solar fleet aggregators, rooftop solar integrators, corporates, and regional energy authorities.

(Continued)

Table 14.3 (*Continued*)

Company	Sector	Fund Target	Estimated Funding Received to Date	Country	Summary
NETenergy	Energy Storage	VC Seed	$750,000	USA	NETenergy is a thermal energy storage company located in Chicago. They have developed a thermal battery using Black Ice technology that stores thermal energy, similar to how an electrical battery functions. By using NETenergy's thermal battery to store cold energy, building owners can save over 30% on energy costs and cut carbon emissions by 50%.
Smart Energy Link	Solar	VC Seed	$685,000	Switzerland	Smart Energy Link (SEL) develops software and provides services for captive power solutions in homes and businesses. SEL helps reduce energy expenses, simplifies service charge accounting, and lowers investment for public power supply.
Cambio	SaaS	VC Seed	$650,000	USA	Cambio is a real estate software aimed at assisting commercial landlords and corporate tenants in reducing carbon emissions from buildings. It was created as a comprehensive platform for major real estate owners and users, who often lack resources to manage the complex sustainability landscape in real estate. Cambio serves as a single solution for carbon emissions analysis and decarbonization plans.

Sample Deep Dive: Energy Efficiency for Buildings

Company	Sector	Fund Target	Estimated Funding Received to Date	Country	Summary
MOVEAIR	Wind	VC Seed	$526,000	Germany	MOVEAIR provides a unique energy system that integrates standardized micro wind turbines, which can be tailored to local needs regarding energy demand, space, and loads. The system utilizes existing infrastructure like masts, bridges, and rooftops for effective integration. MOVEAIR energy systems assist businesses in gaining independence from the public grid and diesel generators, leading to a notable decrease in carbon emissions. Additionally, their advanced wind energy systems come with IoT-based features for smooth integration into modern energy management systems.
Seeder Clean Energy	Services	VC Seed	$438,000	China	Seeder is a rooftop solar financing platform for commercial and industrial buildings in China. Seeder assists building managers in achieving their renewable energy goals and offers services to transform strategic plans into successful projects by vetting and qualifying vendors, partnering with on-the-ground project and supplier resources, supporting contract negotiations and execution, and providing expertise on policy, market, and best practices.

(Continued)

Table 14.3 (*Continued*)

Company	Sector	Fund Target	Estimated Funding Received to Date	Country	Summary
Keren Energy	BEMS	VC Seed	$100,000	Israel	Keren Yeda Energy Ltd. is a company specializing in building energy optimization and savings, as well as managing, controlling, and executing energy-saving projects. Keren's activities include controlling electricity and water consumption and expenses, sharing electricity, water, and energy through a smart sharing device, and providing consulting and support for energy saving.
SolarGik	BEMS	VC Seed	$100,000	Israel	SolarGik provides smart PV tracker solutions that are modular, configurable, lightweight, and simple to install and maintain, offering 20–25% more energy production than fixed-tilt panels. Their trackers can be installed wherever fixed-tilt panels are placed. The "Master Control System" acts as a project-level SCADA/DCS system, calculating and balancing important factors like weather, project details, wind, radiation, degradation, and agricultural needs.

Sample Deep Dive: Energy Efficiency for Buildings

14.17 WHICH EMERGING COMPANIES HAVE BEEN IDENTIFIED AS EMERGING PLAYERS FOR ENERGY EFFICIENCY FOR BUILDINGS (PE TARGETS)?

Table 14.4 lists a (noncomprehensive) list of established players in the EEB space that would be valid targets for private equity investments, ordered by decreasing amount of funding received.

Table 14.4 Emerging players in the Energy Efficiency for Buildings space.

Company	Sector	Fund Target	Estimated Funding Received to Date[11]	Country	Summary
Antora Energy	Energy Storage	PE Established	$230,000,000	USA	Based in the United States, the company uses zero-carbon heat and electricity to power heavy industry. It stores thermal energy by capturing extra solar and wind energy to heat carbon blocks, which can reach temperatures up to 1,500 °C for mining electricity or industrial processes. Antora Energy turns sunlight and wind into continuous heat and power at a cost lower than fossil fuels. In 2018 Antora Energy utilized NREL's facilities to create larger TPV cells and advance its technology with aid from the Advanced Research Projects Agency-Energy (ARPA-E) and the Shell GameChanger Accelerator Powered by NREL (GCxN).

(Continued)

---

[11] As per publicly available data, might be inaccurate/incomplete

Table 14.4 (Continued)

Company	Sector	Fund Target	Estimated Funding Received to Date	Country	Summary
UrbanVolt	BEMS	PE Established	$193,000,000	Ireland	UrbanVolt is an LED lighting company that retrofits commercial spaces with no upfront cost, offering immediate cash and energy savings through their Light as a Service model.
AtomPower	BEMS	PE Established	$174,500,000	USA	AtomPower created the first solid-state circuit breaker, using semiconductors for digital current control, enabling smarter and safer power management.
Ice Energy	Energy Storage	PE Established	$132,000,000	USA	Ice Energy creates Ice Bear, a thermal energy storage system using ice for air conditioning. This system helps lower electric bills for both businesses and homeowners while reducing CO_2 emissions.
Aeroseal	Sealing	PE Established	$119,000,000	USA	Aeroseal seals air ducts and building envelopes to cut down on wasted energy and lower energy bills for buildings.
Malta	Energy Storage	PE Established	$112,900,000	USA	Malta has developed a thermal energy storage system that can collect and store energy from various sources like wind and solar, allowing it to retain energy for long durations. The system can provide electricity on demand from 8 hours to over 8 days. It uses established thermodynamic principles to store energy as heat in molten salt and as cold in a chilled liquid. This innovative technology offers a flexible, low-cost, and efficient solution for utility-scale energy storage, using standard parts and readily available materials such as steel, air, salt, and other liquids.

Sample Deep Dive: Energy Efficiency for Buildings

Company	Sector	Fund Target	Estimated Funding Received to Date	Country	Summary
Ecoworks	Services	PE Growth	$83,000,000	Germany	Ecoworks modernizes multifamily houses with up to four floors in a few weeks using industrial prefabrication, digital processes, and energy systems. The renovation turns the building into "a small, decentralized power plant" by adding photovoltaic systems, heat pumps, and thermal reservoirs.
David Energy	Solar and Storage	PE Growth	$77,500,000	USA	David Energy aims to turn every building into an energy retailer, enhancing customer value from solar and storage systems.
BrainBox.AI	BEMS	PE Growth	$75,100,000	Canada	BrainBox AI uses cloud computing and algorithms for autonomous building technology energy management.
Carbon Lighthouse	BEMS	PE Growth	$67,100,000	USA	Carbon Lighthouse aims to stop climate change by helping building owners cut carbon emissions from energy waste, revealing and fixing hidden inefficiencies for long-term savings and carbon reduction.
Verdigris Technologies	BEMS	PE Growth	$51,500,000	USA	Verdigris Technologies creates AI software for energy efficiency.

(Continued)

Table 14.4 (*Continued*)

Company	Sector	Fund Target	Estimated Funding Received to Date	Country	Summary
Steffes	Energy Storage	PE Growth	$50,000,000	USA	Steffes provides various energy storage products that work with heating and cooling systems based on an efficient Electric Thermal Storage (ETS) method. This system uses cheaper off-peak electricity when demand is low to generate and store heat in ceramic bricks, allowing buildings to benefit from peak performance at lower costs.
Qarnot	Heating	PE Growth	$48,000,000	France	Qarnot creates the Q.rad, a heater that uses microprocessors to generate heat and is linked to the Internet to provide cloud-based computing power.
SolydEra SpA	Energy Storage	PE Growth	$47,000,000	Italy	SOLIDpower creates Bluegen, a stationary fuel cell unit that uses high-temperature fuel cell technology (SOFC) and is well suited for residential and small commercial buildings' energy storage needs.
Blue Frontier	HVAC	PE Growth	$38,000,000	USA	Blue Frontier focuses on sustainable air conditioning systems that ensure comfort and energy storage. Its technology uses liquid desiccants to remove moisture from the air.
cove.tool	SaaS	PE Growth	$36,800,000	USA	cove.tool is a B2B SaaS company focused on improving building energy efficiency and reducing construction costs.

Sample Deep Dive: Energy Efficiency for Buildings

Company	Sector	Fund Target	Estimated Funding Received to Date	Country	Summary
Kel.vin	HVAC	PE Growth	$34,400,00	USA	Kel.vin was founded in New York City in 2013 with the goal of decarbonizing heating and cooling systems in older buildings. In 2016, Kel.vin launched the Cozy system, which controls radiator heat output and has shown to save heating costs by 25% to 40%. Kel.vin also developed a heat pump to replace air conditioners, working with the Cozy system to manage heating and cooling. This approach, called "hybrid electrification," uses mostly electric energy from renewable sources. Kel.vin aims to help buildings decarbonize their systems effectively. Kel.vin has sold more than forty thousand systems.
75F	BEMS	PE Growth	$29,900,000	USA	75F is a smart building automation system that manages HVAC, lighting, and equipment using IoT technology.
MGA Thermal	Energy Storage	PE Growth	$28,800,000	Australia	MGA Thermal, an Australian company, offers thermal energy storage solutions with its unique technology, Miscibility Gap Alloys (MGA). This technology enables Thermal Energy Storage Systems (TESS) to deliver safe, affordable, and durable high-temperature heat or power. As the blocks cool and solidify, they store significant thermal energy through a solid-liquid phase change.

(Continued)

Table 14.4 (*Continued*)

Company	Sector	Fund Target	Estimated Funding Received to Date	Country	Summary
Energy X	Services	PE Growth	$24,500,000	South Korea	Energy X markets a platform for sustainable architecture to build zero-energy buildings.
AeroShield Materials	Windows	PE Growth	$24,100,000	USA	AeroShield Materials is making transparent inserts from Aerogel that improve insulation for windows, saving thermal energy. These inserts are just 4 millimeters thick and, when added to a double-pane window, increase energy efficiency by 65%.
Effy	Services	PE Growth	$21,050,000	France	Effy is an energy renovation company based in France. It focuses on energy renovation for public buildings, residential properties, and industrial facilities.
Fracttal	BEMS	PE Growth	$17,300,000	Chile	Fracttal is a Chilean company that creates Cloud-based enterprise asset management solutions for real-time monitoring of physical assets. Its software includes asset and inventory management, condition monitoring, issue management, and maintenance tasks. By using IoT, it collects data from connected devices and analyzes it to detect anomalies, which are then processed through issue management to prevent potential losses in various industries such as manufacturing, mining, technology, construction, transportation, and food and drinks.

Sample Deep Dive: Energy Efficiency for Buildings

Company	Sector	Fund Target	Estimated Funding Received to Date	Country	Summary
Vaagen Timbers	Building Materials	PE Growth	$15,000,000	USA	Vaagen Timbers aims to be the top producer of cross-laminated and glue-laminated timber in North America. They focus on eco-friendly methods to create strong, beautiful, and versatile wood products for their customers. Their vision is to transform how people perceive their living and working environments while connecting forests and communities through their best products.
Flair	Ventilation	PE Growth	$12,700,000	USA	Flair produces smart vents, wireless thermostats, and advanced software for home heating and cooling.
aedifion	BEMS	PE Growth	$12,630,000	Germany	aedifion creates tools to process operating data from building automation systems in the cloud.
Brilia	Lighting	PE Growth	$12,300,000	Brazil	Brilia makes smart LED lighting products, including LED drivers, bulbs, PAR lights, panel lights, tube lights, candle lights, floodlights, and downlights. The products are made using its own LED technology. They also offer a wifi-enabled LED lighting controller that functions as a plug-and-play product.
Bisly	BEMS	PE Growth	$12,100,000	Estonia	Bisly is a startup from Estonia that creates smart building solutions for managing energy in real estate.

(Continued)

Table 14.4 (Continued)

Company	Sector	Fund Target	Estimated Funding Received to Date	Country	Summary
Solarstone	Solar	PE Growth	$11,050,000	Estonia	Solarstone creates and manufactures building-integrated photovoltaic (BIPV) solutions that support sustainable building practices. These solutions include solar roofs that can be added to existing structures or parking areas.
Aeromine Technologies	Wind Energy	PE Growth	$10,100,000	USA	Aeromine Technologies offers bladeless wind energy solutions for high-rise and large residential buildings, enabling local energy production and reducing grid energy usage.

14.18 WHICH ESTABLISHED PLAYERS EXIST IN ENERGY EFFICIENCY FOR BUILDINGS (PRIVATE CREDIT TARGETS)?

Table 14.5 lists a (noncomprehensive) list of established players in the EEB space that would be valid targets for private credit investments, ordered by decreasing amount of funding received.

Sample Deep Dive: Energy Efficiency for Buildings

Table 14.5 Established players in the Energy Efficiency for Buildings space.

Company	Website	Sector	Fund Target	Estimated Funding Received to date[12]	Country	Summary
Redaptive	https://redaptive.com	BEMS	Private Credit	$916,500,000	US	Redaptive is a provider of Energy-as-a-Service that finances and installs equipment that saves and generates energy, while also managing energy consumption in buildings.
STEM	https://www.stem.com/	BEMS	Private Credit	$582,600,000	US	Stem combines artificial intelligence with energy storage to assist organizations in automating energy cost savings and safeguarding against fluctuating rates.
Tecnoglass	www.tecnoglass.com/	Windows	Private Credit	$300,000,000	Colombia	Tecnoglass manufactures air-insulated windows, providing tempered, laminated, insulated, silk-screened, and curved glasses using techno bend and low e-series technology.
BlocPower	https://www.blocpower.io	BEMS	Private Credit	$266,600,000	US	BlocPower is providing building owners with smart, all-electric heating, cooling, and hot water systems with no upfront payment required.

[12] As per publicly available data, might be inaccurate/incomplete

INDEX

Note: Page numbers in **bold** refer to tables and figures.

4 × 3 investment matrix, **96**

A
abandoned subterranean mines, 268–270, **269**
acute physical risk, 11, **15–16**, **110**, 110
Agricultural Land, Cropland, 321–322
Agricultural Land, Cropland, Irrigated, 322
Agricultural Land, Cropland, Non-irrigated, 322
Agricultural Land, Pastureland, 322
Agent-Based models, 41
airplanes, electric, **181**, 181–183
airplanes, hydrogen, 161–163
aluminum mines, smelters, 210–213, **211**
ammonia, hydrogen, 151–152, 159–160
anthropogenic climate change, 1–9
 atmospheric CO_2, 4–9
 CO_2 levels, **4, 6–8**
 EPICA Dome C temperature, **4**
 Mauna Loa observatory, CO_2 levels, **8**
 temperature, land, **2**, 2–3
appreciation, hardiness zone improvements, 341–347, **342–347**
asset allocation, 80–81, **81**
atmospheric CO_2, **6**

B
back-testing, 71–77
 challenges, **72**
 narratives, 72–73

INDEX

back-testing, *(Cont.)*
  validation, 75–77
benchmarking, 71, 77–78
BECCS, **104,** 171–174, **172–173**
biochar, 174–177, **175**
Bioenergy with Carbon Capture
  and Storage, *see* BECCS
biofuels, **247,** 247–249
bottom-up results, 104
box models, 39
Building Energy Management
  (BEMS) market, 373–376,
  374, 376
building thermal insulation
  market, 376–379, **377–378**

C

Carbon Capture Usage and Storage
  (CCUS), 92, 232, 235–237, **236**
Carbon Dioxide Removal, *see* CDR
  (Carbon Dioxide Removal)
CCLW, *see* Climate Change Laws of
  the World (CCLW)
CCUS, *see* Carbon Capture Usage
  and Storage (CCUS)
CDR (Carbon Dioxide Removal),
  189–190
cheap green hydrogen, 149
chronic physical risk, 11, **110,** 111
Climate Alternatives/Physical
  Assets Plays Strategy
  Fund, 92, 96, **267–268,**
  265–282
  climate sanctuary cities' real
    estate, 279–282, **280**
  Northern Latitudes Farmland
    (NLF), **275,** 275–276
  paper recycling facilities, **277,**
    277–278
  plantation forest, **271,** 271–272
  primary forest, **273,** 273–274
  subterranean mines, abandoned,
    268–270, **269**
climate change, 23–25, **25**
Climate Change Laws of the World
  (CCLW), 66
climate data, 52
  Climate Premium Evaluation
    Model flowchart, **46**
  End-to-End climate
    modeling, **45**
  models, 37–46
  power production changes by
    scenario, **25**
climate driver
  energy efficiency, buildings,
    359–360, **360**
  geothermal energy, 283
  Northern Latitudes
    Farmland, 310
climate liability risk, data quality,
  61–64, **63**

climate litigation, 200–203, **201**
  cases, **63**
  risk, 66–67, 84, **110**, 111
climate modeling, 37–46, **72**
climate pathway, 87
climate risks, **14–16**, 17–18, 28–29, **110**
climate sanctuary cities' real estate, 279–282, **280**
CMIP6 models, 55–56, **56**
CO_2 levels, **4**, **6–8**, 9–25
  acute physical risk, 11, **15–16**
  atmospheric, **6**
  chronic physical risk, 11
  climate change, 23–24
  climate risks, **14–16**
  direct environmental drivers, 17
  EPICA Dome C temperature, **4**
  liability risks, 16
  litigation drivers, 17
  litigation risk, 12
  market risk, 11, **14–15**
  Mauna Loa observatory, **8**
  physical risks, 10–17
  policy drivers, 17
  policy risk, 11–12, **14**
  regulatory drivers, 17
  reputation risk, 13, **15**
  resource-derived drivers, 17
  SENSES Project, 23–25
  Shared Socioeconomic Pathways (SSPs), 19–23, **19–23**
  social/behavioral drivers, 17
  stranded assets, 17–18
  technology risk, 12–13, **14**
  temperature, 18–25
  transition risks, 10–17
coastal areas, novel modeling for, 217–219, **218**
coastal tidal protection, **261**, 261–263
Computable General Equilibrium (CGE), 36
concentration risk, 67, 84
Conference of Parties (COP), 29
contagion risk, 68, 84
copper mines, **213**, 213–214
critical mineral mines, 221–222, **222**
crowdedness, 114–115, **115**, 285, 317, 361–362
customized scenarios, 102–103

D

DAC (Direct Air Capture), 179–181, **180**
dark doldrums, 165
data quality, 53–55
  acute physical risk, **110**
  chronic physical risk, **110**

data quality, (*Cont.*)
   climate liability risk, **110**
   transition risk, **110**
DICE, *see* Dynamic Integrated Model of Climate and Economy (DICE) model
direct air capture, *see* DAC
direct environmental drivers, 17
diversification, 82–85
   climate litigation risk, 84
   concentration risk, 84
   contagion risk, 84
   migration effects, 84–85
   network effects, 84
   physical risk, 83
   stranded assets, 83
   transition risk, 83
drivers, climate risk, **110**, 110–111
DSGE, *see* Dynamic Stochastic General Equilibrium (DSGE)
Dunkelflaute, 165
dynamic allocations, 80–81, **81**
Dynamic Integrated Model of Climate and Economy (DICE) model, 43–45, **44**
Dynamic Stochastic General Equilibrium (DSGE), 36

E

E2E modeling, **191**, 191–193
economic module, 41
ECS, **56**
EDF, 307
electric airplanes, **181**, 181–183
electric grid infrastructure, 237–239, **238**
electric transportation, **215**, 215–217
electrolysis, hydrogen, 146–147
EMICs (Earth-system Models of Intermediate Complexity), 40
emissions-based approaches, 82–85
emissions-free shipping, **228**, 228–229
energy efficiency, buildings, **178**, 178–179, 359–403
   Building Energy Management (BEMS) market, 373–376, **374, 376**
   building thermal insulation market, 376–379, **377–378**
   climate driver, 359–360, **360**
   crowdedness, 361–362
   established players, 402–, **403**
   fixes, 363–369, **363–369**
   funds, 360
   HVAC market, 380–382, **380–382**
   investment benefits, 373
   investment horizon, 361
   investment maturity, 361

Index

investment opportunity, 369–372, **370–372**
long-term vision, 383
market size, 373–382
PE targets, 395–402, **395–402**
root problem, 362
technology readiness, 360
trigger, 383
VC targets, 384–394, **384–394**
energy moisture balance models, 40
energy storage, **239**, 239–241
EPICA Dome C temperature, **4**
ESG investing strategies, 81–82

F
fat tails, 64–69
fixes, for root problems, 118, **118–119**
forest land
  plantation forest, **271**, 271–272
  primary forest, **273**, 273–274
four fund/three strategy approach, 92–96, **93**
  Climate Alternatives/Physical Assets Plays Strategy Fund, 92, 96
  Growth Strategy Fund, 92–94
  Infrastructure Strategy Fund, 92, 95
  Public Strategy Fund, 92, 94–95
  time horizon for transition finance, 93, **94**
fuel cell transportation, hydrogen, 152–154

G
gasoline vs. hydrogen, **142**
GCMs (Global Climate Models, or General Circulation Models), 41, 45–46, **45–46**, 57
geographies, Northern Latitudes Farmland targeted, 356–357, **356**
geothermal energy, **109**, **130–132**, **283**, 283–307
  climate driver, 283
  crowdedness, 285
  established players, 306–307
  fixes, 288–293
  funds, 284
  growth, **292**
  installed capacity, **293–294**
  investment benefits, 296
  investment horizon, 285
  investment maturity, 285
  investment opportunity, 295
  long-term vision, 302
  market size, 296–302, **297**
  NGFS (Network for Greening the Financial System), 288–291

INDEX

geothermal energy, (Cont.)
 NGFS Phase IV scenarios, **289**
 NGFS Phase IV projections, **294–295**
 NGFS Phase V scenarios, **291**
 PE targets, 305–306
 root problem, 286–288
 Technology Readiness Level (TRL), 284
 timeline, 293–295
 trigger, 303
 VC targets, 303–304
geothermal energy generation companies, **242**, 242–243
Global Change Data Lab, 3
greenhouse gases (GHG), 1, **60**
grid energy storage, hydrogen, 163–165
ground transportation, hydrogen, 152–156
growth fund investment theses, 167–205
 BECCS, 171–174, **172–173**
 biochar, 174–177, **175**
 CDR (Carbon Dioxide Removal), 189–190
 climate litigation, 200–203, **201**
 DAC (Direct Air Capture), 179–181, **180**
 End-to-End (E2E) modeling, **191**, 191–193
 electric airplanes, **181**, 181–183
 energy efficiency, buildings, **178**, 178–179
 identifying, **168–171**, 168–171
 methane measure, **183**, 183–185
 MMRV (Measurement, Monitoring, Reporting, and Verification), **185**, 185–187
 novel modeling for hurricane, tornado, and wildfire impacts, **187**, 187–188
 ocean-based CDR, **189**, 189–190
 Voluntary Carbon Markets E2E risk transfer solutions, 193–195, **194**
 Voluntary Carbon Markets exchanges, 195–196, **196**
 Voluntary Carbon Markets insurance, 196–198, **197**
 Voluntary Carbon Markets satellite monitoring, **183**, 183–185
 vertical farming, **203**, 203–205
 workforce retraining companies, 198–200, **199**
Growth Strategy Fund, 92–94

H

hardiness zone improvements, NLF, 341–347, **342–347**

Index

heating, hydrogen, 157–158
higher-dimension models, 40
HVAC manufacturers/installers, 224–226, **225**
HVAC market, 380–382, **380–382**
hydroelectric power generation companies, 243–245, **244**
hydrogen, 139–165
   airplanes, 161–163
   ammonia, 151–152, 159–160
   cheap green hydrogen, 149
   chemistry of, 141–144
   dark doldrums, 165
   electrolysis, 146–147
   fuel cell transportation, 152–154
   gasoline vs., **142**
   grid energy storage, 163–165
   ground transportation, 152–156
   heating, 157–158
   internal combustion engine transportation, 154–155
   kerosene, 163
   manufacturing, 144–146
   methanol, 160–161
   naturally occurring, 149
   pipelines, 150
   pyrolysis, 148
   rail transportation, 156
   shipping, 149–151
   steam generation, 157–158
   synthetic fuels, 155
   transportation risks, 156
   trucking transportation, 156
   zero-emissions heating, 158

I

IAM, optimization-based, **42**
Infrastructure Strategy Fund, 92, 95, **233–235,** 231–263
   biofuels, **247,** 247–249
   CCUS (Carbon Capture, Utilization, and Storage), 232, 235–237, **236**
   coastal tidal protection, **261,** 261–263
   electric grid infrastructure, 237–239, **238**
   energy storage, **239,** 239–241
   geothermal energy generation companies, **242,** 242–243
   hydroelectric power generation companies, 243–245, **244**
   OTEC (Ocean Thermal Energy Conversion), **258,** 258–260
   solar power generation companies, 253–255, **254**
   Sustainable Aviation Fuel (SAF), 232, **245,** 245–247
   sustainable concrete, **256,** 256–258

INDEX

Infrastructure Strategy Fund, (*Cont.*)
  tidal power generation
    companies, **249,** 249–251
  waste, organic, **247,** 247–249
  water, 251–253, **252**
  wind energy, 253–255, **254**
insurance companies, novel
  modeling, 217–219, **218**
Integrated Assessment Models
  (IAM), 41–42, **42**
Intergovernmental Panel on
  Climate Change (IPCC), 18,
  22, 29, 66
internal combustion engine
  transportation, hydrogen,
  154–155
investing in the transition,
  91–92, **91**
investment benefits, 120–121, **121,**
  296, 320–347, 373
investment horizon, 113, 127–128,
  285, 311, 361
investment matrix, **96,** 96–97
investment maturity, 113–114,
  114, 285, 312–316, **313, 315–
  316,** 361
investment portfolios, 99–133, **133**
  bottom-up results, 104
  crowdedness, 114–115, **115**
  customized scenarios, 102–103
  drivers, **110,** 110–111

fixes, 118, **118–119**
investment benefits, 120–121, **121**
investment horizon, 113, 127–128
investment maturity, 113–114, **114**
investment theses, 127–129, **129**
long-term visions, 122–123, **123**
market size, **121–122,** 121–122
model results, 105–107, **106**
NGFS Phase IV, **103–105**
NGFS Phase III, **105**
opportunities, identifying, **109,**
  109–110, 119–120, **120**
overlays, models, 108
overrides, models, 108
pre-prepared scenarios, 101–102
primary funds, 124–126, **126**
primary strategy identification,
  126–127, **127**
risk appetite, 127–128
risk pyramid, **128**
root problem, **116–117,** 116–118
scenarios, 99–103
subject matter expertise,
  108, 108
targets, identifying, 129–133
technology readiness, 111–
  113, **112**
top-down results, 104
transition finance investing
  flowchart, **100**
trigger events, 124, **125**

investment triggers, 124, **125**, 135–138
investment theses, 87–88, 127–129, **129**
investment types, 79–80, **80**

K
kerosene, hydrogen, 163

L
land, *see* forest land and Northern Latitudes Farmland (NLF)
land value, United States, 321–328, **324–328**
liability risks, 16
litigation drivers, 17
litigation risk, 12

M
manufacturing, hydrogen, 144–146
market risk, 11, **14–15**
market size identification, **121–122**, 121–122, 296–302, **297**, 348–354, **349–352**, 373–382
Mauna Loa observatory, **8**
measurement, monitoring, reporting, and validation, *see* MMRV
methane measure, **183**, 183–185
methanol, hydrogen, 160–161
migration effects, 68–69, 84–85
MMRV (Measurement, Monitoring, Reporting, and Verification), 136, **185**, 185–187
models, 33–69, **47–51**, 108
  acute physical risk, data quality, 53–55
  Agent-Based models, 41
  box models, 39
  chronic physical risk, data quality, 55–57
  climate, 37–46
  climate data, 52
  climate liability risk, data quality, 61–64, **63**
  climate litigation risk, 66–67
  climate module, 42
  CMIP6 models, 55–56, **56**
  concentration risk, 67
  contagion risk, 68
  Dynamic Integrated Model of Climate and Economy (DICE), 43–45, **44**
  economic module, 41
  EMICs (Earth-system Models of Intermediate Complexity), 40
  energy moisture balance models, 40
  fat tails, 64–69

INDEX

models, (*Cont.*)
  GCMs (Global Climate Models, or General Circulation Models), 41, 45–46, **45–46**, 57
  higher-dimension models, 40
  Integrated Assessment Models (IAM), 41–42, **42**
  migration effects, 68–69
  need, 33–34
  network effects, 68
  overlays, 108
  overrides, 108
  physical risk, 65
  primitive equation models, 40
  proprietary, 46–51, **47–51**
  quasi-geostrophic models, 40
  radiative-convective models, 39–40
  results, 105–107, **106**
  Spherical Cow Critique, **34**
  SSPs, 41
  statistical dynamic models, 40
  stranded assets, 65–66
  transition risk, data quality, 57–61, **60**, 65
  vendor, 46–51, **47–51**
  zero-dimensional models, 39

N
narratives, 72–73
naturally occurring hydrogen, 149
nested markets **122**
network effects, 68, 84
Network for Greening the Financial System (NGFS), 28–29, 288–291
NGFS Phase III, **105**
NGFS Phase IV, **103–105, 289**
NGFS Phase IV projections, **294–295**
NGFS Phase V scenarios, **291**
Northern Latitudes Farmland (NLF), **275**, 275–276, **310**, 309–357
  Agricultural Land, Cropland, 321–322
  Agricultural Land, Cropland, Irrigated, 322
  Agricultural Land, Cropland, Non-irrigated, 322
  Agricultural Land, Pastureland, 322
  appreciation, hardiness zone improvements, 341–347, **342–347**
  climate driver, 310
  crowdedness, 317
  fixes, 319–320
  funds, 310
  geographies, targeted), 356–357, **356**

investment benefits, 320–347
investment horizon, 311
investment maturity, 312–316, **313, 315–316**
investment opportunity, 320
land value, United States, 321–328, **324–328**
long-term vision, 354–355
market size, 348–354, **349–352**
projections, U.S. market, 352–354, **353**
rental, farmland returns, 328–333, **329–332**
Risk-Adjusted Returns (RAR), United States, 333–341, **333–340**
root problem, 318–319
technology readiness level, 311
timeline, 320
trigger, 355
novel modeling for hurricane, tornado, and wildfire impacts, **187**, 187–188
nuclear reactor manufacturers, 219–221, **220**
NY Climate Week, 29

O

ocean-based CDR, **189**, 189–190
opportunities, identifying, **109**, 109–110, 119–120, **120**
opportunities set,
OTEC (Ocean Thermal Energy Conversion), **258**, 258–260
overlays, models, 108
overrides, models, 108

P

paper recycling facilities, **277**, 277–278
PE targets, 305–306, 395–402, **395–402**
physical risks, 10–17, 65, 83
pipelines, hydrogen, 150
plantation forest, **271**, 271–272
policy drivers, 17
policy risk, 11–12, **14**
positive screening, 88–89, **89**
pre-prepared scenarios, 101–102
primitive equation models, 40
primary forest, **273**, 273–274
primary funds, 124–126, **126**
primary strategy identification, 126–127, **127**
private credit, 92
private equity, 92
projections, Northern Latitudes Farmland, 352–354, **353**
proprietary models, 46–51, **47–51**

415

INDEX

Public Strategy Fund, 92, 94–95, **209–211**, 207–229
   aluminum mines, smelters, 210–213, **211**
   coastal areas, novel modeling for, 217–219, **218**
   copper mines, **213**, 213–214
   critical mineral mines, 221–222, **222**
   electric transportation, **215**, 215–217
   emissions-free shipping, **228**, 228–229
   HVAC manufacturers/installers, 224–226, **225**
   insurance companies, novel modeling, 217–219, **218**
   nuclear reactor manufacturers, 219–221, **220**
   steel, sustainable, **226**, 226–227
   uranium mines, **223**, 223–224
pyrolysis, hydrogen, 148

Q

quantitative investing, 85–88
quantitative models, 86
quasi-geostrophic models, 40

R

radiative-convective models, 39–40
rail transportation, hydrogen, 156
real estate, climate sanctuary cities, 279–282, **280**
regulatory drivers, 17
REMIND IAM model, **105**
rental, farmland returns, 328–333, **329–332**
reputation risk, 13, **15**
resource-derived drivers, 17
Risk-Adjusted Returns (RAR), United States, 333–341, **333–340**
risk appetite, 127–128
risk pyramid, **128**
root problem, **116–117**, 116–118, 286–288, 318–319, 362

S

scenarios, transition, 99–103
SENSES Project, 23–25
Seventh Assessment Report (AR7), 22
Shared Socioeconomic Pathways (SSPs), 19–23, **19–23**
shipping, hydrogen, 149–151
social/behavioral drivers, 17
solar power generation companies, 253–255, **254**

Spherical Cow Critique, 34
SSPs, **19, 23,** 41
   SSP pathways, **19**
   mitigation, **23**
static asset allocations, 80–81, **81**
statistical dynamic models, 40
steam generation, hydrogen, 157–158
steel, sustainable, **226,** 226–227
stranded assets, 17–18, 65–66, 83
subject matter expertise, **108,** 108
subterranean mines, abandoned, 268–270, **269**
Sustainable Aviation Fuel (SAF), 232, **245,** 245–247
sustainable concrete, **256,** 256–258
synthetic fuels, hydrogen, 155

T
targets, identifying, 129–133
Task Force on Climate-Related Financial Disclosures (TCFD), 13–14, 29
technology readiness, 111–113, **112,** 284, 311, 360
technology risk, 12–13, **14**
temperature, 18–25
   CO_2 levels, 9–25
   land, **2**

thematic investment, 89–90, **90**
tidal power generation companies, **249,** 249–251
time horizon for transition finance, **93, 94**
top-down results, 104
transition finance, defined, 26–27
transition finance investing flowchart, **100**
Transition Finance Investment Thesis Identification process, **85,** 85–88
transition risks, 10–17, **110,** 111
   data quality, 57–61, **60,** 65
   diversification, 83
transportation risks, hydrogen, 156
trucking transportation, hydrogen, 156
trigger events, 124, **125,** 303

U
uranium mines, **223,** 223–224

V
validation, 75–77
Voluntary Carbon Markets (VCM)
   E2E risk transfer solutions, 193–195, **194**
   exchanges, 195–196, **196**
   insurance, 196–198, **197**

Voluntary Carbon Markets, (*Cont.*)
satellite monitoring, **183**, 183–185
VC targets, 303–304, 384–394, **384–394**
vendor models, 46–51, **47–51**
venture capital, 92
vertical farming, **203**, 203–205

W
waste, organic, **247**, 247–249
water, 251–253, **252**

wind energy, 253–255, **254**
workforce retraining companies, 198–200, **199**

Z
zero-dimensional models, 39
zero-emissions heating, hydrogen, 158